THE WOMAN WRITER IN
LATE-NINETEENTH-CENTURY ITALY

Gender and the Formation of Literary Identity

THE WOMAN WRITER IN
LATE-NINETEENTH-CENTURY ITALY

Gender and the Formation of Literary Identity

Lucienne Kroha

The Edwin Mellen Press
Lewiston/Queenston/Lampeter

Library of Congress Cataloging-in-Publication Data

Kroha, Lucienne, 1947-
    The woman writer in late-nineteenth-century Italy : gender and the
formation of literary identity / Lucienne Kroha.
        p.   cm.
    Includes bibliographical references.
    ISBN 0-7734-9530-4
    1. Italian fiction--19th century--History and criticism.
    2. Italian fiction--Women authors--History and criticism. 3. Women
authors in literature. 4. Women and literature--Italy-
-History--19th century. I. Title.
    PQ4174.K76 1992
    853'.8099287--dc20   92-12080
                                                                              CIP

A CIP catalog record for this book
is available from the British Library.

The Edwin Mellen Press   The Edwin Mellen Press
        Box 450   Box 67
Lewiston, New York   Queenston, Ontario
     USA 14092   CANADA L0S 1L0

The Edwin Mellen Press, Ltd.
Lampeter, Dyfed, Wales
UNITED KINGDOM SA48 7DY

Printed in the United States of America

Contents

Prefatory Note

Five of the chapters in this book began life as a series of previously published essays. Two have been translated from the original Italian and all have been modified to greater or lesser degrees; the essay on Matilde Serao has been added to substantially. For permission to reprint them here I thank *Esperienze letterarie*, Dovehouse Editions of Ottawa, Casalini Libri of Florence, Olschki publishers of Florence and *The Italianist*. They appeared originally as follows: "La Marchesa Colombi: la scrittura come trasgressione nell'opera di una narratrice dell'Ottocento," *Esperienze letterarie* 13.2 (1988): 17-37; "The Marchesa Colombi's *Matrimonio in provincia*: Style as Subversion," *Donna: Women in Italian Culture*, ed. A. Testaferri (Ottawa: Dovehouse Editions, 1989) 153-173; "Neera: The Literary Career of a Woman of the Nineteenth Century," *Yearbook of Italian Studies* 5 (1984): 77-101; "I segreti di un quadro in un romanzo femminile dell'Ottocento: il ritorno del represso," *Letteratura italiana e arti figurative: Atti del XII Convegno dell'AISLLI*, ed. A. Franceschetti, vol. 2 (Florence: Olschki, 1988) 917-928; "Matilde Serao's *Fantasia*: An Author in Search of a Character," *The Italianist* 7 (1987): 45-62 [rpt. in *Women and Italy: Essays on Gender, Culture and History*, eds. Z. Baranski and S.Vinall (London: Macmillan, 1991) 245-262].

The introductory chapter and the last two essays, "Strategies of Intertextuality in Sibilla Aleramo's *Una donna*" and "Pirandello and the Woman Writer: A Reading of *Suo marito*" appear here for the first time.

Acknowledgements

There are several people to whom I would like to express my gratitude and recognition.The first of these is someone whose contribution goes well beyond the scope of these pages – Emeritus Professor Antonio D'Andrea of McGill University. Without his formative influence, scholarly insight and challenging perceptions, my work would have been much poorer. His intellectual generosity, his patience and rigour where I often lacked both, and his unfailing encouragement have always meant a great deal to me.

I would also like to thank Pamela Stewart and Maria Predelli, once teachers, now colleagues, whose solidarity and support have manifested themselves in both practical and intangible ways, too numerous and various to mention, but none of which have gone unnoticed – or unappreciated.

I am greatly indebted to Zyg Baranski of the University of Reading, UK, for his active interest in my work, in my career and in this book, as well as for his loyalty in difficult times. His concrete suggestions, timely trans-Atlantic phone calls and down-to-earth advice have kept me on course.

Barbara Gabriel of the Department of English, Carleton University, read the entire manuscript and offered important suggestions for improvement, as well as much-needed discussion of questions related to feminist scholarship. Stephen Bornstein took time off from the affairs of state to make valuable comments on parts of the manuscript and has provided continuous suppport – and humor – throughout. Lonnie Weatherby of McLennan Library Reference offered both moral and bibliographic assistance. Irena Murray and Jen Weinstein were patient and encouraging listeners on topics not necessarily confined to literature.

More than anything, I would like thank these people for their friendship over the years and for often putting up with me when it would have been much easier not to do so.

Thanks are also due to Carmela Parzanese who typed most of these essays and whose patience and skill at unscrambling them in their various drafts places her in a class by herself and to Suzy Slavin who generously proofread the manuscript .

The research that went into this project was facilitated by grants from the Social Sciences and Humanities Research Council of Canada and the Faculty of Graduate Studies and Research of McGill University.

Introduction

On the first of January 1907 one of Italy's most influential literary critics, Luigi Capuana, published an article in *Nuova antologia* entitled "Letteratura femminile." It opened by asking quite bluntly whether the new influx of female novelists was really the cause for concern that some of their male counterparts – and competitors – seemed to think it was: "C'è da impensierirsi, come fanno taluni, dell'invadente concorrenza della donna nella letteratura narrativa?"[1]

Capuana's reassurances notwithstanding, the alarm of the male literary community was well-founded. As far back as 1855 Ruggero Bonghi, in his well-known *Perché la letteratura italiana non sia popolare in Italia*, was citing the fact that Italian women read mostly foreign novels to prove that Italian books "son letti poco e solo da letterati o da chi s'immagina d'esser tale."[2] Bonghi's comments were a barometer of the times: indirectly, he was letting his colleagues know that the mass reading public had become largely female. It was not long before there was to be a corresponding increase in the number of women who wrote. The years after 1880 saw an explosion of women writers unlike anything that had ever taken place in Italy before, all the more significant because it took place at a time of considerable social and political turbulence:

> E' un'"infinita schiera di novellatrici"e di intellettuali, di giornaliste, di appendiciste e di poetesse, di educatrici, di favoliste e di scrittrici per l'infanzia, che costituiscono quella galassia sommersa, dai contorni è vero incerti e un po' ambigui ma dall'indubbio spessore quantitativo e anche qualitativo, che era percepita dai contemporanei come uno dei fenomeni più importanti dell'Italia umbertina. La letteratura femminile era infatti seguita con attenzione proprio perché giocava un suo ruolo, non solo e non tanto come "lettura di

evasione," ma come legittimo intervento di analisi e di denuncia sociale, operato da donne per cui la scrittura era diventata uno *status* professionale, e sulle quali l'interesse dei contemporanei si appuntava, anche considerandole in sé come personaggi pubblici, su cui riflettere e di cui discutere: esse in sostanza costituivano una "categoria sociale" a sé, con ben definite peculiarità e caratteristiche.[3]

As if to confirm the anxieties of his fellow *literati*, in 1906 Luigi Pirandello, an acute observer of the times as well of the human condition, began the composition of *Suo marito* (1911), a little-known novel about the devastating personal consequences of a young woman's literary ambitions. Suffice it to say that while Silvia Roncella, the novel's heroine, writes prolifically, her lover, described as one of the most prominent authors of the time, has had writer's block for at least ten years.

The one major critic who managed to show some enthusiasm for the new crop of women writers despite the general malaise of his contemporaries was Benedetto Croce. His *Letteratura della nuova Italia* contains essays on Matilde Serao, Neera, the Marchesa Colombi, Emma, Vittoria Aganoor, Ada Negri, the Contessa Lara, Carola Prosperi, Clarice Tartufari and Grazia Deledda. In his *Storia d'Italia dal 1871 al 1915* (1928) Croce identifies the post-unification movement for the creation of a popular culture as having favored the "personal" voice of women. He also points out what it is that distinguishes the work of these women writers from that of their predecessors: for the first time, female experience, as recounted by women themselves, was finding expression in novelistic form. And yet, for this very reason, his general attitude to these women is more than somewhat patronizing:

Nei raccomandati precetti di "scrivere come si parla," e di "dire quel che si sente" e di essere "spontanei" e "naturali," trovavano condizioni favorevoli le donne, disposte anche troppo da natura all'osservanza di quei precetti, le quali nei secoli innanzi non entravano di solito nel mondo letterario se non prendendo abito virile, coltivandosi nelle scuole, rimatrici petrarchesche, pastorelle d'Arcadia o patriottiche Vellede; e invece ora effondevano il loro cuore e narravano le loro esperienze, come la Serao, Neera, Emma, la contessa Lara e molte altre.[4]

The gender biases evident in Croce's otherwise perceptive remarks, however grating, pale in comparison to those of other critics of the time. Capuana, for example, reassures his readers that women writers do not really constitute a threat, in spite of their burgeoning numbers, since their work is characterized by what he calls "quel contributo di femminilità ... che è speciale caratteristica dell'intelligenza e, più, del cuore della donna":

> ... Esse mettono nella loro opera d'arte un elemento tutto proprio, la femminilità; ma niente di più. E i lettori di romanzi, maschi e femmine, che si equivalgono, se ne trovano contenti. Io poi sono convinto che nell'avvenire, nel lontano avvenire, le donne saranno quel che ora sono gli uomini; ma allora gli uomini saranno tutt'altri; e la distanza rimarrà uguale a quella di oggi. Allora gli uomini lasceranno alle donne l'occupazione di scrivere romanzi, liriche, tragedie, commedie e, se ci avranno preso gusto, poemi; ma esse – aggiungo – non creeranno nulla di nuovo, perché non ci sarà altro da creare nelle forme dell'arte. Sarà un'eterna ripetizione, fino a che non si stancheranno; cosa un po' improbabile: le donne sono ostinate.[5]

In the light of these remarks it comes as no surprise that Capuana's inventory and discussion of novels published by women in the previous year or so makes no mention whatsoever of Sibilla Aleramo's controversial *Una donna* (1906), which had caused such a fuss in the Italian press.[6] Pirandello, not given to this sort of subterfuge, had neither ignored Aleramo's autobiographical novel nor been among its many detractors; in fact he had published a favorable review of it in Turin's *Gazzetta del popolo* on the 27th of December 1906, just a few days before the appearance of Capuana's article.[7]

Capuana was not alone in insisting on the "feminine" character of women's writing, perhaps in an unconscious attempt to neutralize the potential effects of the massive presence of women on the literary scene. In a similar vein, in a major essay on Neera which also appeared in *Nuova antologia* (1901), another critic, Guido Menasci, declares unabashedly his desire to find in the writings of women the confirmation of gender stereotypes. In Neera, one of the most popular writers of the period and a protégé of both Croce and Capuana, he claims to find

> certi graziosi atteggiamenti del pensiero, non so quali raffinatezze di sentimento, [una] tepida atmosfera d'affetto e di tenerezza ... l'associazione strana ma aggraziata di alcune idee ... qualche volta il capriccio, ma un capriccio carino e garbato.... Ecco in qual modo Neera rivela negli scritti la gentilezza donnesca: così come basta a rilevar la presenza della donna nella dimora un nonnulla: un fiore, un ritratto, il fruscio d'una gonna.[8]

One writer whom it was difficult to encapsulate in such definitions was Matilde Serao, perhaps as much because of her boisterous personality as because of anything she wrote. Giovanni Verga, who admired Serao's work, simply solved the problem by declaring her a hermaphrodite! (The context is a letter in which he expresses his annoyance at having been asked, yet again, to express an opinion on the manuscript of an aspiring woman novelist):

> Avevo già immaginato che il romanzo della Sig.a Ferruggia pervenutomi i giorni scorsi fosse quello già da voi annunziatomi per incarico della marchesa Visconti. Non ebbi il coraggio di pregarvi per aiutarmi ad allontanare da me il calice amaro del *giudizio letterario*, e l'ho letto coscienziosamente quantunque, debbo confessarvelo, non abbia molta fede nelle donne scrittrici, o meglio nel loro valore artistico, la Sand compresa, ch'è una seccatrice, e la Serao eccettuata perch'è ermafrodita.[9]

The reactions of readers such as Croce, Capuana, Verga and Menasci are valuable because they document not only the social pressures and gender prejudices to which women who chose to write in this period were subject, but also the extent to which these prejudices could "blind" the most normally insightful critics to the emotion and anger often present in their work. It was not until the nineteen-seventies, when the feminist revival led to a renewed interest in women writers of the past, that some of these writers were to get a second hearing. In this new context, and some seventy-five years after the appearance of Menasci's article, Luigi Baldacci unearths and reprints Neera's *Teresa* (1886). In his introduction (1976) he declares it among the best Italian novels of the late-nineteenth century, and Neera's creative writings in general "documenti essenziali dello spirito feminista."[10] Unfettered by visions of "femininity," Baldacci allows Neera her anger and indignation and acknowledges the seriousness of her enterprise, as well as the challenge to received values it represents. However, undoubtedly because of the groundbreaking nature of his critical gesture, he neglects to explore what I believe are other, more complex and unsettling aspects of her art (which I attempt to bring out in the two essays on Neera in this volume). From this point of view, Baldacci's "feminist" reading of Neera is, in its own way, almost as prescriptive as Menasci's "feminine" one, and exemplifies the limitation of Italian feminist approaches to women writers of this period in general – the tendency to read their work in the light of late twentieth-century ideological expectations, as more-or-less disappointing, unmediated documents of feminine oppression or feminist consciousness. Little or no attention is accorded to the novelty and complexity of their enterprise as women writing in the specific social and literary context of late-nineteenth century Italy, other than to point out that it may have interfered with their ability to take strong feminist positions.[11]

The essays in this collection attempt to address some of the issues left untouched by this often reductive, essentially extra-literary approach. They examine the work of four of the most important and widely-read women novelists of the period – Neera, Matilde Serao, the Marchesa Colombi and Sibilla Aleramo[12] – all of whom were extremely prolific and, to varying degrees, involved in the on-going debate on the changing role of women in Italian society of the time. The texts under consideration span the years between 1880 and 1920. For the most part, however, they inhabit the fertile grey zone between late-Romanticism and naturalism which spawned so many of the popular novels and *racconti* of this period. In looking at the work of these four authors together, this study in part continues the project of reconstructing and mapping out the place of women writers in the English and Continental traditions which feminist critics have been carrying out in the academy for the last two decades.

Any project of this sort invariably confronts the question of whether women writers construct what Elaine Showalter has called "a literature of their own."[13] French theory has argued that women's writing constitutes an *écriture féminine* (which Nancy K. Miller has described as "roughly ... a process or a practice by which the female *body*, with its peculiar drives and rhythms, inscribes itself as text"[14]), a view which in some quarters has been criticized for its essentialist, biological underpinnings.[15] My argument is a less radical one: it assumes that women's experiences in a given historical moment have placed them at the margins of dominant cultural institutions and often outside of dominant discourses. From this premise, it proceeds to ask two basic questions. How does the woman writer mediate between her own experience and those dominant modes of representation and discourse which constitute national literary traditions? How, also, does she "[cope] in a literary form with her social position, the expectations attached to her role as a woman, her fears, desires and fantasies"?[16] In the case of each of the four writers examined I have come up with answers which, however different, contribute to a general argument: that these writers do, in fact, inscribe their experience as women in their work, but indirectly, through recourse to strategies which allow them simultaneously to display *and* to disguise a subversive stance vis-à-vis the literary tradition on the margins of which they find themselves. As writers, they are also inevitably interpreters of their literary heritage, and it is their conditioned, strategic reaction to this heritage which I believe constitutes their shared experience as women writing at this time.[17]

From a methodological standpoint, I have drawn loosely on a variety of sources from the Anglo-American feminist critical tradition. Of these, the most important are Elaine Showalter's extensive discussion of the tension between authorship and womanhood in *A Literature of Their Own: British Women Novelists from Brontë to Lessing*; her "theory of culture" model as elaborated in "Feminist Criticism in the Wilderness," which has as its goal "to plot the precise cultural locus of female literary identity and to describe the forces that intersect an individual woman writer's cultural field," and which recognizes that women's writing is "a double-voiced discourse that always embodies the social, literary and cultural heritages of both the muted and the dominant;"[18] Sandra Gilbert and Susan Gubar's seminal work *The Madwoman in the Attic: The Woman Writer and the Nineteenth-Century Literary Imagination* which examines what it means "to be a woman writer in a culture whose fundamental definitions of literary authority are ... both overtly and covertly patriarchal."[19] I have also kept in mind Lucien Goldmann's theory of homologies which sees the relationship between works of literature and the consciousness of the social "groups" from which they emanate as being articulated in the forms or structures which these works assume.[20] In the case of the women treated here, it is their particular position as a group within a culture that not only lacked a significant female tradition but which, insofar as it conceived of women writers at all, assigned them narrow and debilitating roles, that I see as the determining factor.

II

Before discussing more specifically the results of my investigation, I want to outline something of the historical context, particularly those crises and contingencies that shaped the lives of these writers as women. Since Unification, a number of factors had brought about profound changes in the role of women in

Italian society. The rapid industrialization of northern Italy, the entry of women into the labor force and the rise of the Socialist Party (1892), which became the official champion of the rights of working women, had all contributed to bringing Italian society closer to the level of awareness of women's issues which characterized other European nations.

However, Italian feminism owed its development at first almost exclusively to the efforts of the indefatigable Milanese activist Anna Maria Mozzoni (1837-1920), who was to be the single most important force behind the attempt to create an Italian women's movement.[21] In 1864, in an unsuccessful attempt to influence the revisions to the Civil Code passed in 1865, she published *La donna e i suoi rapporti sociali*, "the first feminist assault on legal inequality in the unified state."[22] Her push for reform, particularly in the area of family law, "which virtually equated women with minors and mental incompetents,"[23] culminated in her translation of John Stuart Mill's *The Subjection of Women*, published in 1870, the same year which saw the secular forces of the Risorgimento present a divorce bill to the Italian parliament. Though the bill failed to pass, the controversy created by its proposal, coupled with the publication of Mill's tract, unofficially inaugurated the national debate on women's rights.

For Mozzoni the "the woman question was not fundamentally economic,"[24] but had to do with concepts of gender roles which invested men and women of all social classes. It was on this point that she was later to enter into conflict with another important feminist leader, the Russian-born Anna Kuliscioff (1857-1925), whose first allegiance was to the Socialist Party. These were years of great social tension in Italy, as the pressure to industrialize and compete in international markets created both a growing need for cheap labor and increasing pressure from the Left for government legislation to regulate working conditions. By the end of the nineteenth century one-and-a-half million women were working in factories in northern Italy, the majority of them in the textile industry. Mozzoni was a socialist herself, and though she continued to maintain that the *questione femminile* was, to a large extent, independent of the *questione sociale*, she eventually realized that if the feminist movement in Italy had any hope at all of reaching women *en masse*, it could do so only by calling attention to the hardships they suffered in the workplace. Correspondingly, from 1878 on, her organizational efforts were directed largely toward women of the working classes.

And indeed, the first really successful attempts to mobilize women in Italy took place in the factories, where the vote for women was promoted as a means of influencing legislation on working conditions. In 1881 Mozzoni organized the famous "Comizio dei comizi" in Rome on the question of women's suffrage. That same year the Left presented a bill in Parliament calling for the replacement of the existing property-based franchise, "which empowered about 80,000 men of a total population of 4,200,000 to elect the lower house,"[25] with universal adult suffrage. The bill was defeated. As a result, the question of women's rights in Italy became even more intertwined with the question of workers' rights than in the past. Thanks largely to the the efforts of Anna Kuliscioff, the first laws regulating the employment of women and children were finally passed in the Italian parliament in 1903, the same year which saw the foundation of the *Consiglio nazionale delle donne italiane*.

In these years women were organizing not only in industry, but also in agriculture, especially in the rice-fields of northern and central Italy, which were the site of a number of violent strikes in the years between 1883 and 1890. White-collar work was also becoming increasingly available, largely in the state bureaucracy and in the schools, though by the 1880's the working conditions of elementary school teachers had become "a public scandal."[26] Women were even beginning to enter the universities, which were officially opened to them in 1874, and a handful were attempting to break into the liberal professions. A *cause célèbre* in these years was that of Lidia Poët, the first woman to be admitted to the Italian bar, but subsequently denied the right to practice by the Italian courts. The year was 1883 and public opinion was divided on whether or not a woman could – or should – be denied this right.

In this context, the *questione femminile* in all its facets became an increasingly volatile subject of public debate. At first the feminist cause found support mainly in such progressive women's journals as *Donna, L'Aurora, Cornelia* and *Missione della donna*, founded by women who had become politicized during the Risorgimento,[27] and opposition or only moderate support in the more conservative female publications such as *Il giornale delle donne*, founded in Turin in 1869, which declared its goal to be "l'istruzione della donna, inculcata senza pedanteria, promuovendo gli affetti familiari e la felicità domestica, nonché il diletto procurato con romanzi e racconti dovuti a penne insigni, e tali da poter essere letti con pari interesse dalle madri e dalle figlie."[28] By the turn of the century, however, the mainstream Italian press had entered the fray and magazines and newspapers were full of articles and even regular columns on questions raised by the feminist movement. *L'Almanacco italiano* published one such column, entitled "Rubrica femminile," to which noted feminists were invited to contribute; in 1903 *La tribuna illustrata* went as far as to launch its own referendum on the vote for women, promising its readers prizes of 50 lire for the best responses for or against.

Women's issues were hotly debated in intellectual publications as well. *Nuova Antologia* ran articles such as "La questione della donna" (F. De Renzis, 1 June 1889), "La donna e il socialismo" (G. Boccardo, 16 February 1892), "La donna e il suo avvenire" (R. Bonghi, 1 May 1892), "Le donne nella scienza" (P. Mantegazza, 16 July 1898). In 1911 it also published an *Inchiesta sul femminismo* with contributions from such names as Bracco, Cian, Croce, Deledda, Di Giacomo, Farina, Labriola, Neera and Pareto.

All this controversy obviously contributed greatly to the high profile of women writers. At a time when the lone female lawyer was still seeking permission to practice, and elementary school teachers were working for a pittance in hardship conditions in remote areas of the country, women writers constituted an "invading horde" who could be neither excluded by overt institutional barriers nor marginalized by the structures of the labor market. Furthermore, by the very nature of their activity, they could not avoid touching on subjects related to both the private lives and the social roles of women. As a result, both press and public automatically identified them with the burning questions of the day and, whether they liked it or not, they were called upon regularly to take stands on such thorny issues as divorce, suffrage and the problems created by the entry of women into the labour market. Inevitably, they also began to reflect, in print, on their own intellectual identity and on the relationship between female subjectivity, the cultural tradition and the literary institutions.[29]

Paradoxically, their positions were, for the most part, anything but radical. Neera and Matilde Serao were both well-known anti-feminists. Even the Marchesa Colombi, who was involved with Anna Maria Mozzoni's alternative education project for women, appears to have been ambiguous in her endorsement of feminist claims:

> Anche nei confronti del contemporaneo svilupparsi del movimento femminista, sono proprio le scrittrici più affermate ad assumere un atteggiamento generalmente negativo. Dalle violente prese di posizione antifemministe di Neera – una delle più note, e indubbiamente quella che si espose di più in campo teorico – a Matilde Serao che nega addirittura che esista una questione femminile o ironizza con toni riduttivi e sprezzanti sulle donne che lavorano, alla Marchesa Colombi che, nella sua rubrica "Colore del Tempo" sulla rivista "Vita Intima" ... e nelle importanti prefazioni che usa premettere alle sue opere, traccia una visione del femminile tutta in grigio, di malinconica compostezza e di segreta ironia: è un coro generale di perbenismo e di moderazione, basta sfogliare i giornali dell'epoca.[30]

How is it possible to explain this contradiction? It is true that the political and social issues women writers were expected to address were not only delicate, they were also potentially damaging to them. Many of them earned a large part of their income from women's journalism and had to tread lightly through the minefield, lest they offend the sensibilities of their readers or their employers. Feminist positions were also associated, in the popular mind, with socialism, especially after the Socialists took over the cause of women in Parliament. But none of this is enough to explain the virulence with which such figures as Neera and Matilde Serao sometimes embraced anti-feminist stances.

Briefly, the late-nineteenth century was an extremely ambiguous period as regards the role of women in Italian society, and the serious woman writer, because of her high profile, was more sensitive than most to the contradictions and pressures created by constrasting social imperatives. On the one hand, opportunities for self-expression were greater than they had ever been before and a variety of economic, political, social and literary forces were pushing women toward forms of consciousness that were profoundly threatening to the *status quo*. On the other hand, serious writing demanded a degree of self-exposure which not many women of the time were prepared to risk: self-exposure conflicted not only with established bourgeois norms of feminine modesty, but also, as we shall see, with the specific Risorgimento image of woman as angel-of-the-hearth, a myth all the more resistant because the family was considered the primary nucleus of the new Italy. This lingering image could not help but influence the female writer's sense of her place in society and tended to block any inclination toward confrontation.

The official rhetoric of the Risorgimento and the ideology it upheld – which lived on well into the years of post-Unification – had assigned women an extremely important moral role in the ideal society of the new Italy. This role, which contrasted drastically with the changing realities of Italian life in this period of social and economic transformation, encompassed two very specific tasks: the emotional support of their husbands and the moral education of their children. By selflessly assuring her husband the warmth and material comforts of a smoothly-run home, the Italian woman was silently helping him to perform his duties as a citizen; and by providing an example of domestic austerity, sacrifice and devotion, she was offering her sons a living example in the private sphere of what was expected of them in the public domain. This latter role was seen as particularly important in a country as desperately lacking in modern and efficient public educational structures as was post-Unification Italy. It also contributed, in part, to the proliferation of women writers, who in this period produced a large number of treatises on every aspect of child-rearing.[31] However, as historian Dina Bertoni Jovine has argued, for all its "importance," in the final analysis the role assigned to women by Risorgimento ideology put them on much the same footing as the working classes:

> Dal popolo dovevano essere tratti lavoratori capaci di adeguarsi alle nuove techniche lavorative e collaborare alla realizzazione degli ideali liberali; nelle donne si doveva formare la capacità di organizzare la vita familiare e l'educazione dei figli in modo da favorire il progresso nazionale. Ma sia nell'uno come nell'altro caso si trattava di forme di cultura avaramente dosate in modo che non intaccassero il sostanziale predominio di coloro che consideravano come legittimo non soltanto il privilegio di dirigere la vita familiare e nazionale secondo i propri interessi ideali e pratici, ma anche quello di possedere in pieno gli strumenti della vita culturale.[32]

This is confirmed by the tone of the debate on the education of women, which immediately became an integral and important part of public discourse on the need for a new, more moral society.[33] Among the many writers and thinkers who pronounced themselves on the subject were personalities as diverse as Cesare Balbo, Silvio Pellico, Niccolò Tommaseo, Vincenzo Gioberti and Antonio Rosmini.[34] Whatever their orientation on other Risorgimento issues, all agreed that the confinement of women to the private sphere was a *sine qua non* for the creation of a new and better society. While this was perhaps to be expected from Catholics such as Gioberti and Rosmini (for Gioberti "la donna ... è in un certo modo verso l'uomo ciò che è il vegetale verso l'animale, o la pianta parassita verso quella che si regge e sostenta da sé"[35]), the same was true of some of the most ardent democrats, whose arguments were essentially the same:

> Le alunne siano preparate, anzitutto, ai domestici uffici. Poiché la vita è lavoro e sacrificio, conviene che vi si avezzino per tempo, che vi si addestrino, che in qualche maniera di opere accrescano il proprio valore, e ciò sentano ed amino fin dai primi giorni. Sai che avverrebbe altrimenti? Ragazze, che la scola [sic] ha rubato alla famiglia, cullate coll'immaginativa di un mondo diverso dal loro, sono affannate, disgustate dalla irrevocabile realtà della loro condizione. Può la scola impedire cotale malattia dello spirito, e lo deve. Oltre i soliti lavori di cucito e di maglia [...][36]

Woman's patriotic duty coincided, then, with her ignorance and isolation. According to one propagandist, she must be educated "a starsene solitaria per attendere ed allevare i figliuoli nella virtù [onde] la crescente generazione prepari a sé e all'Italia miglior fortuna."[37] In the eyes of another, her true glory "non consiste nel vano rumore del mondo, nello splendido trionfo d'un giorno, ma nel rimanere ignorata dalla folla e nota sola ai pochi buoni cui è dato avvicinarla e di ammirare la sua saviezza e bontà."[38] This same writer then goes on to address Italian women directly:

> Voi non pensate a far pompa delle vostre belle doti, ma procurate invece nel santuario della famiglia, ove trovate rifugio e consolazione ... di abbellire e perfezionare sempre più il vostro spirito, di esercitarvi nella pratica delle domestiche virtù, della abnegazione ... per riuscire sempre più gradite a coloro ai quali vi siete interamente consacrate.[39]

Inevitably, this view of the role of women was to spill over into considerations on the role of women writers, particularly in the context of the ongoing debate on the merits and shortcomings of the novel as a vehicle for the education of women. The variety of opinions expressed on this subject reflected not only the diverse ideological positions within the Unification movement, but also the somewhat contradictory roles that the novel was expected to play as a vehicle for the modernization of Italian letters on the one hand and as an instrument of moral education on the other.[40] Modernization and morality did not always go hand in hand, and opening the door to European cultural influences meant admitting every sort of novel, including gothic novels and novels of adultery which did not reflect the pedagogical mandate of the Italian novel. Nonetheless, the more enlightened saw the novel as an appropriate means of education for women, since by temperament, women were thought "naturally" inclined to prefer it to other literary genres.[41] Others, however, in keeping with the time-worn opposite tradition, persisted in considering the novel dangerous, especially French novels, which were often the mainstay of the reading woman's diet.

One of the most stringent opponents of the French novel was Carlo Cattaneo. His frequently cited essay "Sul romanzo delle donne contemporanee in Italia" (1863) clearly denounces French writers, particularly George Sand, for depicting heroines whose passions provoked in them "quello stato di irrequietezza, quel bisogno di ribellarsi alla posizione sociale e di reclamare un'emancipazione."[42] Cattaneo made no secret of the fact that he expected to find "nelle opere letterarie delle nostre autrici contemporanee una scuola di virtù, di gentilezza, di amore."[43] After all, the act of writing for the public entailed a disquieting departure from the silence and shadows to which woman was best relegated and could only be justified in the name of her "true vocation": "Se la donna abbandona il suo silenzio, se si distacca dall'oscurità dove brilla assai più che in qualsiasi splendore di fama, essa deve discendere fra noi come infermiera, come missionaria."[44]

Those who deplored the influence of novels often believed that lyric poetry was less harmful and more suited to the cultivation of those qualities women were expected to display. By the 1880's, although the woman writer had become commonplace, this belief had not changed. Partly as a result, the number of volumes of poetry published still far exceeded the number of novels.[45] Moreover, critics and journalists tended to ignore or gloss over much of the novelistic production of women, favoring instead women's poetry, perhaps because the new opportunities for social analysis and realistic representation provided by *verismo* were as threatening as the romantic passions of George Sand's unstable heroines, if not more so:

> Nel complesso, se seguiamo il dibattito sul romanzo, vivo all'epoca, gli accenni a scrittrici sono contenuti, marginali, anche se numerosi sono i libri di donne ad essere pubblicati. Le citazioni sono per lo più riservate a poetesse.... La poetessa ha un ruolo rassicurante, che pone la donna in uno spazio idealizzato, ricco, anzi eccedente in sensibilità, lontano da eventi concreti. Diversa è invece la posizione delle narratrici, attente con altro sguardo alle trasformazioni del sociale. Appaiono subito sospette per l'adesione a un genere a loro

quasi interdetto già nella conoscenza; sono questi infatti gli anni nei quali un romanzo tra le mani di una donna è segno di emancipazione spregiudicata.[46]

In this context, the opening in the literary system that the emergence of a female audience had created was something of a double-edged sword. While the existence of a "captive" female market certainly facilitated publication for women writers, it created a situation in which women writers were induced to see themselves as catering to a female audience which they were also in a position to influence by virtue of their "authority" – not the best circumstances for unhindered artistic expression. It also tended to confine women writers to a ghetto from which only a few were to emerge. Those who did, and the four writers in question here are among them, understandably did so only with a tremendous amount of ambivalence and trepidation :

> ... mentre nel ghetto dell'appendice e del popolare, delle storie di pura evasione, si costruiscono per la lettura di intrattenimento dei tipi femminili estremi, variamente giocati sul *leitmotiv* del sentimento, recipienti adatti a canalizzare in modo elementare ma efficace il desiderio di fuga dal quotidiano e dalle sue miserie e il sogno di felicità delle masse, rigidamente attenendosi a una struttura di storia a lieto fine, è nelle scrittrici "impegnate" che spesso si rivela una sostanziale dicotomia fra riflessione e scrittura creativa: sicché proprio là dove esse più attentamente rappresentano, nelle loro protagoniste, modelli più realistici di donne, accuratamente esemplati sulla realtà della condizione femminile contemporanea, si intuisce una specie di scarto psicologico, una forma di timore, quasi della loro stessa audacia e dell'influsso che potrebbero esercitare sul pubblico dei lettori.[47]

The failure of the major female writers of this period to confront in an unambiguous manner the questions raised by the changing role of women reflected also the difficulties of working within the confines of a literary tradition which had come late and ill-prepared to the novel, and even later to the major woman novelist. As a result, the depiction of female characters in Italian literature, though it varied over the centuries, had consistently little to do with the social reality of women's lives.[48] When, in the early-nineteenth century, the novel finally did arrive, it made of the female character, in keeping with official Risorgimento ideals, the exclusive custodian and symbol of domestic values and virtues:

> Nella figura della donna confluiscono tutti i requisiti moralmente apprezzabili (nobiltà e mitezza di carattere e comportamento, virtù

domestiche, ecc.) le qualità estetiche (bellezza in genere, che comprende i vari segni: capelli, occhi, pelle, delicatezza del viso, portamento), le qualità aggiuntive o complementari (vestiti, colori, acconciatura) e i temi tipici della condizione femminile: l'amore come dedizione, la virtù materna e domestica, l'educazione dei figli e dei cittadini, il sacrificio, ecc.[49]

Q. D. Leavis, in an essay entitled "The Englishness of the English Novel," comments on the narrow range of action and the restricted roles assigned to female characters in the Italian novel of the period, as compared to the case of the more "permissive" English novel. She points out that "as the English novel is the product of an essentially Protestant culture ... its heroines, though modest, sensitive and domesticated, are in any crisis prepared to act in defiance of the conventions of their society if their sense of what is just prompts them to do so." She goes on to say that "this is a very different concept of virtue from what we find in Continental girl heroines of esteemed novels of the same period, for instance, *I promessi sposi* or *Eugenie Grandet*." While English heroines were allowed to be "bravely heretical ... the Latin heroines were characteristically required to be morally docile and blindly obedient to authority."[50] Or, as De Donato puts it, with more emphasis on the specifics of the Italian situation,

> ... la donna-Ottocento-made-in-Italy, ebbe tratti distintivi non confrontabili con quelli della letteratura europea: gli scrittori infatti, quando anche come i democratici, si trovino dislocati su di un terreno ideale più avanzato, sono trattenuti dal grado di sviluppo della società, dal moderatismo diffuso anche in letteratura e dal ristretto 'orizzonte di attese' tracciato dai moderati attorno alla figura-emblema della donna, al di qua di quell'universo femminile ricco di presenze inquiete che incomincia a prendere vita in Europa proprio con il processo di formazione della società capitalistica moderna.[51]

With the possible exception of Ippolito Nievo's Pisana in *Le confessioni di un italiano* and the female protagonists of Rovani's *Cento anni*,[52] this is as true of the women in the vast array of popular *racconti* and novels of the period as it is of those in works by authors of major stature (such as Manzoni, whose Lucia remains the archetype of the "donna-angelo"[53]). In both cases, "unica alternativa alla cieca ubbidienza sempre positiva e pagante, rimangono il castigo e l'emarginazione, simbolicamente presenti nelle metafore della pazzia, della monacazione forzata, della morte."[54]

By the end of the century, the virtuous woman had yielded the literary limelight to her opposite sister – the *femme fatale*. While the dilemmas of female characters in other literatures at this time were often symptomatic of deeper disturbances in the old European social order, the Italian novel managed to avoid such issues altogether, by reducing female sexuality to a simple biological function. Though drawn with varying degrees of complexity and subtlety, the often diabolical, erotically-motivated *belle dame sans merci* appears in the work of almost all the major and minor writers of the latter part of the nineteenth century.[55] In fact, according to an American critic of the turn-of-the-century, she provides the one recurring face of woman as she appears in the Italian novel of the time:

> En général, on n'a vu en elle qu'un être pervers et mal équilibré, hanté par un seul désir, incapable d'éprouver autre chose qu'un seul sentiment et qui, par suite, n'est apte qu'à suggérer une seule émotion. Inutile d'analyser les autres aspects de son caractère, inutile de discuter les nombreux problèmes qui se rattachent à elle.... De là, dans les romans italiens, cette continuelle répétition de l'eternelle situation, toujours ressassée, jamais epuisée; de là, cette ressemblance monotone, de tous les personnages féminins, copiés d'après natures, mais vus à travers des préventions aveuglantes.[56]

III

Women writers of this period, independently of their feminist or anti-feminist stances on other issues, unanimously rejected the traditional literary depiction of women and of women's experiences. However they were unable, for the most part, to express this dissent in a forthright manner. Fear of exposure was undoubtedly one factor contributing to their reticence. As Sigrid Weigel has pointed out, the traditional exclusion of women "from economics, politics and culture implies that authentic women's literature at first could only give voice to 'merely' personal and subjective feelings and concerns" ("effondevano il loro cuore," as Croce puts it), and this was not without its consequences, for their personal lives as well as for their art:

> The publication of woman's subjectivity is ... not equivalent to her liberation, for it has consequences (often unpleasant ones) for her personal happiness. As far as women are concerned, no distinction is made between the *writer* and the *person*. Woman's desire for

public involvement and equality in the cultural sphere is thus broken by the desire to protect her own self.[57]

In order to understand fully what Ecker means when she says that for women "no distinction is made between the writer and the person" one has only to imagine the consequences for a woman of a phrase like Flaubert's notorious "Madame Bovary c'est moi." Recourse to literary clichés may have offered women what they perceived as a false representation of their reality, but at the same time it afforded them protection from the exposure that more direct self-expression necessarily entailed. As late as 1910, a journalist and writer known by the pseudonym Donna Paola, whose main interest lay in examining the transformations that had taken place in women's lives in the years since Unification, was to point out that it was still far easier for women to write silly love stories than to express their thoughts about their condition as women:

> Io penso che il narrar delle storielle d'amanti sia ben meschina audacia a confronto di quella che occorrerebbe ad una donna per esporre al pubblico non già il solo lato della sua intimità personale, ma tutto l'intero prisma del suo pensiero e della sua coscienza; tutte le idee, tutte le convinzioni, tutti i giudizi, tutte le delusioni e le speranze che il suo vivere odierno nel bel mezzo della mischia sociale, morale, politica, l'ha obbligata a elaborare, a formulare, a soffrire. Questo è davvero il suo giardino segreto....[58]

Fear of exposure was compounded by a profound sense of writing as an unfeminine, even transgressive activity. There were no George Eliots, George Sands, Jane Austens, Mme. de Staëls or Brontë sisters to stand behind the fledgling female novelist in late-nineteenth-century Italy. As the article by Capuana cited at the beginning of this introduction clearly indicates, the woman writer of this period was perceived as nothing less than a trespasser invading a masculine domain – unless of course she confined herself to the pedagogical writing which the dominant culture had designated as the only appropriate vehicle for the female voice.[59] Writing novels in this prescriptive climate was difficult enough and a source of conflict in and of itself; going so far as to challenge canonical representations was an anxiety-provoking experience which called women writers into question as both women and writers. To shield themselves from this anxiety, as well from the watchdogs of public morality, they devised strategies which can be said to be the hallmark of their work and which the essays in this volume attempt to delineate.

These strategies allowed them to express their subversive impulses toward the tradition without completely abandoning a facade of "feminine" submission. As such, they reflect an inordinate degree of both personal and literary self-consciousness.

By the latter I mean that all four writers deliberately engage at least as much with previous literature as with "reality" itself. While Neera and Sibilla Aleramo seem content to simply re-write aspects of the traditional, and even not-so-traditional, depiction of women, Matilde Serao and the Marchesa Colombi share a very modern and precocious awareness that literary language and structures are not mimetic and transparent, and that they filter and *construct* images of reality rather than reflecting reality directly: metafiction, parody, pastiche, authorial intrusion all testify to this awareness. This insistence on literature as literature may reflect, in part, a desire to avoid confronting major social issues of the period head-on. Most certainly it marks a search for literary identity through the critical appraisal of those aspects of the tradition experienced as most inauthentic and even as damaging to women.

The first essay in this volume, "The Marchesa Colombi: The Madwoman vs. Manzoni" begins by examining the various ways in which this author's experience of writing as a transgressive act is inscribed in her work; then, through a close reading of a little-known novel, *Il tramonto di un ideale*, it brings to light her suppressed desire to subvert the influence of Alessandro Manzoni's *I promessi sposi* on the Italian novel. This desire is projected onto a destitute, barely articulate, "minor" character known as the Madwoman, whose rudimentary knowledge of the alphabet leads to her unwitting interception of her master's correspondance with his beloved and to the sabotage of their marriage plans. A second essay on the same writer, "The Marchesa Colombi's *Un matrimonio in provincia*: Style as Subversion" demonstrates how she finally found a narrative voice of her own, despite the anxieties caused her by the wish to overthrow the authority of patriarchal plots and styles. An analysis of *Matrimonio*, as well of the two novels leading up to it, shows how she slowly came to grips with and discarded the major narrative models of her time to forge a startlingly modern, pre-expressionistic style which brings to mind that of the contemporary writer Natalia Ginzburg. More than any of our writers, the Marchesa Colombi confirms Elaine Showalter's belief that "the feminist content of feminine art is typically oblique, displaced, ironic, and subversive; [that] one has to read it between the lines, in the missed possibilities of the text."[60]

"Neera: The Literary Career of a Woman of the Nineteenth Century" traces the development of this writer's career over a period of forty years and demonstrates that its trajectory was determined, above all, by her desire to protect her identity and reputation as a woman, which she saw as seriously threatened by her role as a novelist. As we shall see, for Neera, writing novels was an experience equal in peril and intensity only to love of the most subversive kind: adulterous passion. In order to diminish the conflicts this caused her, she began to devote herself assiduously to moralistic essay-writing and journalism. These activities mitigated but did not completely erase her anxieties, which remain embedded in her writing in the most cryptic and fascinating manner. A second study, "The Search for Literary Mothers: Neera's *Teresa*" uncovers the conscious and unconscious strategies she devised to connect herself covertly to three of the most prominent and controversial women writers of her century (George Eliot, George Sand and Mme. de Staël) despite overt devaluations of their persons and achievements in her non-fiction.

"The Early Matilde Serao: An Author in Search of A Character" provides a different answer to the question of why Serao's literary achievements, so promising at first, slowly yielded completely to the demands of the popular market, and why, though she broke new ground as a woman, she was unable to transpose this spirit into her writing in a sustained fashion. It concentrates on her early attempts to combat the stereotypical literary representation of women and love, and shows how these efforts finally came to naught with the waning of the naturalist movement. It also shows how the meta-fictional sub-text of an early novel, *Fantasia*, inscribes both her insecurities about writing and her hostility to her literary heritage.

"Strategies of Intertextuality: Sibilla Aleramo's *Una donna*" proposes a new reading of this controversial novel which emphasizes not its autobiographical elements but its attempt to re-write and distance itself from previous literary solutions to the dilemma of the woman in an unhappy marriage. From this perspective, it emerges less as the profoundly revolutionary text it is usually thought to be, and more as a sort of *Doll's House* re-written for a Catholic society by a woman still full of conflict and ambivalence about her decision to "speak openly" of her desires.

The closing essay, "Pirandello and the Woman Writer: A Reading of *Suo marito*" examines the fictional portrayal of a woman writer of the turn-of-the-century as constructed by arguably the most important Italian author since Unification, playwright, novelist, essayist and acute observer of the times, Luigi Pirandello. As it traces Silvia Roncella's troubled evolution from "secret scribbler" to high-profile writer, *Suo marito* not only exposes the problems creativity and professionalism posed for women in Italian society of the time, it also gives voice to the culture's anxieties about the emergence of women from their long-held place in the shadows of society. Pirandello's sensitivity to the complexities of his female character's situation makes this novel an extremely important contribution to the understanding of the conflicts, acknowledged and otherwise, that plagued literary women of the time.

Three of the writers in question here, Neera, the Marchesa Colombi and Matilde Serao were fortunate enough to have enjoyed a brief respite, if not from their anxieties as such, at least from the crippling influence these anxieties could exert on their work. The moment was fleeting and coincided with the influence of *verismo*, the Italian version of naturalism, as a liberating force for Italian writers in general, still locked into themes and forms no longer adequate to express the new post-Risorgimento realities. For the women in question here, *verismo* provided the opportunity to put aside the adultery theme, which dominated the bourgeois novel of the time, and to represent instead the lives of women frustrated in their quest for emotional and sexual fulfillment by societal and familial restrictions. All three do this by turning largely to the plight of the younger, unmarried woman as an alternate source of inspiration: Neera in *Teresa* (1887), the Marchesa Colombi in *Un matrimonio in provincia* (1885) and Matilde Serao in *Il romanzo della fanciulla* (1885).

What *verismo* allowed these writers was, more than anything, direct access to their own preoccupations, and often, as a result, to their own potential for art. *Verismo* functioned as a means of escape from the prisonhouse of literary stereotypes for male writers too, as in the case of Verga, for whom it provided access to the peasant culture in his own Sicilian backyard. The way in which women writers needed to be liberated was somewhat different, however. Verga had only to be freed from the literary past; women had to be freed from their own fear of exposure as well. Benedetto Croce has suggested that the rise of socialism and the literary institutionalization of many of its preoccupations and constituencies in naturalism legitimized, in part, the new focus on women's problems by the women writers of *verismo*.[61] The implications of this suggestion are greater than they seem: *verismo* did not make women aware of their problems, but it did provide a "discourse" or framework within which to bring them out. This took a part of the onus off the woman writer as an individual speaking for *herself* as she exposed the difficulties encountered by her sex. In other words, whatever fears she may have had of being personally or politically implicated are, if not entirely allayed, certainly diminished, as she camouflages her concerns in the "protective colouration" of the rhetoric of oppression. This in fact is confirmed by Neera, in an article published in 1888 entitled "Le donne che piangono":

> Noi rechiamo alla luce del sole i derelitti e gli sventurati presentandoli alla vostra pietà.... La causa che meglio abbisogna di quest'opera paziente è la causa della donna.... Ecco la donna – noi diciamo – ecco le sue lagrime.... Mi si disse ingiusta, pessimista, partigiana del mio sesso, quando in lavori scritti col più ardente amore del prossimo osai difendere la donna, la donna pura, la donna caduta, quella che ama e quella che non ama, la donna sempre, per ciò solo che è donna, vale a dire oppressa.[62]

If the social discourse of the moment provided one sort of camouflage, *verismo*'s ideology of the writer as *impersonal* observer offered another: like the male pseudonym in earlier times, it afforded "the *formal* possibility of overcoming the contradiction between self-protection and self-expression."[63] Paradoxically, the more she felt protected, the more the woman writer felt free to turn to her own preoccupations as a source of literary inspiration: in other words, the more "personal" she became. The paradox in fact is such that Serao, in *Il romanzo della fanciulla*, recognized as the best work of her naturalist phase, offers us some glimpses of *herself* as a young girl, the only ones, in fact, that we have. When she writes about the life of a journalist and the world of journalism (*Vita e avventure di Riccardo Joanna*), she hides behind a male protagonist, but in the *Romanzo* we see her directly, as a rambunctious, somewhat ungainly young woman, given to reading literary periodicals under her desk as a student in *Scuola normale femminile* and as an operator in *Telegrafi dello stato*. Similarly, Neera, in *Teresa*, often interferes in the narration to express openly her indignation about the lot of women caught between "il ridicolo della verginità e la vergogna del matrimonio di convenienza."[64] And in *Un matrimonio in provincia* the Marchesa Colombi, for the first time, uses a first-person female narrator when, in the past, she had used the female voice only as one of several voices in the epistolary novel, or not at all, preferring to hide behind male first-person narrators.

By emphasizing the felicitous influence of *verismo* on the female voice of this period I do not mean to suggest that this did, in fact, allow women writers to represent "realistically" the condition of women – literary characters and situations are obviously never the direct projection of historical and social ones, and cannot be used as documents, whatever the intentions of their creators. Women's texts are, however, documents of the condition of women as writers, provided one can decode the complex mediations through which this condition expresses itself. What I hope emerges clearly from the attempt to do so represented by these essays, is that the primary concern of these writers was the contemporary legitimization of their persons as *women* and of their endeavours as *artists*: a contradictory process so fraught with tensions and ambiguities that it often drowned out their voices. What *verismo* provided was temporary relief from the impossible pressures of these contrasting imperatives.

Notes

[1] The article has been reprinted, with an introduction and a postscript, as a small volume entitled *Letteratura femminile*, ed. G. Finocchiaro Chimirri (Catania: C.U.E.C.M., 1988). The paragraph cited here is on page 19. On the proliferation of women writers in this period and on some of the characteristics of their work see A. Arslan, "Ideologia e autorappresentazione: Donne intellettuali fra Ottocento e Novecento," *Svelamento. Sibilla Aleramo: una biografia intellettuale*, eds. A. Buttafuoco and M. Zancan (Milan: Feltrinelli, 1988) 164-177. See also the introductions to the following anthologies: A. Santoro, *Narratrici italiane dell'Ottocento* (Naples: Federico & Ardia, 1987); G. Morandini, *La voce che è in lei: Antologia della narrativa femminile italiana fra '800 e '900* (Milan: Bompiani, 1980); also, A. Nozzoli, "La letteratura femminile in Italia tra Ottocento e Novecento," *Tabù e coscienza: La condizione femminile nella letteratura italiana del Novecento* (Florence: La nuova Italia, 1978) 1-40.

[2] R. Bonghi, "Lettera a Celestino Bianchi (9 marzo 1855)," *Lettere critiche: Perché la letteratura italiana non sia popolare in Italia* (1856), ed. E. Villa (Milan: Marzorati, 1971) 66-69.

[3] Arslan 164.

[4] B. Croce, *Storia d'Italia dal 1871 al 1915*, tenth ed. (Bari: Laterza, 1953) 89.

[5] Capuana 21-22.

6 The glaring omission of any mention of Aleramo is also pointed out by Chimirri in her Postscript to the article, pp. 76-77. Moreover, in order to avoid taking responsibility for these and other remarks, Capuana attributes them to the scientist and writer Angelo Camillo De Meis (1817-1891), with whom he claims to have had an exchange on the subject many years previous.

7 This particular review of Pirandello's has been reprinted in S. Zappulla Muscarà, *Pirandello in guanti gialli* (Caltanisetta: Salvatore Sciascia, 1983) 219-225.

8 G. Menasci, "Neera," *Nuova antologia di scienze, lettere ed arti* 16 Sept. 1901: 267.

9 Letter to Paolina Greppi, 21 February 1890 in G. Verga, *Lettere a Paolina*, ed. G. Raya, (Rome: Fermenti, 1980) as cited in F. Bruni, Introduction, *Il romanzo della fanciulla*, by M. Serao (Naples, Liguori, 1985) x.

10 L. Baldacci, Introduction, *Teresa*, by Neera (Turin: Einaudi, 1976) vii.

11 Nozzoli, in discussing writers of this period, emphasizes "l'assenza nella letteratura della nuova Italia di ogni accenno al problema della emancipazione femminile," as a result of which any criticism of the work of women writers "dovrà in primo luogo insistere sulle falsificazioni e gli pseudovalori diffusi attraverso l'opera letteraria [delle donne]" (pp. 2-3); from this perspective Neera and the Marchesa Colombi emerge as "portatrici di una inconfessata, rancorosa, repressa coscienza del proprio asservimento" (p. 5). Arslan, writing as recently as 1988, also insists repeatedly on the fact that the major female writers of this period were unable to take strong positions on the role of women in their novels: "E se nei loro romanzi ... è indubbio un intento di denuncia sociale ... e si avverte l'eco del grande dibattito sulla questione femminile della fine del secolo ... si percepisce anche il riflesso di tante malinconiche costatazioni sull'inevitabilità della sconfitta finale delle protagoniste, in un 'ritorno all'ordine' vissuto con rancorosa soggezione, attraverso la riconferma delle norme sociali. Le norme di una società che è organizzata secondo prospettive completamente maschili, e che invano le eroine di queste opere hanno sfidato – o tentato di sfidare" (pp. 168-69).

12 Matilde Serao (1857-1927) is best known as a representative of the Italian naturalist movement *verismo*, at least in the early stages of her career, and as the first high-profile Italian female journalist, co-founder of two major newspapers, *Il Giorno* and *Il Mattino*; Sibilla Aleramo (Rina Faccio, 1876-1960), is the author of the explosive autobiographical novel *Una donna* (1906), considered a feminist manifesto as well as a milestone in the history of women's writing in Italy. Neera (Anna Radius Zuccari, 1846-1918) is the subject of two major essays by Croce who, in 1942, brought out a collection of her major works in a volume published by Garzanti. Since Luigi Baldacci's 1975 Einaudi reprint of her most important novel *Teresa* (1886), there has been considerable renewed interest in her work and other reprints have followed. The Marchesa Colombi (Maria Antonietta Torriani Torelli, 1849-1920) was, for a brief period, the wife of Eugenio Torelli-Viollier, founding editor of the *Corriere della Sera*, Italy's most prestigious daily newspaper. Her work has come to the attention of contemporary critics since the 1973 Einaudi reprint of *Un matrimonio in provincia*, introduced by Natalia Ginzburg, and with a brief critical assessment by Italo Calvino. In 1988, another novel, *Prima morire* (1881), was re-issued by Lucarini, with an introduction by Giuliana Morandini.

13 E. Showalter, *A Literature of Their Own: British Women Novelists from Brontë to Lessing* (Princeton: Princeton University Press, 1977).

14 N. K. Miller, "Emphasis Added: Plots and Plausibilities in Women's Fiction," *The New Feminist Criticism*, ed. E. Showalter (New York: Pantheon, 1985) 341. This essay first appeared in *PMLA* 96 (1981): 36-48.

15 For an account of feminist literary history which favors the French see T. Moi, *Sexual/Textual Politics: Feminist Literary Theory* (London: Methuen, 1985); for the Anglo-

American historically-based perspective see J. Todd, *Feminist Literary History* (New York: Routledge, 1988).

[16] S. Weigel, "Double Focus: On the History of Women's Writing," *Feminist Aesthetics*, ed. G. Ecker, trans. H. Anderson (Boston: Beacon Press, 1985) 60.

[17] In her well-known essay "Emphasis Added: Plots and Plausibilities in Women's Fiction," Nancy K. Miller locates the sign of feminine difference in literature in what she calls "demaximization." By this she means a sort of subversive change of emphasis brought to bear by women writers on traditional genre conventions, defined by Gérard Genette as "a body of maxims and prejudices which constitute both a vision of the world and a system of values," but which normally "function like a system of natural forces and constraints which the narrative obeys as if without noticing them, and *a fortiori* without naming them." (G. Genette, "Vraisemblance et motivation," Figures II [Paris: Editions du Seuil, 1969], as translated by and quoted in Miller 343.) I quote from Miller's essay inasmuch as it provides an accurate, though not complete, formulation of my own findings in this study: "In what is perhaps the best-known statement of contemporary French feminist thinking about women's writing, 'The Laugh of the Medusa,' Hélène Cixous states that, 'with a few rare exceptions, there has not been any writing that inscribes femininity.' On the contrary, what she finds historically in the texts of the 'immense majority' of female writers is 'workmanship [which is] in no way different from male writing, and which either obscures women or reproduces the classic representations of women (as sensitive-intuitive-dreamy, etc.).' I think this assertion is both true and untrue. It is true if one is looking for a radical difference in women's writing and locates that difference in an insurgence of the body, in what Julia Kristeva has called the irruption of the semiotic. And it is true if difference is sought on the level of the sentence, or in what might be thought of as the biofeedback of the text. If, however, we situate difference in the insistence of a certain thematic structuration, in the form of content, then it is not true that women's writing has been in no way different from male writing. I consider the 'demaximization' wrought by Mme de Lafayette to be one example of how difference can be read." (Miller 341)

[18] E. Showalter, "Feminist Criticism in the Wilderness," *Critical Inquiry* 8.2 (1981): 179-206 now in *The New Feminist Criticism*, ed. E. Showalter (New York: Pantheon, 1985) 243-270.

[19] S. Gilbert and S. Gubar, *The Madwoman in the Attic: The Woman Writer and the Nineteenth Century Literary Imagination* (New Haven: Yale University Press, 1979) 45. See, in particular, chapter 2, "Infection in the Sentence: The Woman Writer and the Anxiety of Authorship."

[20] L. Goldmann, *Pour une sociologie du roman* (Paris: Gallimard, 1964).

[21] On Mozzoni and the rise of the feminist movement in Italy see the rich and extremely detailed volume by F. Pieroni Bortolotti, *Alle origini del movimento femminile in Italia, 1848-1892* (Turin: Einaudi, 1963) and, also by F. Pieroni Bortolotti, *Sul movimento politico delle donne. Scritti inediti*, ed. A. Buttafuoco (Rome: Utopia, 1987). Unless otherwise indicated, the information contained in this section derives from these volumes, as well as from the chapters on Italy in G. Parca, *L'avventurosa storia del femminismo* (Milan: Mondadori, 1976).

[22] J.J. Howard, "The Civil Code of 1865 and the Origins of the Feminist Movement in Italy," *The Italian Immigrant Woman in North America*, Proceedings of the Tenth Annual Conference of the American Italian Historical Association, eds. B. B. Caroli, R. F. Harney, L. F. Tomasi (Toronto: The Multicultural Historical Society of Ontario, 1978) 16.

[23] Howard 17.

[24] L. Chiavola Birnbaum, *Liberazione della donna: feminism in Italy* (Middletown: Wesleyan University Press, 1986) 19.

[25] Chiavola Birnbaum 14.

[26] J.J. Howard, "Patriot Mothers in the Post-Risorgimento," *Women, War and Revolution*, eds. C.R. Berkin and C.M. Lovett (New York: Holmes and Meier, 1980) 243.

[27] See Howard, "Patriot Mothers..." for a most interesting and informative account of the lives, activities and accomplishments of these women.

[28] As quoted in Parca 75.

[29] M. Zancan, "La donna," *Letteratura italiana*, vol.5, ed. A. Asor Rosa (Turin: Einaudi, 1986) 822.

[30] Arslan 171.

[31] See G. De Donato, "Donna e società nella cultura moderata del primo Ottocento," *La parabola della donna nella letteratura italiana dell'Ottocento*, by G. De Donato *et al.* (Bari: Adriatica, 1983) 11-96. This essay deals with "la interazione tra il livello dell'organizzazione economico-sociale, con i suoi bisogni e le sue domande, e la definizione dei modelli ideologici e dei ruoli funzionali assegnati alla donna (e i conseguenti risvolti nella letteratura) lungo il corso storico del processo unitario" (p. 15). It also offers a wealth of bibliographical information and citations regarding the debate on the education of women. On the duties of women see pp. 53-63; see also Santoro 18-19.

[32] D. Bertoni Jovine, "Funzione emancipatrice della scuola e contributo dells donna all'attività educativa," *L'emancipazione femminile in Italia. Un secolo di discussioni 1861-1961* (Florence: La Nuova Italia, 1963) 223 ff., cited in F. Pieroni Bortolotti, "A proposito del dibattito risorgimentale sull'educazione femminile," *Sul movimento politico delle donne. Scritti inediti* 119.

[33] See De Donato 17-53.

[34] C. Balbo, *Pensieri ed esempi* (Turin: Unione tipografica edit., 1857); S. Pellico, *Dei doveri degli uomini. (Discorso a un giovane)* (Naples: Gammella, 1834); N. Tommaseo, *La donna* (Milan: Agnelli, 1872); V. Gioberti, *Il gesuita moderno* (Naples: Battelli, 1848-49), all cited in De Donato.

[35] As cited in Parca 58.

[36] As cited in Pieroni Bortolotti, "A proposito del dibattito risorgimentale sull'educazione femminile," 122.

[37] C. Franceschi Ferrucci, *Degli studi delle donne* (Florence: Le Monnier, 1876) 382, as cited in De Donato 19.

[38] G. Calvi, "Le donne italiane," *Rivista europea* 23-24 (1840): 455, as cited in De Donato 18.

[39] Calvi 455, as cited in De Donato 56.

[40] See De Donato 76. Also Zancan 813-817.

[41] Among the supporters of the novel were Giovanni Berchet and Silvio Pellico, both of whom considered the novel an excellent means of providing women with appropriate scenes of domestic harmony. On their participation in this debate, see De Donato 68-74.

[42] C. Cattaneo, "Sul romanzo delle donne contemporanee in Italia," *Scritti letterari, artistici, linguistici e vari*, ed. A. Bertani (Florence: Le Monnier, 1946) 363.

[43] Cattaneo 389.

[44] Cattaneo 362.

[45] Santoro 10.

[46] Morandini 44.

[47] Arslan 168.

[48] On the depiction and function of female characters before the nineteenth century, see Zancan 768-777, 788-803; on the nineteenth century, 813-817. For more specific analyses, M. Pagliara Giacovazzo, "Remissività e trasgressione nel romanzo storico," *La parabola della donna* 171-231, and S. Ghiazza, "La donna nella novella sentimentale," *La parabola della donna* 97-169.

[49] Pagliara Giacovazzo 176.

[50] Q. D. "The Englishness of the English Novel," *Collected Essays*, vol. I, ed. G. Singh (Cambridge: Cambridge University Press, 1983) 318.

[51] De Donato 67.

[52] See Pagliara Giacovazzo 177-181.

[53] On Lucia see Zancan 817 and V. R. Jones, "Lucia and her Sisters: Women in Alessandro Manzoni's *I promessi sposi*," *Women and Italy: Essays on Gender, Culture and History*, eds. Z. Baranski and S. Vinall (London: Macmillan,1991) 209-223.

[54] Pagliara Giacovazzo 182.

[55] See G. Zaccaro, "Da angelo a medusa: le donne della Scapigliatura," *La parabola della donna*, 307-327; A. Cavalli Pasini, "La donna 'fin-de-siècle' tra isteria e misticismo," *La Scienza del romanzo. Romanzo e cultura scientifica tra Otto e Novecento* (Bologna: Patron, 1982) 203-257; Nozzoli 1-19; B. Dijkstra, *Idols of Perversity: Fantasies of Feminine Evil in Fin-de-Siècle Culture* (Oxford: Oxford University Press,1986.); and, of course, M. Praz, *La carne, la morte e il diavolo nella letteratura romantica*, 1930 (Florence: Sansoni, 1976), in particular the chapter entitled "La belle dame sans merci," which treats at length the work of Gabriele D'Annunzio.

[56] J. S. Kennard, "La femme dans le roman italien," *The Colonnade* 14 (1922): 6-7. This is a lecture originally delivered in English in 1904; the works discussed all belong to the late-nineteenth century.

[57] S. Weigel, "Double Focus: On the History of Women's Writing," *Feminist Aesthetics*, ed. G. Ecker (Boston: Beacon Press, 1986) 66.

[58] Donna Paola, *Io, e il mio elettore. Propositi e spropositi di una futura Deputata* (Lanciano: Carabba, 1910) 5, as cited in A. Buttafuoco, "Vite esemplari. Donne di primo Novecento," *Svelamento* 148.

[59] "Dopo l'Unità la maggior parte della produzione letteraria femminile ha intenti pedagogici non solo perché la nuova classe dirigente ha improntato di sé tutta la cultura del tempo e questa prevede appunto un 'ammaestramento' generale alla nuova ideologia ma perché alle donne specificamente (che nel frattempo erano con veemenza uscite dal privato) viene assegnato un *luogo* letterario e una precisa *missione* che è quella dell'educazione, secondo la solita pratica di incanalare le forze eversive" (Santoro 17).

[60] E. Showalter, "Toward a Feminist Poetics," *The New Feminist Criticism: Essays on Women, Literature and Theory*, ed. E. Showalter (New York: Pantheon,1981) 138.

[61] Croce, *Storia d'Italia dal 1871 al 1915* 83.

[62] Neera, "Le donne che piangono," *Fanfulla della Domenica* 15 April 1888, as cited in Arslan 174.

[63] Weigel 67.

[64] Neera, *Teresa* 180.

The Marchesa Colombi: The Madwoman vs Manzoni

Among the many theoretical positions to have emerged in the course of the past thirty years on the specific nature of women's writing, few I believe have been as fertile for students of the nineteenth century in particular as those elaborated in Sandra Gilbert and Susan Gubar's controversial classic, *The Madwoman in the Attic: The Woman Writer and the Nineteenth-Century Literary Imagination*.[1] Gilbert and Gubar focus their attention on nineteenth-century female narrators and poets writing in the English language. Their method is, broadly speaking, psycho-analytic, their point of departure Harold Bloom's theory of literary history as expounded in his well-known volume *The Anxiety of Influence*.[2] Bloom suggests that literary history is really the story of a continuous struggle between fathers and sons, in which sons undergo the influence of their fathers and at the same time attempt to throw it off, in order to finally take their places beside them. If this is the case, wonder Gilbert and Gubar, how does the woman writer fit into this process? Or does she at all?

If, for the nineteenth-century woman novelist, the act of writing for the public represents a break with the silence of the past, and the appropriation of a traditionally male privilege, then she is substantially a writer without a "tradition of her own," to quote Elaine Showalter.[3] The literary models she has at her disposal derive, for the most part, from the male imagination (and this is even more true for Italy than it is for England). Suffocated by an abundance of "fathers," but almost completely bereft of "mothers" – that is to say of behavioural and artistic models capable of legitimizing her own endeavours – the woman writer of the nineteenth century almost inevitably suffers from what Gilbert and Gubar have called "the anxiety of authorship," provoked by the ground-breaking nature of her enterprise. This anxiety invariably leads to a conflictual relationship with the act of writing, which in turn determines, to a large extent, the nature of her work.[4]

In what follows I will attempt to analyze this phenomenon in the work of Maria Antonietta Torriani-Torelli (1840-1920), *nom de plume* La Marchesa Colombi, best known today for her long novella *Un matrimonio in provincia* (1885).[5] The analysis is conducted in three parts: the first attempts to demonstrate how the anxiety of authorship manifests itself in her texts at the most superficial level, and discusses the use of irony as a wilful sign of detachment on her part vis-à-vis her work, which she herself clearly considers inferior. The second part analyzes a story about the place of creative endeavour in a woman's life, and shows how, notwithstanding affirmations to the contrary, Torriani herself has difficulty in conceiving creative activity as anything but an either/or proposition with respect to woman's "true" vocation, love and marriage. The third part focuses on a little-known novel entitled *Il tramonto di un ideale* (1882) and in particular on a meta-literary sub-text which demonstrates the extent to which a lack of prestigious female role models and literary models interferes with her ability to find a narrative voice. In this sub-text the author engages in a veiled attack on Alessandro Manzoni's *I promessi sposi* which betrays both her hostility toward the Italian mainstream narrative tradition as well as her difficulty in finding alternatives to it.

The social and psychological pressures incumbent upon women writers of the time are nowhere as clearly visible as in the work of Torriani. Particularly important are the recurring prefaces and introductions in which she addresses her readers directly. Like Neera and Serao,[6] Torriani used these prefaces to situate herself vis-à-vis her public, to appear as she wished to appear, and not as she might were she judged only by the tenor of her fiction, most of which conforms to the norms of the mass-market novel, specifically conceived for a burgeoning female readership.

The most curious of these prefaces, by far, is the lengthy introduction to a collection of short stories entitled *La cartella n. 4* (1901), in which Torriani sees fit to reassure her readers, in an almost obsessive fashion, that her literary endeavours have but one goal: to enable her to provide her nieces and nephews with appropriate and much longed-for Christmas gifts:

Crescemmo tutti col culto delle strenne; e quando passammo dallo
stato sereno e spensierato di figli di famiglia, a quello più grave assai
di capi di casa, non fu più la parte piacevole di ricevere doni che ci
dette da pensare, ma quella più difficile di farli. Tanto più difficile
poi, per chi deve cavarli dai magri frutti della sua penna.
Io ci penso tutta l'annata. Ed appena passata la burrasca d'un capo
d'anno, mi preparo una cartella nuova, dove raccolgo man mano i
miei lavori brevi per farne un volume, al capo d'anno seguente.
Quella cartella è il mio salvadanari; è la strenna dei miei nipoti; è, per
me, la gioia dei loro desideri appagati, dei loro baci, dei loro sorrisi;
del tripudio dei bambini, delle soddisfazioni vanerelle delle
giovinette, dei loro spassi, delle loro letture. E' per loro una
promessa lungamente aspettata, il realizzarsi d'una speranza, una
prova del mio affetto. E' per tutti un giorno di allegria; una festa in
famiglia.
E che ansietà negli ultimi mesi dell'anno! Grandi e piccini tutti
sappiamo che i doni del capo d'anno sono là in quella cartella in
quegli scartafacci della zia. Ma quelle carte, non sono biglietti di
banca; e perché subiscano questa metamorfosi, occorre un editore.
E se l'editore non capitasse?
E' una minaccia che ci impensierisce tutti, e me più di tutti.
E mi figuravo i visi imbronciati delle mie nipotine capricciose; la
delusione malinconica delle più buone; lo stupore dei bambini, il
loro risentimento dinanzi alle scarpette rimaste tutta la notte al freddo
sul balcone e trovate al mattino vuote raggrinzate dal gelo....
Ma, per fortuna, l'editore non mi manca mai. E' il dono di ceppo
alla zia; forse la provvidenza lo concede alle preghiere dei bambini.
Per tutti i cavallini e le carrozzelle e le armate internazionali di legno
e di piombo che faranno impazzire di gioia i miei bimbi, per tutte le
bambole e le casine e le cucinette ed i corredini, che ispireranno alle
bambine le prime idee casalinghe e materne, pei vezzi, pegli abiti,
pei buoni libri che faranno sorridere o palpitare le giovinette, io
auguro al mio nuovo editore che questo libro gli porti fortuna.[7]

The lady doth protest too much. Whether this is an attempt to disown her
writing, by claiming it is only a means to an end, or merely an attempt to justify it,
the will to write is clearly being camouflaged in terms more socially acceptable for a
woman than undiluted literary ambition; moreover, the fact that she requires seven
pages to say what could easily have been said in one, leads us to believe that we are
dealing here with something more than simply an ironic posture.

Further evidence of such ambiguity is to be found in the preface to another
volume of stories entitled *Dopo il caffé* (1880), a highly ironic "aside" to her female
readers, whom she encourages to use her stories to entertain themselves while their

husbands, absorbed in their newspapers, are busy conducting the affairs of state in the bourgeois comfort of their armchairs: "*Dopo il caffé* tutte le famiglie debbono raccogliersi in un religioso silenzio, dinanzi al kilo ed alle gravi preoccupazioni del capo di casa, che pondera nella sua alta saviezza i destini dei popoli." She assures her audience that her stories are totally unpretentious and suitable for family reading: "Sono storiette semplici; sono le idee e i sentimenti che, poco su poco giù, si scontrano ad ogni uscio; la vita di tutti i giorni. Sono cosuccie che possono leggere anche le loro figliole." On the other hand, Torriani needs to differentiate herself from the public for whom she imagines herself to be writing, and she does this by adopting a somewhat patronizing tone which underscores the fact that she is the first to recognize the limitations of her own work: "Ed i miei personaggi non hanno la pretesa d'insegnare nulla a nessuno, né di sciogliere tesi sociali; e quanto a scopo umanitario, si propongono soltanto quello di aiutare le mie graziose lettrici a sopportare più facilmente l'ora tediosa dopo il caffé."[8]

Distancing devices which are the product of a consciousness that rejects what it is producing, which tell the reader "I am not what I write" are also to be found in the body of her fiction. One such device is to be found at the end of a particularly insipid tale entitled *Un sogno azzurro* (1880), whose happily-ever-after dénouement is alluded to, but not rendered explicit, in such a way as to suggest that the author herself is casting some doubt on the validity of her own creation and seeking complicity with the reader clever enough to see through her stratagem: "Io non amo i particolari, gli epiloghi e le conclusioni che finiscono i romanzi a coda di sorcio. I lettori intelligenti comprendono la fine senza che io metta i punti sugli *i*. E gli altri – peggio per loro."[9]

The same ironic or distancing frame is to be found elsewhere. In more than one case, Torriani claims to be transcribing a story sent to her by someone else, and hence not of her own invention: for example, in *Skating Ring*, the narrator closes by making a direct reference to the author, thus introducing a distinction between the two: "Mando copia del mio manoscritto alla Marchesa Colombi, una vecchia signora che ho conosciuto a Milano, perché lo traduca, se crede, nella sua lingua."[10] Another story, *I morti parlano*, is preceded by a letter from Torriani to the editor of *Fanfulla della domenica*, in which the story is said to have been first published. Torriani claims to be including the letter for the sake of "truth," but her repeated insistence on the origins of the story (ostensibly a word-for-word transcription of two other letters sent to her from America) leads us to believe that what we have here is another distancing device.[11]

A final element worth considering is the pseudonym with which Torriani chooses to submit herself to the public eye: Marchesa Colombi is the feminine form of the name of the most popular character of a very well-known comedy of the time – the Marchese Colombi of Paolo Ferrari's satire of Settecento mores *La satira e Parini* (1856). According to theatrical histories, the Marchese is presented as a fool, the personification of vacuous aristocratic conformity, whose reactions provoked the unmitigated hilarity of the play's audiences and endeared him to them more than any other character.[12] The choice of this pseudonym tells us something about how Torriani saw herself: as a silly, harmless entertainer of mass audiences. It is also, however, a sign of her detachment vis-à-vis this role, clearly assumed as a "mask." But there is more. Most women writers of the nineteenth century adopted pseudonyms that were either clearly masculine or clearly feminine: George Eliot, George Sand, Neera, Contessa Lara, Bruno Sperani, etc. Torriani makes a hybrid choice: a woman's name which alludes clearly to a well-known male fool, as if to suggest that if in taking pen to paper a woman assumes a masculine role, it is only to appear foolish in the process.

That Torriani's *malaise* as a writer derives to a large extent from her doubts as to the legitimacy of feminine literary or artistic ambitions is further substantiated by a long novella entitled *Impara l'arte e mettila da parte* (1897). Here she appears to be reassuring her readers that a woman can undertake some sort of artistic endeavour without necessarily casting doubt on her identity as a woman. As the title itself makes amply clear, she is hardly espousing an extremist viewpoint, but the suggestion of even a slight shift in the economy of a woman's life is deemed so threatening that the novella's conclusion actually transmits a highly ambiguous message which belies even its very tame premise.

The protagonist of the story is Odda, an orphan and amateur artist, still unmarried at the age of twenty-eight. One day, Odda, who lives alone, decides to spend some time with the family of an elderly uncle, which includes his marriageable daughter and his forty-year-old widowed and childless sister. Of the three women, only Odda has something to take her mind off the onerous task of finding a husband, though when her uncle reminds her that "l'arte delle donne ... è di essere buone mogli e buone mamme," she answers in the following fashion:

"Ma crede che, se avessi trovato un uomo come l'avrei voluto, non l'avrei preferito ai pennelli ed alla tavolozza? E che il mio babbo non avrebbe approvata quella preferenza? Ma che! Le pare? Il babbo ha voluto che imparassi un'arte, e se l'avessi preferito mi avrebbe fatto imparare una scienza, o tutt'altra cosa, unicamente per prepararmi una passione di ripiego."[13]

This very cautious and conservative approach to the question might be attributed to Torriani's desire to avoid alienating her readers by putting forth a role model too far removed from prevailing mores: art or science or any interest as a hobby then, as a means of distraction or, in the worst case, as a fall-back position should the occasion for marriage not present itself:

"Le ragazze si mettono in testa d'essere al mondo soltanto per trovare un marito, e non pensano che a quella X incognita e sospirata....
Diamo loro un'occupazione nobile e seria, che le appassioni per se stessa, indipendentemente dall'idea del marito. Se il marito verrà, lo ameranno malgrado la loro occupazione; se non verrà, continueranno a lavorare e ad amare il loro lavoro.... Ecco quel che diceva il babbo." (pp. 11-12)

However, were things really so clear and unequivocal in Torriani's mind, the logical thing would have been to develop the story around the character of Odda and have it unfold in one of two directions: Odda marries and continues to cultivate painting as a hobby, or Odda fails to marry and continues to paint. Instead, Torriani introduces into the economy of the tale the two minor female characters, both without husbands and without "alternatives." The entire plot is centered on the love lives of the three women and on their attempts to alter their situations, and it is from the juxtaposition of their fates that the contradiction inherent in Torriani's thesis emerges. For if her intention is, as it appears to be, to demonstrate that women can pursue other interests without jeopardizing their chances at marriage, then how does one account for the fact that both the cousin and the aunt (neither of whom has cultivated anything other than the fine art of patience and would seem destined, according to Torriani's prescription, for lives of quiet desperation or marriages of convenience) marry the men whom they love while Odda is left holding her paint brushes with Prince Charming nowhere in sight? In fact, as if to add insult to injury, Odda discovers that the man she secretly loves through his art though she does not know him, is the same man who loves her young cousin and eventually marries her.

What is the moral of the tale? That depends where one chooses to focus one's attention. It is true that at first the young cousin, terrified of remaining an "old maid," would have consented to a loveless marriage to an older man had Odda not intervened, whereas Odda herself had turned him down graciously with no qualms. It is also true that the widowed aunt, whose first marriage had been a loveless one as well, says to Odda "non so che fare di me stessa; mi sento vecchia e non mi ci so rassegnare; mi sento inutile al mondo; non so a chi voler bene," (p. 161) while Odda is never quite so desperate. Nonetheless, both the aunt and the cousin finally marry for love, while Odda remains the odd-woman-out, with only her art to console her. It is almost as if the cousin and the aunt were being rewarded for having remained faithful to the traditional feminine role, while Odda is being punished for having attempted to escape it.

Whether or not this dénouement is a purely conventional one representing an apparent concession to prevailing mores and nothing more, it remains that it is as ambiguous as everything else relating to Torriani's view of herself as a writer. It seems superfluous to point out that no one would ever dream of asking the young male artist who marries her cousin the same question that her uncle asks Odda: "E tu, senza figlioli, senza sposo, sola nella tua casa deserta, sei felice perché fai dei quadri?" (p. 117). Men are not spared romantic disappointments in Torriani's narrative universe, but their lives have another dimension as well and it is the right to this second dimension that Torriani seems to be claiming for women, however timidly. And yet, in practice, her ambivalence is so strong that she feels the need to "punish" Odda somehow, even though Odda is merely an amateur painting in the privacy of her home.

If it is true that Odda represents Torriani's ambivalences and conflicts about writing as a career for women, then it is the novel *Il tramonto di un ideale* which illustrates the repercussions of these conflicts on the nature of her art.

The novel's plot is deceptively simple. Giovanni, the son of a poor country doctor, is in love with Rachele, the daughter of a wealthy landowner, but Rachele's father refuses to accept Giovanni as a son-in-law because of his inferior social and economic status. A series of misunderstandings finds Rachele still faithful to Giovanni many years after their paths have diverged, though Giovanni, now himself a wealthy, socially-prominent Milanese lawyer, is totally unaware that his first love is slowly withering away in the provinces awaiting his return. One day, after the death of his father, Giovanni does return to his hometown and discovers, much to his surprise, that Rachele, like himself, is still unmarried. Having had nothing but a series of adulterous affairs, he is finally ready to settle down and allows himself to dream for a while - about the lovely, innocent young woman he courted and loved in his youth. He seeks her out only to find, quite predictably, that she is no longer the Rachele he once knew. Years of isolation and inactivity have turned her into an old maid, a mere ghost of the image he had been carrying around in his mind. Disappointed and depressed, Giovanni returns to Milan to resume the life of an aging but attractive and successful bachelor. Rachele remains a prisoner of her home, devastated by the death of her dream.

If the surface plot of this apparently unexceptional novel is entirely conventional, the same cannot be said of the minor character or of the circumstances responsible for the early misunderstanding between the ill-fated lovers, and for the fact that their paths cross again only when they are too old to be appropriate protagonists of a proper "love story." The character in question is a curious one, a young orphan girl known to everyone as "La Matta" – the Madwoman. She arrives at Giovanni's father's home, no one is quite certain how, at the age of thirteen, becomes the family servant and falls in love with her young master. Her love, however, remains secret, since she is considered semi-demented, and has difficulty communicating effectively. Before coming to work for the doctor, we are told, she had worked for seven years in a cloth factory, and had become almost deaf. Though the doctor often beats her, she is uncomplaining. Occasionally he praises her, but she answers only by shrugging her shoulders and mumbling "I don't know":

> Intontita dai sette lunghi anni che aveva passati in mezzo ai rumori forti, incessanti, della filanda, rimaneva spesso a bocca aperta dopo aver ricevuto un'istruzione, come se non capisse....
> Se il Dottorino la picchiava, perché anche lui aveva le sue ore nere e doveva pure sfogarsi con qualcuno, la Matta si curvava, si rattrappiva sotto le busse, urlava quando sentiva male; ma non faceva lagnanze, non domandava ragione di quel trattamento. Se invece il padrone lodava le sue cucinature e le diceva: "Hai fatto bene" si stringeva nelle spalle come per dire che non c'entrava, oppure rispondeva: "Io non so."[14]

Though Giovanni never stoops to beating her himself, he is as insensitive to her as his father. Nonetheless, La Matta is in love with him, and even resorts to typically feminine wiles to endear herself to him, such as allowing him to win at the games in which he frequently engages her to pass the time. One day, in a fit of boredom, Giovanni decides to try to teach her to read, but he finally gives up, because she learns to recognize only the letter "o": "La serva si prestò volentieri a quel gioco tranquillo e dopo parecchie lezioni riuscì a conoscere l'*o*.... Ma le altre lettere incontrarono maggiori difficoltà ed il fanciullo, impazientito, si disgustò dell'insegnamento, e cercò altri passatempi" (p. 22).

Eventually Giovanni leaves home to study law at Torino. La Matta falls into a depression so severe that she is almost unable to work, and "sarebbe diventata una cattiva massaia, se non avesse avuto un padrone energico, il quale anche a costo di eccitarsi i nervi e farsi del cattivo sangue, seppe correggerla in modo che ne portò le traccie per un pezzo, e comprese la necessità di tornare ai suoi doveri," (p. 25) but no one – certainly not Giovanni's father – is aware that this madwoman has an internal life of her own.

It is during one of Giovanni's visits home from Torino that he meets and falls in love with Rachele. The occasion is a dinner party in her father's home to which Giovanni has been invited along with a group of the town's first citizens. Giovanni is taken with Rachele's blonde beauty immediately, but is made quite self-conscious by the social and economic distance between them. In order to diminish his discomfort, he resorts to a neutral topic of conversation, literature, more precisely *I promessi sposi* and the improvements in the second edition. Rachele, though familiar with the novel, is unaware of the difference between the first and second editions, and proclaims her overwhelming desire to read the corrected version of the novel. Giovanni offers to bring it to her, and so their "love story" begins, apparently under the auspices of the most famous betrothed couple in Italian literature:

> Egli stava sulle difese, ed assumeva modi riservati, serii, da gentiluomo. Avviò colla sua vicina un discorso sulla letteratura; ed essendo romantico e puritano, sparlò dei novatori, e fece un lungo elogio dei *Promessi sposi*, insistendo sui miglioramenti della seconda edizione. La Rachele aveva letto i *Promessi sposi* in collegio, ma non aveva badato all'edizione e non sapeva che differenza ci fosse fra la prima e la seconda.

> Immaginandosi di fare cosa grata al suo ospite, disse che aveva letto
> la prima edizione, e che si struggeva di conoscere la seconda. Si
> mostrò anzi desolata di esser giunta alla sua età senza aver letto i
> *Promessi sposi* corretti. Giovanni le offrì premurosamente di
> portarglieli, ed ella diede segni di grande gioia. (pp. 47-48)

However, Giovanni and Rachele are not to be as "fortunate," in the long run, as Renzo and Lucia. When Giovanni finally works up the courage to ask Rachele's father for her hand, he finds himself categorically rejected as socially unsuitable. On the eve of his departure for Torino, desperate to obtain a promise from Rachele in spite of her father's veto, Giovanni decides to send La Matta to Rachele's home under the pretext of asking her to return the second edition of *I promessi sposi*. In his note to her, Giovanni asks Rachele to wait until he has established himself as a lawyer and can ask for her hand from a position of strength. He asks her to communicate her positive answer by writing "Yes" on a sheet of paper she is to hide between the pages of the novel:

> "... se mai, se nel tuo cuore, c'è forza bastante per questo sacrificio,
> metti una parola, un sì nel volume dei *Promessi sposi*, che ti prestai
> e che la Matta ridomanderà per avere un pretesto di presentarsi in
> casa tua, dove io sarei discacciato." (p. 100)

Rachele complies. La Matta, however, refuses to act as a simple messenger. Though she does not know exactly what is transpiring, her instincts tell her that her own interests are at stake, and she removes the sheet of paper to attempt to decipher the message on it.

Giovanni, meanwhile, is bursting with impatience. Instead of waiting at home for La Matta to return, he dashes out to meet her. As soon as he sees her he tears the volume of *I promessi sposi* from her hands, unaware that La Matta has had to hide the piece of paper she was scrutinizing in her apron, since there was no time to replace it. Finding no reply to his request, Giovanni returns to Torino thinking himself rejected. The rest is a foregone conclusion: though armed with the best intentions – he still wishes to pursue his goal of establishing himself in order to ask for Rachele's hand with or without her promise – he finally yields to the temptations of life in the big city and forgets her. Only after many years, and a major romantic disappointment, do his thoughts turn again to Rachele. Quite coincidentally, shortly afterward, his father dies. La Matta, who is still in love with him, and thinks that she will now be able to live with and serve Giovanni as in the past, turns up on his doorstep in Milan with all the furniture from his father's home, including the old bookcase containing the second edition of *I promessi sposi*, a reminder of his ill-fated "love story." In a fit of nostalgia, he picks up the volume and leafs through it, only to come upon the piece of paper he had expected to find some twenty years earlier:

> Giovanni rimase sbalordito, convulso. Era certissimo che quella lettera non era nel libro quando la Matta glielo aveva riportato.
> "Quella stupida donna!" pensò. "L'avrà tolta fuori per la curiosità di cercare gli *o* sulla soprascritta. Poi l'avrà rimessa a posto troppo tardi...."
> E si perdé a fantasticare da che piccole cause dipendono i nostri destini; e che cosa sarebbe stato di lui, se da bambino non gli fosse venuta l'idea di insegnare ad una serva scema le lettere dell'alfabeto....
> E' tutto quel romanzo alla Dickens d'amor puro, di gioie intime, di vita casalinga che sarebbe stata la sua vita senza quella circostanza affatto casuale, gli si presentò alla mente e gli parve un sorriso di cielo. (pp. 232-235)

The significance of this "love story" gone awry, subverted by dint of fortuitous circumstance and as a result of the interference of a character known as the Madwoman is, I believe, best understood in the light of Gilbert and Gubar's observations on the role of such figures in women's novels of the nineteenth century. In their view, the Madwoman is a character to whom the women writer resorts when she is unable to accept her own desire to rebel against patriarchal institutions and conventions. By projecting feelings of anger and insubordination onto a character who is already "condemned," so to speak, she condemns the part of herself reflected in the Madwoman without however having to renounce these feelings: in other words, the Madwoman represents a sort of "compromise formulation" of difficult-to-acknowledge feelings.[15] This identification on the part of the writer with her also explains why, in women's writing, the Madwoman is almost always represented as having a very rich interior life, as opposed to the vacuous Madwoman evoked by male writers.[16] Moreover, this interior life is depicted as a dimension which completely escapes the male characters by whom she is surrounded.

In her portrait of La Matta, Torriani repeatedly calls our attention to the abyss that separates Giovanni's and his father's perceptions of her, and her actual emotional and psychological states. When, on account of Giovanni's imminent departure, she is so upset that she is no longer able to work, Giovanni thinks only that "forse c'era qualcuno malato in casa della sua balia" (p. 82); similarly, during a conversation with Giovanni, Rachele catches a glimpse of La Matta spying on them, but Giovanni dismisses her anxieties by saying "non badarci. E' la Matta" (p. 91). For Giovanni La Matta is not only harmless, she barely exists. In fact, when she turns up on his doorstep in Milan with the family furniture, it never crosses his mind to inquire after her motivations and it certainly never occurs to him that she may now wish to re-establish their old ties. La Matta, on the other hand, is only too aware of his indifference, and reacts like any woman scorned by the man she loves:

> Era una sentenza definitiva. Non voleva tenerla con sé. Era finita, non c'era più speranza. Il lungo sogno della sua povera vita svaniva, il suo grande amore da schiava era respinto dal padrone. In quella immensa rovina parve alla Matta che il mondo crollasse intorno a lei, che la spingessero sola in un immenso deserto. (p. 199)

If La Matta's love for him escapes his notice completely, this does not, as we know, diminish its importance as a factor contributing to the outcome of his "love story" with Rachele. If they are "betrothed" in her eyes only, it is precisely because of the servant girl's interference in their affairs. Both their destinies are dictated by La Matta's love for Giovanni and by his total indifference to her, and hence his lack of awareness of her as a possible agent in his "love story." Not only is the "promise" of Rachele to Giovanni not protected by providence, divine or otherwise, it is subverted by ill-fortune, that is by the fortuitous coincidence in time of La Matta's interfering gesture and Giovanni's own impatience:

> E si ricordò con una lucidezza fenomenale tante circostanze che gli erano sfuggite allora. L'improvviso voltarsi della Matta per evitarlo quand'egli era andato, nella sua impazienza amorosa, ad incontrarla per via; il suo imbarazzo, la resistenza a dargli il libro, l'insistenza con cui reclamava ancora di portarlo lei quand'egli lo aveva già ripreso; e finalmente l'averla trovata nella sua camera col libro in mano quand'era salito l'ultima volta per pigliare il baule. Coll'abitudine delle induzioni e delle ricerche acquistata nella sua lunga carriera legale, tutto questo gli risultò chiaro, e disse:
> "Allora aveva riposta la lettera nel volume."
> E si perdé a fantasticare da che piccole cause dipendono i nostri destini; e che cosa sarebbe stato di lui, se da bambino non gli fosse venuta l'idea di insegnare ad una serva scema le lettere dell'alfabeto.... (pp. 234-235)

La Matta's love is never presented as an obstacle, surmountable through patience or through the interference of a powerful third person: on the contrary, it is an extraneous element, a malign *deus-ex-machina*, which interrupts the course of their relationship and then has it momentarily resume, much later, only to bring out the fragile and "illusory" nature of the feelings on which it was based. In fact, when Giovanni sees Rachele again after many years we discover that he has loved not Rachele, but an image of Rachele. Once this image is no longer possible to sustain, his love for her falters as well: "Era ancora Rachele, ma non era più il suo ideale; ed il cuore di Giovanni rimaneva freddo e calmo nel ritrovarla" (p. 255). In any case, by this time at least a third of the novel has been dedicated to Giovanni's adulterous adventures in Milan. It is too late for their relationship to resume, especially on the more-idealized-than-ever literary terms in which Giovanni now imagines it:

> Rachele doveva essere ormai una donna affascinante. Ed era orfana; l'avrebbe accolto sola coll'ospitalità d'una castellana.
> Dopo tanto tempo forse non lo sperava più. Che commozione doveva provare al rivederlo! Doveva essere una scena da medio evo, rappresentata da una bella donnina moderna e da un *lion*. Si figurava di giungere a cavallo, sollevando un nembo di polvere, e di vedere la sua dama salita sull'alto della torre come la moglie desolata di Malborough, *pour voir s'il reviendra*.
> S'addormentò in mezzo a quelle fantasie rosee, e sognò sogni di poesia e d'amore.
> La mattina si alzò presto, impaziente di correre a Fontanetto, di rientrare in quel romanzo d'amore giovanile e puro, di portare quella *sorpresa di piacere* alla donna onesta e fedele che lo aveva aspettato. (pp. 237-238)

Keeping in mind the insistence with which Torriani repeatedly underlines the literary nature of Giovanni and Rachele's idyll, it is perhaps possible to conclude that La Matta's unrequited love for Giovanni, aimed at interrupting that idyll, may have a meta-literary dimension, above and beyond its superficial narrative function. It may in fact be a sign of Torriani's intolerance of and hostility toward the social and cultural values of which Manzoni's *I promessi sposi* was still considered, at the time, the highest and most venerated expression. In fact La Matta's love for Giovanni is never presented as having any possibility of realization; its only function, from the very beginning, is to interrupt and later to discredit the love story between Rachele and Giovanni. To this end, it operates slowly and unobtrusively throughout the novel as a sort of subversive sub-text which, without ever actually supplanting the surface text, certainly undermines it, by preventing it from unfolding according to the well-known Manzonian parabola.

This interpretation is supported not only by Torriani's generalized intolerance toward the "sacred cows" of the patriarchal literary tradition,[17] but also, and more specifically, by a rather cutting remark about *I promessi sposi* and Manzoni's much-touted realism to be found in another novel. The fact that this rather abrupt dismissal of the great novelist's portrayal of Lucia is attributed to the female protagonist of *Prima morire* (1881), described as an avid reader of contemporary novels, only serves to cast on it the degree of ambiguity necessary to authenticate it:

> Per quanto il Manzoni lo affermi, dai fatti e dal contegno di quei due si capisce che non si amano. Una donna che ama non farebbe mai quello stupido voto di Lucia, di non sposare il suo Renzo. Potrebbe imporsi qualunque sacrificio, ma non quello; l'amore è la sua speranza, la sua vita; a cosa le serve di vivere e di serbarsi pura se non dev'essere pel suo amante? Allora tanto faceva che si fosse uccisa per sottrarsi a quel pericolo.[18]

Torriani's *antimanzonismo* is certainly not unique in this period: to cite only one other example (but a particularly significant one for our purposes) in 1895, Cletto Arrighi, a member of the Milanese Scapigliatura, announced the imminent publication of a work entitled *Gli sposi non promessi. Parafrasi e contrapposti dei promessi sposi*. The work never did appear but Arrighi's goal was to "radicalmente trasformare personaggi, ruoli, modelli, valori dell'universo manzoniano, coerentemente con la sua strategia di dissacrazione del mondo borghese e della tradizione culturale di cui Manzoni è appunto, a parer suo emblema."[19] It is to be noted that while Arrighi speaks openly of transformation, Torriani, plagued by the conflicts and ambivalences that derive from her experience of writing as an infraction of normative behaviour, depicts her intolerance of received values as a form of deviation: this interpretation is supported not only by her description of La Matta, but also by her need to explicitly insinuate that La Matta may be the illegitimate child of a black servant, among the most marginal and least "reassuring" characters imaginable in a conventional literary universe:

> Era bruna di carni, con molti capelli d'un nero carbone, che, a forza di ungerli, riduceva come una massa compatta e levigata. Aveva dei grandi occhi neri infossati con le ciglia lunghe e folte, e le sopracciglia esagerate che si riunivano sopra il naso corto e un po' monco alla punta. Gli zigomi sporgenti, le mandibole larghe, e le

labbra grosse, che lasciavano vedere dei grossi denti bianchi, le davano l'aria d'una mulatta. A Novara, a ricordanza della vecchia Lucia, c'era stato un negro al servizio d'una famiglia nobile, che sfoggiava quell'oggetto di curiosità dietro la carrozza di parata. La Lucia aveva sempre sospettato che la Matta fosse figlia di quel negro. (pp. 27-28)

Seen from this perspective, the character of Rachele also acquires a dimension which overrides her narrative function. Like that of La Matta, her attitude becomes a metaphor for one of the terms of Torriani's conflict: if La Matta represents the desire to rebel, Rachele, the daughter of an authoritarian father whose orders she obeys without flinching, obviously represents the desire to conform to patriarchal directives. In fact, it is Rachele herself who is responsible for her life of solitude and renunciation. Her passivity and unconditional obedience to the wishes of her father force Giovanni to call on La Matta as a messenger in order to communicate with her; this intromission of La Matta into their relationship will, of course, be the cause of its failure to unfold as expected. Torriani's description of Rachele's traditional and entirely banal beauty – "i capelli d'un bel biondo d'oro, gli occhi azzurri, le labbra vermiglie" (p. 31) – carries more than a touch of irony, which resonates again in a later clandestine midnight exchange between the two young lovers. Here again, Torriani takes advantage of the situation to underline the literary and artificial nature of this "love story":

Alzò tutte e due le mani, come per implorare di stringere le sue malgrado la distanza. Ella si sporse, si curvò sul parapetto; ma non si raggiunsero.
Allora Giovanni si sentì preso da scoraggiamento al vedersi così diviso da lei, e le disse:
"Oh Dio! E se il tuo babbo mi dicesse di no?"
"Per carità; non pensarlo," rispose Rachele. "Sarebbe terribile."
"Ma se mai, di', cosa faresti?"
"Morirei," sussurrò la giovinetta.
"No, no. Questi sono romanzi, disse Giovanni con impazienza. E poi, io non voglio che tu muoia. Voglio che tu viva e che tu sia mia ad ogni costo. Di', lo sarai?"
"Sì."
"Anche se tuo padre non vuole?"
"Questo è impossibile." (p. 89)

The Torriani case would seem to confirm the destiny of the woman writer deprived of female models and condemned to search for a literary voice in a male tradition. In *Il tramonto di un ideale*, she articulates precisely this dilemma: the difficulties encountered by the "motherless" woman writer, incapable of imagining alternatives which are neither the norm (Rachele) nor a deviation from the norm (La Matta).

A final observation brings us back to Torriani's perennial ambiguity, a particularly significant example of which is to be found in the curious origin she attributes to the nickname "La Matta":

> Quando, appena nata, aveva fatto il suo malinconico ingresso nell'ospizio dei trovatelli, doveva essere stata accolta da una monaca sentimentale, che le aveva imposto il nome tenero di Amata.
> La contadina che l'aveva presa a balia e tutta la sua famiglia, l'avevano chiamata la Matta alla prima, e malgrado tutte le correzioni della monaca ... avevano continuato a dir sempre quella loro storpiatura....
> Una volta Giovanni ... le domandò:
> "Perché ti chiamano la Matta?"
> "Non so," rispose la serva.
> "E' il tuo nome?" disse ancora Giovanni.
> "No. Il mio nome è la Mata."
> "La Mata non è un nome."
> "Io non so."
> Giovanni riuscì ad avere una spiegazione da qualche compagno di scuola o dalla maestra, ed al ritorno andò in cucina tutto trionfante per ripeterla alla serva. Ma questa disse:
> "La Matta o la Mata fa lo stesso."
> "Ma non è la Mata, è Amata che ti chiami; si dice l'Amata."
> "Io non so," concluse la Matta. Ma guardò lungamente il fanciullo con occhio intenerito, e sorrise in silenzio. (pp. 13-14)

"La Matta" is none other than a deliberate mispelling of "Amata." By choosing a name which suggests, emblematically, two difficult-to-reconcile meanings, Torriani again brings to light her fundamental ambiguity at every level. At the same time, however, and perhaps more importantly, she betrays her affection for this strange creature and validates the hypothesis of her own identification with her.

Notes

[1] The volume by Gilbert and Gubar was published by Yale University Press in 1979. It has since generated considerable discussion and criticism. See in particular, T. Moi, *Sexual/Textual Politics: Feminist Literary Theory* (London: Methuen, 1985) 57-69; J. Todd, *Feminist Literary History* (New York: Routledge, 1988) 26-30.

[2] Bloom's volume was published by Oxford University Press in 1973. Gilbert and Gubar explain his theories in the following terms: "Applying Freudian structures to literary genealogies, Bloom has postulated that the dynamics of literary history arise from the artist's 'anxiety of influence,' his fear that he is not his own creator and that the works of his predecessors, existing before and beyond him, assume essential priority over his own writings. In fact, as we pointed out in our discussion of the metaphor of literary paternity, Bloom's paradigm of the sequential historical relationship between literary artists is the relationship of father and son, specifically that relationship as it was defined by Freud. Thus Bloom explains that a 'strong poet' must engage in heroic warfare with his 'precursor,' for, involved as he is in a literary Oedipal struggle, a man can only become a poet by somehow invalidating his poetic father" (Gilbert and Gubar, *Madwoman* 46-47).

[3] E. Showalter, *A Literature of Their Own: British Women Novelists from Brontë to Lessing* (Princeton: Princeton University Press, 1977).

[4] "For our purposes ... Bloom's historical construct is useful, not only because it helps identify and define the patriarchal psychosexual context in which so much Western literature was authored, but also because it can help us distinguish the anxieties and achievements of female writers from those of male writers.... Certainly if we acquiesce in the patriarchal Bloomian model, we can be sure that the female poet does not experience the 'anxiety of influence' in the same way that her male counterpart would, for the simple reason that she must confront precursors who are almost exclusively male, and therefore significantly different from her. Not only do these precursors incarnate patriarchal authority (as our discussion of the metaphor of literary paternity argued), they attempt to enclose her in definitions of her person and her potential which, by reducing her to extreme stereotypes (angel, monster), drastically conflict with her own sense of self, that is of her subjectivity, her autonomy, her creativity. On the one hand, therefore, the woman writer's male precursors symbolize authority; on the other hand, despite their authority, they fail to define the ways in which she experiences her own identity as a writer. More, the masculine authority with which they construct their literary personae, as well as the fierce power struggles in which they engage in their efforts of self-creation, seem to the woman writer directly to contradict the terms of her own gender definition. Thus the 'anxiety of influence' that a male poet experiences is felt by a female poet as an even more primary 'anxiety of authorship' ... an anxiety built from complex and often only barely conscious fears of that authority which seems to the female artist to be by definition inappropriate to her sex" (Gilbert and Gubar 48-51).

[5] Reprinted by Einaudi in 1973 with an introduction by Natalia Ginzburg.

[6] See "Neera: The Literary Career of a Woman of the Nineteenth Century" and "The Early Matilde Serao: An Author in Search of a Character," both in this volume.

[7] Marchesa Colombi, Preface, *La cartella n. 4* (Milan: Baldini e Castoldi, 1901) 82.

[8] Marchesa Colombi, Preface, *Dopo il caffè*, 2nd ed. (Bologna: Zanichelli, 1880) 3-6.

[9] Marchesa Colombi, "Un sogno azzurro," *Dopo il caffé* 142-143.

[10] Marchesa Colombi, "Skating Ring," *Dopo il caffé* 386-387.

11 Marchesa Colombi, "I morti parlano," *La cartella n. 4* 82.

12 Entry on Paolo Ferrari, *Enciclopedia dello spettacolo* (Rome: Le Maschere, 1958), vol. V, 192; entry on *La satira e Parini, Dizionario letterario Bompiani* (Milan: Bompiani, 1972), vol. VI, 523.

13 Marchesa Colombi, "Impara l'arte e mettila da parte," *Serate d'inverno*, 2nd ed. (Milan: Galli, 1897) 111. All subsequent quotations from this work will have page numbers following them in the text.

14 Marchesa Colombi, *Il tramonto di un ideale*, 2nd ed. (Milan: Galli, 1896) 12-13. All subsequent quotations from this work will have page numbers following them in the text.

15 "As we explore nineteenth-century literature, we will find that this madwoman emerges over and over again from the mirrors women writers hold up to both their own natures and to their own visions of nature. Even the most apparently conservative and decorous women writers obsessively create fiercely independent characters who seek to destroy all the patriarchal structures which both their authors and their authors' submissive heroines seem to accept as inevitable. Of course, by projecting their rebellious impulses not into their heroines but into mad or monstrous women ... female authors dramatize their own self-division, their desire both to accept the structures of patriarchal society and to reject them. What this means, however, is that the madwoman in literature by women is not merely, as she might be in male literature, an antagonist or foil to the heroine. Rather she is usually in some sense the *author's* double, an image of her own anxiety and rage. Indeed, much of the poetry and fiction written by women conjures up this mad creature so that female authors can come to terms with their own uniquely female feelings of fragmentation, their own keen sense of the discrepancies between what they are and what they are supposed to be" (Gilbert and Gubar 77-78).

16 "All the nineteenth and twentieth-century literary women who evoke the female monster in their novels and poems alter her meaning by virtue of their own identification with her. For it is usually because she is in some sense imbued with interiority that the witch-monster-madwoman becomes so crucial an avatar of the writer's own self. From a male point of view, women who reject the submissive silences of domesticity have been seen as terrible objects – Gorgons, Sirens, Scyllas, serpent-Lamias, Mothers of Death or Goddesses of Night. But from a female point of view the monster is simply a woman who seeks the power of self-articulation" (Gilbert and Gubar 79).

17 "Quando uscii dalle scuole tecniche dopo l'ultimo esame da cui venni rimandato, sapevo a memoria parecchi canti dell'Ariosto; ripetevo per benino molte novelle del *Decameron*; ed avevo, circa la letteratura moderna, certe opinioni ben chiare, che mi ero formate col mio criterio personale senza aiuto di maestri; ed erano: – Che i romanzi italiani sono generalmente noiosi, e però mancano al loro scopo ch'è il diletto; ed in conseguenza valgono meglio i francesi, i tedeschi, gli inglesi, i quali divertono.... – Che i *Tre moschettieri* di Alessandro Dumas sono quattro. –Che i libri seri del padre Bresciani fanno ridere, e l'umorismo di Cervantes fa piangere. – E, finalmente, che non c'è di meglio del romanzo storico, – il quale fa agire personaggi ideali in fatti veri, – per confonder le idee a chi sa la storia, e darne di false a chi non la sa" ("La cartolina postale," *Dopo il caffè* 264-265).

18 Marchesa Colombi, *Prima morire*, 5th ed. (Milan: Galli, 1896) 53. This novel was re-issued in 1988 by Lucarini of Rome with an introduction by G. Morandini.

19 G. Zaccaro, "Da angelo a medusa: le donne della Scapigliatura," *La parabola della donna nella letteratura italiana dell' Ottocento*, by G. De Donato *et al.* (Bari: Adriatica Editrice, 1983) 307.

The Marchesa Colombi's *Un Matrimonio in Provincia*: Style as Subversion

Were it not for Einaudi's or perhaps Italo Calvino's decision in 1973 to reprint *Un matrimonio in provincia* (1885), the "Marchesa Colombi" (Maria-Antonietta Torriani-Torelli, 1840-1920) might well have remained yet another of the seemingly hundreds of women writing in nineteenth-century Italy whose names – and novels – have by now all but passed into oblivion. In a blurb on its back cover, Calvino informs us that the novel was brought to his attention by Natalia Ginzburg, and in fact the current edition carries a nostalgic introduction by Ginzburg in which she recalls her first encounter with the book as a young girl; it tells us at least as much about *Matrimonio*'s subsequent influence on her own work as it does about the novel itself and, unwittingly perhaps, makes an excellent case for the idea of a female literary tradition – but that is another issue.

Since then, certain feminist critics, operating on a naive mimetic model, have interpreted the novel as a nineteenth-century tirade against marriage.[1] Not only is their assumption questionable, it also mercilessly reduces a small literary masterpiece to the status of an ideological tract. It is Calvino, I believe, who captures *Matrimonio*'s real spirit most accurately as he points out precisely what it is that makes this novel so unusual and so immensely readable at the same time:

> A contestare il mito della donna romantica con l'evidenza prosaica della fatalità piccolo-borghese, la narrativa tardo-ottocentesca italiana – dalla Serao a Neera – non mette avanti eroine alla Madame Bovary (anche il "bovarismo," in Italia, sembra privilegio maschile): più che alla provincia di Flaubert si direbbe che la nostra sia vicina a quella di Cechov: drammi silenziosi nelle esistenze senza avvenimenti di

donne di casa frustrate nell'autonomia dei sentimenti. La Marchesa Colombi appartiene a questo filone ma è anche qualcosa di molto diverso: perché quando rappresenta la ristrettezza, la noia, lo squallore lo fa con una spietatezza di sguardo, una nettezza di segno, una deformazione grottesca da dare l'effetto del massimo di tristezza col massimo d'allegria poetica.

Torriani herself would undoubtedly have been very pleased had she known what one of Italy's great writers was to say about her novel almost a century later; for in one of her other *racconti*, she makes – through one of her characters – what might well be considered a *dichiarazione di poetica* curiously reminiscent of Calvino's own impressions of her writing. He speaks of her ability to evoke "la noia, lo squallore ... l'effetto del massimo di tristezza col massimo d'allegria poetica"; she declares herself in favour of a literature inspired by "un modo di considerare la vita che la poetizza senza trasportarla dal campo pratico alle regioni ideali."[2]

What I would like to demonstrate, by way of introduction to *Matrimonio* and by way of response to those critics who have read it as a feminist tract against marriage, is that this is indeed a novel whose construction foregrounds questions of gender. It does so, however, not by attacking bourgeois institutions directly, but in a complex mediation between established literary conventions and the experience of the writer, a mediation which results in a simultaneous absorption and revision of conventional narrative patterns. What makes this mediation especially complex is that it operates within and upon an already revisionist task: the rewriting of the nineteenth century late-Romantic bourgeois novel in the new conventions of *verismo*.

Maria Antonietta Torriani-Torelli was born in Novara in 1840, studied to become a *maestra*, but devoted herself instead to journalism and fiction.[3] Her marriage was a brief one, to the well-known journalist Eugenio Torelli-Viollier, founding editor of the *Corriere della sera*. If nothing else, it served to introduce her to the Milanese literary circles in which she came to maturity as a writer precisely in the years when the debate on *verismo* was at its peak. *In risaia* (1878), the story of a young peasant girl's failure to find a husband because of a disfiguring disease contracted in the rice fields of the Po Valley, is obviously her attempt to produce a socially-conscious naturalist novel. Though entirely forgettable at the literary level, *In risaia* did attract considerable attention at the time of publication because of its implicit plea for better working conditions for the poor. Quite early in her career, Torriani became an active feminist and campaigned for women's rights alongside Anna Maria Mozzoni; at one point, she also taught literature in a Milanese *liceo* founded specifically to offer "alternative education" to women.[4]

And yet, for all her feminist leanings, Torriani seems to have been unable to escape the fate of producing, for the most part, what George Eliot so eloquently termed "Silly Novels by Lady Novelists,"[5] precisely the sort of reading that her pupils at the Liceo M. G. Agnesi ought *not* to have been doing, if they wished to escape the traps and roles lying in wait for them outside the doors of their institution. Among the factors contributing to this curious, though not inexplicable, contradiction none, I believe, weigh as heavily as the two handicaps Torriani shared with all Italian women writers of the nineteenth century: a lack both of prestigious feminine role models for herself, as a woman engaged in an unusual activity, and of solid feminine literary models for her own experience as a woman.[6] It is precisely this absence of significant precedents which led Neera, one of Torriani's contemporaries, to look beyond the confines of Italian literature, to George Eliot and George Sand, when searching for literary "mothers."[7]

It also accounts, I believe, for the fact that, in spite of Matilde Serao's own highly successful career as a journalist and novelist, "there were no Matilde-Serao-lady-journalists"[8] in her work. Clearly, it was far easier to *be* Matilde Serao, lady journalist, than to write about her. In much the same manner, it must have been easier to be Maria-Antonietta Torriani-Torelli, feminist and *femme de lettres*, than to carve out a place for her as a character in a literary tradition replete largely with languishing virgins and avid adulteresses.[9]

And yet, as has already been suggested, Torriani was not at all lacking in opinions about literature: its function, its shortcomings, its relation to life, were all subjects which she managed to treat, albeit indirectly, in her novels and short stories. Like many of her contemporaries, Torriani's strongest objection to the literature of her time was its lack of any relationship to "reality": *verismo*, the historical novel, Manzoni are all categorically dismissed as misleading in one way or another.[10] Torriani's own particular "thirst" for realism is born of the conviction that there is an entire area of human experience – the banal, the *quotidiano*, the non-exceptional – that has been largely excluded from literature which, as a result, promotes a falsely romantic view of life in all its aspects. If there is in fact a leitmotif that runs through her myriad novels and stories, it is constituted by the infinite number of observations based on the oppositions life/literature, prose/poetry, reality/illusion, marriage/love, all aimed at pointing out literature's refusal to paint "il quadro prosaico della vita d'ogni giorno,"[11] to convey "la prosa della vita pratica,"[12] to evoke "quei sentimenti calmi e sereni che non somigliano punto alle tempeste dei romanzi, e però non giungono mai all'ultimo capitolo."[13]

Yet it should be noted that, in spite of her strenous objections to the romanticized view of life presented in novels, Torriani sees entertainment, not education, as the novel's main function: "Una cameriera che non sa gli interessi dei vicini di casa è un personaggio non riuscito, una cosa che non ottiene il suo scopo, come un romanzo che non diverte."[14] In fact, she considers Italian novels to be "generalmente noiosi [perché] [m]ancano al loro scopo, ch'è il diletto, ed in conseguenza valgono meglio i francesi, i tedeschi, gli inglesi, i quali divertono."[15] However, if novels must entertain, they must not foster in the reader any *illusions* about life. The phrase cited at the beginning of this essay as her "dichiarazione di poetica" is perhaps worth repeating at this point: literature must reflect "un modo di considerare la vita che la poetizza senza trasportarla dal campo pratico alle regioni ideali."[16]

None of Torriani's meditations on the subject of literature are particularly profound, and they certainly echo, in a reductive, often stereotyped and irreverant fashion, the debates going on in intellectual circles at the time; if I have mentioned them in this context it is because they provide the conceptual framework, or the matrix which, in turn, generated *Un matrimonio in provincia*. Torriani did not, of course, arrive at *Matrimonio*'s particular style without a considerable struggle. An examination of the two novels leading up to it, *Prima morire* (1881)[17] and *Il tramonto di un ideale* (1883), reveals an open attempt on her part to lay to rest the two competing narrative models of the time, both of which she perceived as inadequate, neither of which she could ignore: the late-Romantic bourgeois novel on the one hand, the newer naturalist one on the other.

Prima morire is an epistolary novel which explicitly pits the two genres against each other by telling two separate stories, each of which self-consciously mimics a specific narrative model. The first story is that of Eva Malvezzi, a young woman married to a wealthy older businessman who loves her but provides none of the excitement she longs for and reads about in the novels that constitute her only form of stimulation. The first letter in the novel, addressed by Eva to her best friend along with the latest book she has borrowed from a "gabinetto di lettura," sets the stage for the story about to unfold:

> Non so se abbiamo diritto di leggere in due, pagando un solo abbonamento. Alla prima confessione esporrò il caso al confessore. Il guaio è che i confessori sono inesorabili sull'argomento dei romanzi, e specialmente di questi dello Zola....
> Preferisco pagare il doppio abbonamento.
> Questa volta però sono certa la mia lettera ti riuscirà più interessante del romanzo; sembra il principio d'un romanzo anch'essa; ma d'un romanzo vero....[18]

One day Eva meets a struggling young musician, befriended and introduced into the household by her trusting husband as a piano teacher for her daughter. Like Emma Bovary, Eva begins to project onto the young musician all her dreams of passion, epitomized by her reaction to Chateaubriand's famous *Atala*: "... è una lettura che esalta, che dà la febbre. Si vorrebbe non avere più, né marito, né casa, né figli, né tetto, per vagare in quella vastità di deserto, sotto quegli ardori di cielo, ed essere amate a quel modo, ed inebriarsi di quel gran sogno e di quella gran disperazione."[19]

When, after much agonizing, she and the musician finally decide to run away together to Switzerland, they both discover, not surprisingly, that they do have scruples after all – and that once all the barriers to their love have been removed, it provides less joy than they had anticipated: "Cessato il delirio dell'amore combattuto, mi si era ridestato nell'anima quel profondo scontento di me, che mi aveva turbato il giorno inanzi. La mia felicità aveva qualcosa d'incompleto. Mi mancava la gioia di sentirmi felice."[20]

Almost immediately they receive word that Eva's daughter has taken ill and Eva returns home completely repentant. Her husband, in the meantime, has been shattered by the discovery of this double betrayal of his trust. He and Eva are left to continue their lives on this new and very shaky basis, while the young musician, consumed by guilt and remorse, eventually dies.

This re-writing of the novel of adultery is curious not only because it punishes the lover and not the married woman, but also because it unfolds at the same time as another story in another genre, with its own unusual twist as well. While the musician is carrying on his affair with Eva he is corresponding with a friend, an aspiring young writer who serves as his confidante and who has recently taken a position as a private tutor in a quiet provincial town. Through the writer's letters we learn that, "faute de mieux," he has gradually befriended the family of the town pharmacist, father of three daughters, "una specie di padre Grandet che sagrifica le sue figlie all'avarizia."[21] The first two daughters have been sent to convents, but the third is too strong-willed to give in to the father's pressures. The two suitors who ask for her hand are both rejected by the father because he is too stingy to give his daughter any sort of dowry:

> Da allora cominciò per la povera Mercede un'esistenza miserabile, una lotta sorda e continua. Il padre, a forza d'imporle privazioni, umiliazioni e fatiche, cerca di stancarla e di farla risolvere a farsi monaca per togliersi a quelle vessazioni; lei oppone un silenzio freddo e sopporta tutto, pur di non farsi monaca.[22]

The young writer, after much deliberation, finally decides to marry Mercedes himself, in spite of the fact that he does not love her, in order to save her from a life of isolation, humiliation and deprivation. Initially, their relationship is strained, but gradually he learns to love her "come non [avrebbe] amata mai quell'idealità della [sua] fantasia"[23] because "la sua anima è pura, e la virtù è innata nel suo cuore."[24] The long descriptions of life in this "piccolo villaggio, perduto sulla riviera dove torreggia il suo vasto castello isolato e silenzioso"[25] and of the situation of the pharmacist's daughter, proverbially sacrificed to her father's avarice, constitutes the naturalist story that contrasts so sharply with the late-Romantic tale of adultery being lived by Eva and the young musician in Milan.

Prima morire is also remarkable for the number of direct references it contains to other authors, literary works and situations: *King Lear*, *Faust*, Balzac, Zola, Foscolo, Paolo and Francesca, the English realist novel ("Anch'io li sogno, i paesi che finiscono in *shire* e vorrei essere un *clergyman*...")[26] are only a few of the references that occur. Equally numerous are the allusions to the literary nature – or not – of the experiences being evoked: "Così, nei romanzi, entrando nel salotto d'una signora...,"[27] or "avevo bisogno d'un paesaggio più grandioso ... la poesia del cielo e della terra, per rialzarmi da quel abbattimento."[28]

An analogous though less insistent self-consciousness, as well as the identical opposition of the late-Romantic novel of adultery to the naturalist tale of the young woman withering away in the provinces, reappears in *Il tramonto di un ideale*, published two years after *Prima morire*. The *trait-d'union* between the two novelistic worlds is provided here by the use of a common protagonist, Giovanni, a young man who leaves his native village to pursue a successful legal career in Milan. It is here that he lives his "romanzo d'amore" with the lovely young wife of an aging aristocrat. This "novel" comes to an end because his mistress fails to accept the fact that adulterous affairs, too, are subject to the tedium that inevitably befalls marriages that go on for "too long." Though Giovanni is devoted to her, he cannot continue, after years, to provide the attention and excitement that accompany love in its early stages. The young woman's illusions about love are, again, the product of "too many novels" and eventually lead to the downfall of the relationship:

> La bella Gemma ... s'era fatta delle idee da romanzo; sognava la passione esclusiva ed eterna, non poteva rassegnarsi a quel cambiamento di Giovanni.... Giovanni, in realtà, non aveva fatto nessun cambiamento. Egli, che l'aveva sempre amata ad un modo, e soltanto aveva smessa un po' la galanteria e le dimostrazioni ... non capiva di che cosa ella si lagnasse, la trovava esigente ed ingiusta.[29]

In the meantime, in his native village in the Piedmontese countryside, Rachele, the daughter of a wealthy landowner who had refused her permission to marry Giovanni many years before, languishes away, still committed to a promise requested by him on the eve of his departure for Milan. Due to a misunderstanding provoked by the unexpected interference of the servant who had acted as the messenger between them, Rachele is unaware that Giovanni had left thinking himself rejected by her, and is determined to await his return:

> Né prima della morte del padre né poi, non aveva voluto saperne di prendere marito....
> Alla prima s'era lasciata intimidire dall'autorità del padre.... Ma col tempo aveva trovata la forza di resistere.... Si sapeva amata, aveva fede nel suo innamorato, e rimaneva fanciulla per aspettarlo.[30]

Many years later, after the end of his adulterous affair in Milan, Giovanni hears that Rachele is still unmarried and decides to return to his home town, naïvely hoping to revive this old "love story" at the point where it had been interrupted. In the days leading up to the encounter with Rachele he allows his imagination to picture her as "una donna affascinante" who would receive him "coll'ospitalità d'una castellana": "Doveva essere una scena da medioevo, rappresentata da una bella donna moderna e da un 'lion.' Si figurava di giungere a cavallo, sollevando un nembo di polvere, e di vedere la sua dama salita sull'alto della torre come la moglie desolata di Malborough, 'pour voir s'il reviendra.' "[31]

Instead, the Rachele he finds "era ancora Rachele, ma non era più il suo ideale; ed il cuore di Giovanni rimaneva freddo e calmo nel ritrovarla."[32] Idle young women, it appears, are not the only ones subject to excesses of the imagination: successful young lawyers read too many novels as well. In any case, the abyss between reality and expectations is clearly an obsessive preoccupation of Torriani's and, as a popular writer for women drawing on a meagre repertoire of characters and plots, she is keenly aware of the fact that she risks reinforcing this abyss in the minds of her readers. In the works examined thus far, Torriani has expressed her disapproval of these plots and characters by calling attention to their literary nature, and by creating situations which depict – à la *Madame Bovary* – the distortions and disasters wrought by "unrealistic" literary expectations of life. With *Un matrimonio in provincia* she finally succeeds in finding a narrative voice which allows her to abandon the self-conscious posture of previous works and actually transcend the tired plots and characters to which she has thus far been confined.

The novel is narrated by its protagonist, Denza, a housewife and mother of three children, who tells us exactly how she came to marry the man who is now her husband. Her story is that of her *education sentimentale*, of the death of her adolescent dreams of love and marriage to a man she had idealized, and of her awakening to the social and economic realities of woman's lot. It is told in a style totally devoid of sentimentalism or of any dramatic effect other than the sardonic wit, or irony, generated by the constant implicit juxtaposition of the "sublime" and the "ridiculous," the sublime, of course, being the expectation, the ridiculous, the reality. This juxtaposition is achieved by the use of a first-person retrospective narration which allows Denza to tell her story with hindsight and from within the tale itself: the irony thus emanates not from an omniscient narrator located outside the story, but from its very nerve-centre, the *prise de conscience* that stands between the time of action (Denza as a young woman) and the time of narration (Denza as a matron with three children). Behind every image, generated obviously at the time of narration, there stands another image, implicitly attacked but never explicitly expressed, associated either with Denza's expectations at the time of action or, more importantly, with the *reader's* expectations of this and related genres. *In other words, behind the story told, there lurks a story not told, a sub-text continuously suggested which the reader herself supplies and sees subverted at the same time.* The end result is a sort of *romanzo anti-letterario* which, by virtue of its totally irreverent style and imagery, constantly challenges literature's depiction of reality: as Denza confronts her own romantic expectations of life, the reader is forced to confront her own expectations of the novel. The story contains many of the *topoi* associated with its genre (the naturalist tale of the young woman on her way to spinsterhood) as well as some late-Romantic ones, but it distorts them in such a way as to undermine them completely, and to suggest that reality is not nearly as dramatic as it is grotesque and thoroughly banal – and that it is precisely this aspect of life that literature most often fails to capture.

The implicit opposition of text and sub-text that generates a second level of meaning in this novel represents the "natural" outcome of Torriani's gradual movement towards the liquidation of the late-Romantic and naturalist stereotypes that plagued her two previous novels: both *Prima morire* and *Il tramonto di un ideale* pitted the two opposite genres against each other in a highly self-conscious attempt to point out their failings, but stopped at that. In *Prima morire* the two plots are connected by the conventions of the epistolary novel: two friends recount their respective tales to each other, thereby creating a totally artificial link between two effectively independent story lines. In *Tramonto* the two plots remain essentially separate, but are linked in a slightly less artificial manner, by the use of a common protagonist, the young lawyer, Giovanni. In *Matrimonio* the opposition is maintained but is transformed and totally internalized, in keeping with Torriani's belief that both options are equally artificial, and that the real choice is not between naturalist and late-Romantic conventions, but between "reality" and "literature." In *Matrimonio* Torriani's *own* version of naturalism ("reality") provides the "text," while conventional naturalism ("literature") and, to a lesser extent, some late-Romantic *topoi* constitute the implicit sub-text. One might also say, *grossomodo*, that the conventional naturalist sub-text is provided by the reader's thwarted expectations of the genre while Denza's rather more vague but equally undermined fantasies make up a sort of Romantic sub-text, but this must be taken in the loosest sense.

In order to convey effectively the novel's unique character, it is perhaps opportune to compare it briefly to a more conventional work in the same genre, written by another woman at approximately the same time, Neera's *Teresa* (1887). Luigi Baldacci considers it a "feminist manifesto" of its time, as well as one of the best novels of the last two decades of the nineteenth century.[33] At one level, *Teresa* tells a story very similar to that evoked by *Matrimonio*, the story of a marriage which fails to take place. Teresa loves Orlandi, a handsome but as yet unestablished young man. Her father, whose avarice is second only to his ignorance, refuses them the permission to marry, since Orlandi is not rich and the union would be of no direct benefit to the family. Teresa continues to dream of Orlandi but refuses his offer of elopement, since she cannot bring herself to defy the conventions and the authority she has been brought up to revere. She slowly withers away in increasing isolation, depression and even hysteria, until her father, whom she nurses ever-obediently to the end, finally dies. At this point, *deus-ex-machina*, she receives a letter from Orlandi, now ill and penniless in Milan, begging her to join him. In what may be interpreted either as a gesture of rebellion, or of continuing submission to her nurturing vocation, she finally closes down her home and embarks upon her "new life." According to Luigi Baldacci, this dénouement is "unrealistic": had Teresa remained true to her passive nature she would literally have remained a prisoner of her father's home, regardless of his death or of Orlandi's reappearance.[34]

Torriani would certainly have shared Baldacci's view about the novel's "unrealistic" ending. However, unlike Baldacci, for whom realism appears to be a form of internal psychological consistency, she would have had Teresa act in a way having nothing to do with her own nature, and everything to do with practical realities: she would have had her marry the widower Luzzi, one of the less-than-attractive suitors proposed to her by the *pretora*, her neighbour and confidante, whose down-to-earth advice Teresa finds so irksome and intolerable: "Un Luzzi che sposa è sempre superiore ad un Luminelli che non sposa ... o sposa un'altra."[35] For this, in fact, is the solution Denza finally opts for when her own "prince," Onorato Mazzucchetti, finally marries another young woman whose wealth and social position, unlike Denza's, match his own. Mazzucchetti, in fact, had never given her any reason other than his long, mournful gazes to believe that he would ask for her hand at all. "Sposa la Borani"[36] – these are the words that bring down Denza's castles in the air, as well as her pride and self-image. The anguish and isolation she experiences as a result are not very different from the feelings Neera ascribes to Teresa as she slowly realizes that Orlandi has forgotten her. "Mi pareva che tutti i vincoli che avevo colla vita si fossero spezzati ad un tratto, e che dopo quella grande rovina, dovessi morire; che fosse finita," (p. 88) are Torriani's words; Neera, in the case of Teresa, speaks of "una malinconia sottile ... un senso di isolamento, d'abbandono, come se il mondo si sfasciasse intorno a lei, ed ogni cosa viva allontanandosi, ella rimanesse sola in un gran buio freddo."[37] However, while Teresa withdraws more and more into her trance-like passivity, refusing any compromises with reality, Denza makes the necessary adjustment. After several years of boredom and humiliation, when finally presented by her family with the option of marrying a well-to-do notary some years her senior whose most salient characteristic is a large wart on the forehead – "Ha una verrucca, sai, un porro, un po' grosso, qui sulla tempia" (p. 95) – she literally jumps at the chance, in spite of the fact that it spells the end of her romantic dreams:

> Ero sconfortata, perché dinanzi a quell'uomo positivo e nella nebbia delle sue risaie, vedevo svanire i miei sogni sentimentali. Ma però ero resoluta a sposarlo per non restar zitellona.
> Tutti uscirono sul balcone colle chicchere sorseggiando il tè, persuasi che quei pochi minuti fossero bastati per farci decidere di tutta la nostra vita.
> Infatti erano bastati. Avevo deciso. (p. 99)

Wart and all, the middle-aged notary offers a more palatable alternative than the isolation and humiliation of spinsterhood, as epitomized for Denza by the life of her unmarried aunt, presented to the reader in the novel's very first paragraph as "una zitellona piccola, secca come un'arringa, che dormiva in cucina dove aveva messo un paravento per nascondere il letto, e passava la vita al buio dietro quel paravento" (p.3). The total lack of sentimentality with which Torriani evokes the lot of the unmarried woman by no means lessens the impact of her plight on the reader: if anything, it intensifies it. The aunt remains nameless throughout and has no "story" as such in the novel, but simply appears intermittently in "flashes" that repeatedly remind us, more powerfully than any polemical tirade, of the tremendous social injustice suffered by unmarried women in nineteenth-century Italian society, and hence of the tremendous pressures brought to bear upon young girls of marrying age. Perhaps the most poignant of the aunt's appearances is the one Torriani has her make, almost as an afterthought and yet so ominously, at the height of Denza's amorous delusions. Assuming, mistakenly, that her uncle has come to call on her father in order to transmit Mazzucchetti's offer of marriage, Denza is unable to contain herself any longer and rushes behind the screen ("entrai nel paravento") to confide in her aunt: "La zia si allegrò tutta, e si raccomandò che la facessi venire in campagna con me, almeno un mese all'anno, *perché non pareva*, ma era lunga l'annata dietro quel paravento" (p. 79).

The same tendency to use almost visual, expressionistic images that go straight to the heart of things, that show rather than tell – evinced in the images of the *paravento* as a symbol of social ostracism and of the *verrucca* as the literal and metaphorical wart that makes a "frog" of Denza's prince – is to be found in the depiction of every major character in the novel. They range from Denza's heart-throb Mazzucchetti, to her father, the ineffectual, mild-mannered notary, to her stepmother, "una vecchia signora ... [che] masticava perpetuamente un pezzo d'anice stellato per la digestione ... [e] s'era fatta radere i capelli sul cucuzzolo perché erano molto diradati e sperava di farli crescere più fitti, ma non erano cresciuti più, e portava sempre un parrucchino sulla parte rasa" (p. 12).

What these characters share is that they are stereotypical figures of the genre they inhabit, but drawn in such a way as to make it clear that the author's intention is, first and foremost, to *break* with the characteristics usually associated with these stereotypes. In Neera's novel, Orlandi, the young man whom Teresa loves, is depicted, according to our expectations, as charming, handsome and even glib. Since he later turns out to be somewhat irresponsible, we can conclude that Teresa has been taken in by appearances. Onorato Mazzucchetti, on the other hand, is portrayed in such a way as to make it impossible for the reader to believe that Denza has been deceived by anything other than her own pressing emotional needs and volatile romantic imagination. A most unlikely prince, Mazzucchetti is in fact described, quite bluntly, as "una specie di elefante":

> Ero tutta turbata. Quella mole superava ogni mia immaginazione. Sì, lo avevano detto che era grasso, lo sapevo; ma avevo sempre cercato di attenuare la cosa, di conciliare la pinguedine colla gioventù, colla sveltezza.... Invece era un coso tutto d'un pezzo, colle spalle poderose, alte, quadrate, il petto sporgente, il collo corto ed una grossa testa coi capelli neri neri, lisci lisci, e gli occhi neri, grossi, sporgenti. Mi parve un vecchio. (p. 41)

But the thought of abandoning the newly-found feeling of being "loved" – since her cousins have assured her that Mazzucchetti had eyes only for her at the theater where he first caught a glimpse of her – is so painful for Denza that she gradually allows her original doubts as to his appeal and his intentions to be erased:

> In sostanza, mi parve un po' freddo e mi sentiì umiliata e malinconica ... [e] il pensiero che m'avesse guardata poco mi perseguitava ... [ma] l'idea che tutto quell'amore fosse stato un sogno mi affliggeva profondamente. Mi affliggeva al punto che dimenticavo la sua grossezza, e la prima impressione spiacevole che ne avevo ricevuta. (pp. 42-43)

In a short time, her cousin's rationalizations – "Ma è bello, sai. Ha un'aria da gran signore" (p. 42) – and the monotony of her own life, combine to break down any resistance she may have had:

> Più ci pensavo nella nostra solitudine uggiosa, nella monotonia dei giorni piovosi, e più mi sentivo intenerire.... Quel giorno avevo finito d'innamorarmi. D'allora la sua pinguedine, il collo corto, i capelli lustri e lisci, tutto mi parve bello, e sentivo uno struggimento di tenerezza nel rivederlo col pensiero, e lo rivedevo sempre. (p. 44)

Equally unlikely characters are the father and the stepmother. While Teresa's father is a sort of Père Grandet (like the fathers in Torriani's own two previous novels), miserly, blustering, ignorant and authoritarian, Pietro Dellara, a widower and notary, is as far removed as possible from the classic figure of the father whose avarice condemns his daughter to a life of misery and solitude. If Denza is without a dowry, it is not because her father is miserly, but simply because he is largely inept: "Ho detto che il babbo era notaio; ma il suo studio non era preso d'assalto dai clienti" (p. 6). Well-meaning, undemanding and hardly effectual enough to be cruel, his only obsession is "il moto" and his only imposition on his daughters that they accompany him on his daily walks:

> La mattina ci faceva alzare prestissimo, ci dava appena il tempo di vestirci e via; lasciando la casa sossopra, i letti disfatti, s'andava giù giù, lungo una strada maestra qualsiasi, senza scelta, senza scopo. A lui non importava che i luoghi fossero belli; non ambiva di fare delle escursioni alpine; punto. La sua passione era proprio di mettere un piede avanti all'altro, per molte ore di seguito e di poter dire al ritorno "si son fatti tanti chilometri." (p. 7)

All of this changes, of course, when the father decides to remarry and Denza and her sister acquire a stepmother, as curious a figure in this case as one is likely to encounter in any novel, and surely one of the few female literary characters of the nineteenth century to escape spinsterhood at forty-three, bear her first child at forty-four ("quell'uggioso marmocchio ... colla sua faccia vecchia da figlio di vecchi," p. 21), and live happily ever after. In fact, not only does she not appear to have withered away at all in her maiden state, once married, unlike the classically oppressed wives and mothers in *Teresa* (and so many other female literary characters for whom marriage is either submission, misery or boredom) she flourishes and provides Denza and her sister with the model of a happily-married woman:

> Poi una sera tornò il babbo con sua moglie, sana, forte, che non masticava più l'anice stellato, che mangiava polenta e fagioli, e citrioli ed ogni sorta di cose indigeste e camminava come un portalettere.... Insomma quegli otto giorni di viaggio, ed il "cambiamento di stato" come diceva lei, l'avevano rimessa tutta a nuovo. Era piena di brio e di vita. (pp. 13-14)

Full of "buon senso borghese," the stepmother's main concerns, like those of the society in which she lives, are economic. Her reflections on Denza's situation are well-meaning, but inadvertently puncture every one of her romantic notions, from those concerning the role of beauty in a woman's life – "Vedi io sono brutta ed anche vecchia, ed ho trovato il più buon marito del mondo, e poche mogli sono più amate di me" (p. 20) – to her belief that Mazzucchetti will one day ask for her hand – "Un giovane che avrà forse un milione! La guarderà finché non avrà altro da fare, poi sposerà un'altra" (p. 65).

The dry wit and irreverent tone so evident in the presentation of the novel's characters extend also to the manner in which Torriani evokes other *topoi* of the nineteenth-century novel: the *salotto*, the love-letter, the unhappy childhood, the *fidanzamento-a-vita* are all subject to the same reductive presentation which takes all the drama or emphasis out of them and situates them on an uneventful, banal continuum, characterized at best by an element of the grotesque. The *salotto* becomes a storehouse for supplies: "E la sala s'andò coprendo d'uno strato di polvere sopra le vecchie lenzuola che coprivano i mobili, e si trasformò definitivamente in magazzeno. Pareva fatta apposta, perché non aveva né stufa, né camino, ed era fredda come una cantina. Le patate vi gelarono" (pp. 17-18). The love letter is part of a hyper-realist *nature morte* that can only be described as unorthodox: "Eravamo tutte e tre in piedi, noi due e la matrigna, intorno alla tavola della cucina. La lettera era là, tra il pacco della carne aperto, ed un cavolo tutto bagnato che le sgocciolava sopra" (p. 70). The unhappy childhood, without being negated, is presented as minor in comparison with the suggested later miseries of adolescence: "Queste sono le memorie rosee dell'infanzia, l'età dei sorrisi, delle gioie, di tutte quelle cose che si dicono e si scrivono. Poi venne la gioventù" (p. 11); the *fidanzamento-a-vita*, in this case followed by the death of the bride a year after her long-awaited marriage, is referred to in matter-of-fact terms which make it almost comical in spite of its tragic outcome: "La figlia di un farmacista di contro a noi aveva aspettato il figlio d'un notaio per tredici anni, poi l'aveva sposato. E' vero che era morta di una malattia di nervi, dopo poco più di un anno di matrimonio; ma questo a me non poteva accadere" (p. 69).

Torriani's particular brand of *verismo* is unique in that it punctures not only the occasional Romantic stereotype, but also the orthodox naturalist *topoi* that a writer like Neera exploits to the fullest. She does this either by means of a sort of expressionistic irreverence that privileges the visual and the concrete, thereby reducing verbal rhetoric to a minimum, or by adopting a tone that is undramatic and deadpan to a fault, particularly in reference to issues that have traditionally been highly dramatized in literature. Where others, such as Neera, see tragedy and injustice, Torriani sees only the often absurd, implacable logic of life, as it continually fails to live up to our inflated expectations; hence, while Neera polemically divides human beings into male and female, Torriani divides them only into dreamers and realists, into those who suffer from these expectations, and those who don't. As a writer whose audience is primarily female, she is well aware, of course, that because of their restricted sphere of activity, women are particularly vulnerable to romantic misconceptions of life (Eva in *Prima morire* and Denza both suffer from an inordinate lack of stimulation and focus in their lives); she also realizes that she herself risks contributing to the perpetuation of literary myths that undermine women's ability to come to grips with the reality of their lives. In works previous to *Matrimonio* she continues to use these myths, but situates herself *outside* of them either by explicitly calling attention to their literary nature or by ironically distancing herself from them in the ways described above, thus displaying both her intolerance of prevailing literary norms and her inability, or lack of desire, to replace them. In other words, paradoxically, she remains a prisoner of precisely those models she is attempting to criticize. In *Matrimonio*, however, she finally finds a narrative voice able to accommodate her contradictions, her need to conform as well as her need to dissent, without being forced to discredit her own story.

It is interesting to note that it was *verismo*'s theory of impersonality which allowed Torriani, as it did Neera, to find a narrative voice amidst the multiple pressures – commercial, literary, psychological – that made writing so problematic for women in this period. In the case of Neera, whose greatest problem was overcoming her fear of being identified with the characters she created, Capuana's theory of impersonality allowed her to explore woman's lot in a far more genuine manner than the bourgeois genre in which she made her literary debut and to which she was later to return.[38] For Torriani, as evidenced by the two novels leading up to *Matrimonio*, the greatest difficulty lay in deflating what she perceived as the equally false conventions provided by the two major literary models of her time, *without however making any radical breaks with them*. She accomplishes this in *Matrimonio* by adopting a first-person narrator, not in the autobiographical vein, but in the naturalist sense, much as Luigi Capuana himself did in *Profili di donne* (1877), to give the reader "un'impressione non di seconda mano, ma immediata." Since Torriani has used first-person narration before (as in the epistolary novel *Prima morire*), this fact in and of itself would be meaningless, were it not for the additional fact that Denza, unlike previous narrators, *has had little or no exposure to literature*. In *Prima morire*, the adulteress, the young musician and the fledgling novelist are all characters steeped in literature; Denza, on the other hand, is a housewife with three children who divides her time between Novara and her husband's rice fields in the Po Valley. Moreover, given her father's eccentric ways, she has had no formal schooling, and her literary education is summed up as follows:

> [Il babbo] non ci mandava neppure a scuola, perché diceva che tutte quelle ore d'immobilità sono micidiali. C'insegnava lui di quando in quando a leggere, scrivere e far di conto. E durante le nostre passeggiate faceva la nostra educazione letteraria.
> Almeno, lui lo credeva, perché ci raccontava l'*Iliade*, l'*Eneide*, la *Gerusalemme*. Si animava, gesticolava narrando di eroi che si battevano soli contro un'armata ... e quando finiva quelle narrazioni, il povero babbo era tutto ansimante ed in sudore, come se quelle gesta le avesse fatte lui.
> Noi non dividevamo punto la sua ammirazione. Prive dell'attrattiva della forma, dette così fra due campi di granoturco, quelle cose ci parevano stravaganze, e non ci riusciva di capire come potessero

costituire la nostra educazione letteraria. Le confondevamo con certe
fole bislacche che ci raccontava la zia nelle sere di pioggia, e non le
trovavamo neppure più belle. (pp. 7-8)

The fact that Denza is practically a stranger to literature is no mere detail: it is the
pretext Torriani uses to leave behind the entire repertoire of literary models and
conventions she finds so insidious and so confining and to develop her own voice
without abandoning a genre she is bound to by psychological and commercial
pressures. Whether or not Denza has read novels in the years since her marriage is
something we are not explicitly told; we do know, however, that her formative
years were not "contaminated" by literature. If she is now a reader of novels (as one
might assume, given the fact that she has chosen to write one herself) the
circumstances that led to her own marriage, and her rather cold-blooded view of
them, are such that it would be difficult for her to be deceived by them. In fact,
Matrimonio could even be construed as her response to them, as suggested also by
a remark of Torriani's on the literary potential of non-literary women:

> Bisogna avere, come ho la fortuna di aver io, un'immensa
> corrispondenza con le signore, per farsi un'idea del gusto, della
> grazia, dell'eleganza che ci mettono. Nella loro modestia son dei
> piccoli capolavori. E i pedanti e i puristi vanno dicendo che in Italia
> non si sa scrivere! Chi non sa scrivere? Loro e noi letteratucoli (mi
> metto tra questi) che, a forza di studiare parole nei vocabolari,
> perdiamo il filo delle idee e diventiamo imbecilli.[39]

In conclusion, I would like to return to those critics who have interpreted
Matrimonio exclusively as a tirade against marriage. To say that Torriani's irony is
directed against "quanto di mistificato e discriminatorio sia presente nella
imposizione coniugale"[40] or that in the novel "la donna si riconosce nella misura in
cui avverte criticamente il rapporto con l'istituzione, soprattutto con il contratto
matrimoniale,"[41] is to ignore the fact that the only example of marriage put forth in
Matrimonio – that between the father and the step-mother – is in fact a happy one. It
is true that the novel closes on an ambiguous note with respect to Denza's own
situation as a married woman – "la matrigna pretende che io abbia ripresa la mia aria
beata e minchiona dei primi anni. Il fatto è che ingrasso" (p. 103) – but this, again,
is a reference to the *images* of marriage Denza may have had as a young girl –
"Così, dopo tutti quegli anni d'amore, di poesia, di sogni sentimentali, fu concluso
il mio matrimonio" (p. 103) – and not to the actual institution of marriage. There are

no mystifications or idealizations in Torriani's presentation of marriage, which is depicted as a contractual agreement entered into largely for practical purposes: Denza's father marries because he feels his daughters need a stepmother, the stepmother marries because she wants an heir, Scalchi wishes to marry Denza because he needs companionship in the rice-fields. What mystifications there are, are clearly presented as existing in the mind of Denza and as having been generated by her own pressing desires and volatile fantasies. As she tells her story in retrospect, she undoes these mystifications one by one. Torriani, at another level, undoes the mystifications created by literary images of reality: the role of the theme of marriage in all this can be said to lie somewhere between narrative *topos* and narrative pretext.

Because it does not deal directly with marriage as an institution, it might be said that *Matrimonio* is actually reticent, or even ambiguous at an ideological level. If this is true, the converse may also be true: that it is this ambiguity which caused Torriani to contain her dissent within the limits of the purely literary in the first place. In turn what we find in Torriani is a more modern and more "subversive" narrative voice than that of other women of her time, who may have been writing from more explicit ideological positions.

Notes

1 See notes 40 and 41.

2 "Un'avventura di un giornalista," in *Dopo il caffè*, 2nd ed. (Bologna: Zanichelli, 1880) 218.

3 G. Morandini, *La voce che è in lei: antologia della narrativa femminile italiana tra '800 e '900* (Milan: Bompiani, 1980) 390. The most complete source of information on Torriani appears to be the preface by Morandini to a recent reprint of *Prima morire* (Rome: Lucarini, 1988). Morandini claims that Torriani was born in 1840 and not in 1846 as previously thought.

4 F. Pieroni Bortolotti, *Alle origini del movimento femminile in Italia 1848-1892* (1963; Turin: Einaudi, 1975) 91.

5 G. Eliot, "Silly Novels by Lady Novelists," *Westminster Review* Oct.1856: 442-461, reprinted in *Essays of George Eliot*, ed. T. Pinney (New York: Columbia University Press, 1963) 300-324.

6 On the effects of the lack of role models for nineteenth-century women writers see S. Gilbert and S. Gubar, *The Madwoman in the Attic: The Woman Writer and the Nineteenth-Century Literary Imagination* (New Haven: Yale University Press, 1979).

7 See, in the present volume, "The Search for Literary Mothers: Neera's *Teresa*."

8 J. J. Howard, "The Feminine Vision of Matilde Serao," *Italian Quarterly* 71 (1975): 68-69.

9 See A. Nozzoli, "La letteratura femminile in Italia tra Ottocento e Novecento," *Tabù e coscienza: la condizione femminile nella letteratura italiana del Novecento* (Florence: La Nuova Italia, 1978) 1-40; also A. Arslan Veronese, *Dame, droga e galline: romanzo popolare e romanzo di consumo* (Padua: CLEUP, 1977).

10 "La scuola verista, come l'intendono taluni, è la scuola dei poveri di spirito.... I veristi sono l'analisi inanimata" (*Prima morire*, 5th ed. [Milan: Galli, 1896] 158); "... non c'è meglio del romanzo storico ... per confondere le idee a chi sa la storia, e darne di false a chi non la sa" ("La cartolina postale," *Dopo il caffè* 265); "Una donna che ama, non farebbe mai quello stupido voto di Lucia, di non sposare il suo Renzo...; a cosa le serve di vivere e di serbarsi pura, se non dev'essere pel suo amante? Allora tanto faceva che si fosse uccisa per sottrarsi a quel pericolo" (*Prima morire* 53).

11 *Prima morire* 95.

12 *Prima morire* 113.

13 "Un sogno azzurro," *Dopo il caffè* 102.

14 *Prima morire* 9.

15 "La cartolina postale," *Dopo il caffè* 264.

16 "Un'avventura di un giornalista," *Dopo il caffè* 218.

17 In the introduction to a recent reprint of *Prima morire* (Rome: Lucarini, 1988) Giuliana Morandini claims that the novel was first published in 1887. My own research shows that it was first published by A. Morano in Naples in 1881 (*National Union Catalogue*, Vol. 597, 480). In addition, the *Catalogo generale della libreria italiana*, ed. A. Pagliani (Milan: Associazione tipografica libraria italiana, 1903) lists a third edition of the novel as having been published by Galli of Milan in 1887.

18 *Prima morire* 6.

19 *Prima morire* 8.

20 *Prima morire* 216.

21 *Prima morire* 87.

22 *Prima morire* 92.

23 *Prima morire* 263.

24 *Prima morire* 264.

25 *Prima morire* 30.

26 *Prima morire* 117.

27 *Prima morire* 107.

28 *Prima morire* 209.

[29] *Il tramonto di un ideale*, 2nd ed. (Milan: Galli, 1896) 215.

[30] *Tramonto* 229-230.

[31] *Tramonto* 237-238.

[32] *Tramonto* 255.

[33] L. Baldacci, Introduction, *Teresa*, by Neera (Turin: Einaudi,1976) v.

[34] Baldacci xi.

[35] Neera, *Teresa* 71.

[36] La Marchesa Colombi, *Un matrimonio in provincia* (Turin: Einaudi, 1973) 88. All subsequent references will be to this edition, and page numbers will appear in the text.

[37] Neera, *Teresa* 108.

[38] Neera, *Teresa* 108.

[39] L. Capuana, *Profili di donne*, 2nd ed. (Milan: Brigola, 1877) v.

[40] Nozzoli 22.

[41] Morandini 16.

Neera: The Literary Career of a Woman
of the Nineteenth Century

In 1976, Luigi Baldacci, undoubtedly spurred on by the new wave of feminism which had taken hold in Italy, brought to the attention of contemporary readers a relatively unknown novel, *Teresa* (1886), which he introduced as "uno dei più bei romanzi dell'ultimo ventennio del secolo passato."[1]

Its author, Anna Radius Zuccari (1846-1918), or Neera, as she was known to the public, was among the most popular and prolific female writers of her time. Many of her short stories and articles, as well as many of her novels appeared – the novels serialized – in such periodicals as *Nuova antologia, Rivista d'Italia, Il pungolo della domenica, Illustrazione italiana, La lettura, L'idea liberale*. For a while she also published a regular column in *Fanfulla della domenica*. Almost all her works were translated into German, the later ones also into English, French and Russian.[2]

What did Neera write about? Benedetto Croce, to whom Neera owes much of her reputation, put it quite succinctly: "Il problema della donna e quello dell'amore hanno formato l'oggetto principale e quasi unico del suo studio."[3] In fact, all of Neera's work evokes, directly or indirectly, her concern about the role of women, particularly in relation to the changes brought about by the rise of industrialism, socialism and feminism.

Despite the occasional insight, for the most part the tone of her writings, especially of her essays, remains one of bourgeois *perbenismo* and confirms the popular view of her today: "Una delle più accese avversarie del femminismo fu Anna Radius Zuccari ... popolarissima come autrice di romanzi nei quali esaltava l'amore materno, l'amicizia platonica, la mortificazione dei sensi, la dedizione e il sacrificio come tratti significativi della femminilità."[4] Or, as a recent, authoritative literary history puts it, "... tutta l'opera di Neera è opera di moralista, una vera e propria polemica per illuminare con la giusta luce l'insostituibile missione della donna."[5]

It is precisely this aspect of Neera's literary personality which accounts for Croce's warm, if somewhat patronizing, appraisal of her work: "Neera ha una assai solida e compiuta filosofia morale. Ella scorge accuratamente che la radice di tutte le false idee e falsi giudizi morali è in ciò che chiama, con ben appropriate parole, *il concetto materialistico della felicità.*"[6] "Nemic[a]," by her own avowal, "delle macchine, dell'eguaglianza, di tutte le cose piatte e volgari,"[7] Neera was clearly a woman after Croce's heart: "E mi piace di chiedere e di ottenere la mia parte in quel dispregio che onora, e di sentirmi 'borghese' nella buona compagnia di molti grandi scrittori borghesi, e in quella della mia vecchia e venerata amica Neera."[8]

Croce, however, chose to see only one facet of her literary personality; for while Neera the essayist and moralist certainly shared his worldview, Neera the artist was hardly as categoric – or as clear. Among her novels, *Un nido* (1880) has been cited as an unambiguous example of the bourgeois novel: one critic even goes so far as to call it a model of the genre.[9] *Teresa*, on the other hand, is celebrated in Baldacci's essay as both a naturalist novel and a feminist manifesto of its time.

Recent criticism, aware of the "two faces" of Neera, has tended, however, to polarize her work into fiction and non-fiction, depicting the latter as representative of a theoretical conservatism, the former of an "intuitive" feminism. Sergio Pacifici has focused on "the contradictions between the critical and creative work of Neera,"[10] while Luigi Baldacci has spoken of the "contraddittorietà ... che si pone tra la scrittrice d'invenzione e la saggista."[11] According to Baldacci, "sulle idee di Neera non è comunque il caso di soffermarsi troppo.... Se nei suoi scritti saggistici Neera tende a presentarsi come anti-femminista ... i suoi romanzi invece, e segnatamente *Teresa*, si rivelano come documenti essenziali dello spirito femminista" :

> Vale a dire che dove Neera rappresenta, la donna le si rivela per quello che è, come classe subalterna e, in quanto tale, repressa nella sua vita istintiva e materiale; dove invece *teorizza*, la stessa donna le si rivela come ideale, termine fisso di sublimazione di ogni istintualità umana, vittoriosa sulla vita dei sensi e disposta quindi a

quell'amor platonico per il quale non c'è davvero posto in un romanzo come *Teresa*, ma c'era posto, e come, nella vita della donna di lettere e di piccola galanteria quale fu Neera.[12]

Unfortunately, Baldacci's dichotomy, however appealing, is far truer to his own aesthetic biases than it is to the complexities of Neera's art. In reality, Neera's contradictions are to be found not only in the incompatibility of fiction and non-fiction, but within the fabric itself of both these components of her work. In fact, as shall be demonstrated in what follows, it is these contradictions that characterize her literary consciousness and determine the trajectory of her career as a writer.

Simone de Beauvoir, commenting on what often distinguishes the works of women from those of men, has pointed out that "a man would never get the notion of writing a book on the particular situation of the human male.... A man never begins by presenting himself as an individual of a certain sex; it goes without saying that he is a man."[13] The point is particularly pertinent to the case of Neera, whose most important collection of essays is eloquently entitled *Le idee di una donna* (1903). It contains a series of what could almost be called "position papers" on the condition of women. Of these, three are directly concerned with the role of women in relation to literary production.

La donna scrittrice is the most significant of these essays: it brings to light Neera's own self-consciousness and anxiety as a woman writer in an essentially masculine profession. After dismissing the majority of women writers as misguided victims of feminism, it goes on to warn of the special hardships awaiting the few possessed of a true literary vocation. Hostile, perfunctory critics, skeptical publishers and fickle readers are but minor concerns in the face of the most formidale obstacle of all – the hostility of writers of the opposite sex:

> Ognuno di essi era ben disposto a festeggiare la scrittrice quando nel suo interno la considerava come un leggiadro pupazzetto del suo medesimo sogno, inoffensivo, divertente, forse inutile. Ma è tutt'altra cosa se la donna diviene una rivale nella concorrenza....
> Al punto in cui la lotta si impegna seriamente, la differenza del sesso è cagione di astio maggiore. E' allora che la scrittrice si sente straniera in mezzo a quegli uomini inaspriti che hanno gettato la maschera della galanteria, ripresi dalla atavica brutalità dell'animale in guerra. E' il momento supremo. Se le forze, signore, vi hanno sorrette fin qui; se l'umiliazione, il dolore, lo scoramento, lo scetticismo, l'odio, non vi abbatterono sul fatale gradino dal quale

nessuno si alza più, resisterete ai colpi dei vostri fratelli? (pp. 832-833)

Under these circumstances, the challenge to a woman writer becomes not the serious art of writing, but, unfortunately, the delicate art of being a professional and remaining a "lady" in spite of it. The two conditions, as it were, appear to be mutually exclusive:

> A scrivere per sé ogni donna intelligente riesce a meraviglia. Scrivere per il pubblico è tutt'altra cosa ed è cosa difficilissima.... Guardiamo quante signore, recitando in casa propria per i loro amici, o altrove in serate di beneficenza, ci meravigliano per la grazia, il calore della loro recitazione; ci sembra che esse non avrebbero da far altro che salire i gradini di un vero palcoscenico per essere pareggiate alle attrici più in voga. Ma ci inganniamo. Portate fuori dal loro ambiente, dal circolo ossequioso che le sorregge, dalla libertà e dalla limitazione della loro parte ... dalla sicurezza che qualunque cosa accada non rischiano nulla di quella posta e che resteranno anche dopo le signore di prima; cambiati tutti gli accessori, e il lavoro, e il pubblico e lo scopo; vorrei vedere quante di loro si salverebbero! (pp. 833-834)

In this same collection of essays, in a piece entitled *La parte della donna*, she reveals the full extent of her anxieties on the subject by falling prey to an apparently inexplicable contradiction. Rather than continue the vehement polemic of *La donna scrittrice*, she does a complete about-face:

> Appoggerò qui una tesi alla quale accennai già altrove, cioè che tutta la forza impiegata dalla donna per i lavori, dirò così esterni, della intelligenza, vanno a detrimento del lavoro intimo, sublime, inimitabile che lei sola può compiere, sacrificando la sua personalità all'uomo che deve nascere da lei. Sotto questo aspetto è facile scorgere quanto e la Eliot e la Sand poco diedero alla umanità in confronto alle oscure madri di Leonardo e di Dante. Compiangiamo, anziché invidiare la donna che, spinta da occulti destini, fallisce la sua missione di olocausto al sesso da cui esce il genio. (p. 802)

In another of her essays, published many years later, this thesis is carried a step further:

> ... quasi mai il genio passa direttamente da uomo a uomo; sembra che la sua condizione di vita sia quella di maturare in un caldo e appassionato cuore di donna.... Ed ecco una ragione per frenare le donne nella loro smania di produrre opere di mente: ogni conquista da esse fatta in questo campo è un furto all'uomo futuro.[14]

In reality, contradictions such as these are no more paradoxical than those to be found in her *Confessioni letterarie* (1891), a literary memoir dedicated to Luigi Capuana which explains at great length how and why she turned to writing. Not surprisingly, it reads more like a justification – and even an apology – than a confession:

> Leggere, scrivere, pensare: ecco il riassunto della mia giovinezza. Erano le sole gioie che avevo alla mia portata e le prendevo avidamente.... Senza madre, senza sorelle ... differente in tutto dalle mie coetanee ... straniera in grembo alla mia famiglia.
> I miei fratelli avevano gli studi, le passeggiate, gli amici, e poi furono per molti anni all'Università. Essi ridevano qualche volta. Io mai.... Immobile ... silenziosissima, avevo l'unica risorsa di fuggire per la porta sempre aperta della fantasia. (pp. 876-877)

Clearly gifted with a strong imaginative drive, Neera feels compelled to attribute its development – and that of the consequent will to write – almost exclusively to a childhood of emotional and intellectual deprivation. The contribution of these negative stimuli is emphasized to the total detriment of intelligence or talent:

> Sono convinta che la vita interiore, come l'ho vissuta io, pochi la conoscono: ed a questo contribuì certo, oltre la naturale disposizione, l'ambiente singolarissimo, mistura stridente di provincialismo e di vivere cittadino ... dove io stavo continuamente in compagnia di Foscolo e di Byron per liberarmi dalla presenza dei bottegai e delle cameriere in ritiro, alle quali non sapevo che cosa dire.
> Se fossi stata circondata da una semplice parvenza di vita intellettuale e geniale ... avrei sofferto molto meno. Vi prego di ponderare la parola "sofferto" alla quale dò molta importanza. Se avessi avuto i baci ... il sorriso ... il chiacchierìo ... le occupazioni ... le distrazioni ... chi sa? avrei forse scritto ugualmente, ma la tortura psicologica non sarebbe entrata così profondamente in me da formare quasi una seconda natura.... La penna mi calmava. (pp. 878-879)

Curiously enough, a mere few paragraphs later, *what had begun as a consolation, indeed almost a drug, suddenly turns into an invincible will to write*: "Tutto intorno a me era contrario alla mia passione. L'educazione incompleta, l'ambiente ristretto ... niente emulazione, niente stimolo, niente aiuto.... Ci voleva proprio una vocazione irresistibile per vincere tutto ciò" (p. 885).

Equally significant are Neera's deliberate attempts to deny her attraction to the self-assertive and competitive aspects of writing as a profession. The following passage is perhaps one of the most striking examples of the extent to which she had internalized the social pressures incumbent upon an ambitious woman:

> E' certo che allora, quando leggevo avidamente le appendici del *Pungolo*, non mi sarei mai immaginata di dovere un giorno comparire io stessa sulle colonne dei giornali e tra i fogli di un libro. Non ho mai compreso la vanità letteraria, anzi il mio orrore della notorietà era così forte, che allorquando mi trovai al punto di scendere nell'arena, presi uno pseudonimo, colla ferma convinzione di innalzare una barriera inaccessibile fra me e l'opera mia. (p. 890)

This vehement declaration of feminine modesty and total extraneousness to literary ambition resurfaces in an ironic vein in one of Neera's later novels, *Anima sola* (1894). Its narrator, an actress writing a memoir, feels compelled to begin her tale with the following reassuring reminder to her readers: "I am not a *letterata*, one of those women so justly antipathetic to men."[15] An analogous remark crops up in an earlier novel, *Lydia* (1887): the heroine, when urged by her uncle to take up writing as a hobby, asks whether he is trying to make of her "una letterata, una di quelle orribili donne che fanno fuggire gli uomini" (p. 217).

Clearly, Neera is not the nameless narrator of *Anima sola* and much less Lydia. However, as Elaine Showalter has pointed out in *A Literature of Their Own*, for most women of the nineteenth century the decision to write professionally did require "a genuine transcendence of female identity."[16] In Neera's case, as demonstrated by the eloquently entitled *Idee di una donna*, the transcendence is never quite accomplished: unwilling to abandon her traditional role as a woman, she is equally unable to separate it from that of her role as a writer. As a result, her work is characterized by an almost obsessive awareness of herself *as a woman writer*, profoundly and personally implicated *as a woman* in everything that she wrote.

Nowhere is this confusion of roles, this sense of personal implication, as apparent as in the cycle of novels constituting the first phase of her career: the roles and fates she assigns to her female characters are never just that – her own reputation as a woman, as *una donna onesta*, is always at stake as well. Characterized by such ominous titles as *Addio!* and *Il castigo*, they are all centered, in one way or another, on the theme of adultery or, more accurately, on the adultery/punishment motif, a particularly extreme variant of the desire/duty conflict which underlies all her fictional works. The illicit passions and harsh punishments to which Neera repeatedly subjects her heroines in these first novels can only be explained in terms of the acute role-conflict – and role-confusion – she is experiencing when she first begins to write.

Addio! (1877) is the story of Valeria, a young aristocratic woman who marries a much older man for whom she feels respect and admiration but no attraction. She says later of this marriage: "Avevo vent'anni e credevo che il dovere bastasse a riempire tutta una vita."[17] She remains untroubled until she meets Massimo, a younger man with whom she falls in love though she makes every effort to resist. Suddenly her husband falls ill and dies, leaving her childless. On his deathbed, he releases her from her vows and encourages her to remarry. She, however, decides firmly that she will have no other man after him.

To Massimo, whom she is legally free to marry, she explains her decision by way of reference to their adulterous though unconsumated passion: "Questa donna che tu ami, non puoi stimarla."[18] Finally, she puts an end to things by leaving the country. "Era possibile resistere a quell'assalto di carezze, a quell'urto dei sensi da cui già sprigionavansi infocate le mille scintille del desiderio?"[19] asks Neera. Clearly not. Valeria pays her tithe to society several times over: first by repressing her adulterous instincts in the course of her marriage, then by refusing to give in to them when they are no longer adulterous, finally by going into exile thereby sacrificing country, home, family, every form of comfort.

Il castigo (1881) transposes the tale of Valeria from the aristocracy to the petty bourgeosie. Laura has married a man whom she does not love, though, unlike Valeria, she has done so out of exhaustion rather than innocence: "Adesso Laura si maritava per finirla. Era stanca di soffrire e di combattere. Anelava a una cosa sola – la pace."[20] The stifling atmosphere of the provinces provides the backdrop for Laura's adulterous passion for her husband's young dynamic nephew, Ugo, the first man ever to reciprocate her love. She yields to him and bears a child, unaware that her husband has been suffering silently in the knowledge that the child is not his. In time, Ugo falls ill and dies. Shortly afterward the same fate befalls her daughter. Her husband's words to his stricken wife close the story on a bitter note: "Il castigo è tremendo ... ma anche per me la vita fu un castigo ... e non avevo nulla da scontare!"[21]

As in *Addio!* it is difficult to reconcile the harshness of the punishment with the crime; however, as in *Addio!* Neera also makes few concessions to her public's *pudore*, at least in her descriptions of the violence of the passions involved:

> Laura non era più padrona di sé stessa. Nel suo interno una marea montante di desideri pazzi, di illusioni stravaganti la soffocava. Un cerchio opprimente le stringeva il cervello, come se avesse odorato del muschio. Si sentiva le ali alle spalle; ai piedi una voluttà morbosa, qualche cosa di molle e di pesante, come devono provare i mangiatori di oppio o i tisici destinati a morire.... Lunghi progetti di seduzione le trottavano nella fantasia. Avrebbe voluto vendicarsi degli uomini; farli soffrire come ella aveva sofferto – e vendicarsi delle donne anche: mostrar loro che questa morta seppellita, questa zitellona maritata per grazia le superava tutte. Voleva vivere! Vivere![22]

La freccia del parto (1883) and *Il marito dell'amica* (1885) follow *Il castigo* at two-year intervals. In *La freccia* a young widow virtuously resists the attentions of a married man to whom she is very attracted, but in a chance encounter with his clearly deranged wife she forgets her own pain and shows kindness and understanding. She is soon rewarded by the wife's death, which leaves the husband free to marry her.

Il marito dell'amica returns to the theme of renunciation. Maria is a young widow who has just returned to Milan after years of living in Brazil. When circumstances inadvertently reunite her with her first and only love, Emanuele, she discovers that her passion for him is still alive. She is sorely tempted to yield to his advances, until the presence of his child reminds her of the sanctity of the tie she is about to violate. Her virtue and Emanuele's marriage both still intact, she leaves immediately for Brazil. The immensity of her sacrifice is emphasized by her return to a foreign country where she has only memories of a cold and sterile marriage, and by pages and pages of flashbacks recreating her youthful passion for the man she is leaving behind.

Virtue is rewarded, disobedience punished, in some cases virtue must suffice as its own reward: though this is the moral of these tales of adulterous passion, it is hardly their only point. In reality, the adultery/punishment motif and its variations serve a two-fold purpose, one conscious, the other unconscious. On one level, the harsh punishments Neera inflicts on her transgressing heroines allows her to avoid having herself identified with them and with their misadventures; that is, it allows her to espouse the outward conservatism so necessary to her as a woman, as she undertakes the highly unorthodox task of writing novels. This is confirmed by Neera herself in the original preface to *Addio!*:

> Nel succedersi delle leggi e dei costumi noi abbiamo vista la donna adultera condannata a morte, e la vediamo libera e impunita regnare nel disonorato talamo.
> Dov'è la giustizia? Essa si trova certamente fra i due estremi.
> L'umanità fa grazia della vita ma la morale reclama il castigo.
> Ecco il mio tema. Tema contrario a quella riabilitazione tanto di moda che pareggia la donna pentita alla donna pura. Il perdono assolve, non muta il passato.
> Dedico questo libro alle donne oneste.[23]

Not surprisingly, her critics were unconvinced by Neera's declarations. In a later preface she tells us: "... al primo apparire di questo volume quasi tutta la critica italiana si slanciò su di esso e su di me con una veemenza veramente straordinaria (trattandosi di un autore giovane e di una donna)."[24] She takes up their accusations in terms that confirm the importance of the heroine's intensity of conflict:

> La morale oltraggiata, voi dite? Ma se dalla prima all'ultima parola è tutto un inno alla morale? – se accanto alle frasi più appassionate c'è sempre il grido della coscienza, egualmente vero, egualmente forte?...
> All'accusa che mi si fece di aver dato un carattere troppo sensuale a questo amore, risponderò che ... non credetti di palliarne le tinte per non togliere il contrasto che sta appunto nell'ardore della passione coll'ardore della virtù. Una Valeria fredda avrebbe delirato meno, questo è certo, ma non avrebbe nemmeno compiuto un così gran sacrificio.[25]

Elsewhere in the same preface she also betrays her personal sense of identification with her heroine, whose role as an "adulteress" appears totally beside the point:

> In genere i critici che sono avvezzi a trovare nei romanzi le passioni convenzionali, si ribellano davanti a questo caso di amore spontaneo, davanti a questa donna che è una vera donna di carne e di sangue e (lo dico perché i miei avversari fanno apposta a volerlo dimenticare) di nobilissima anima.
> Un fatto curioso è che a tutte le donne piacque l'*Addio*; gli uomini quasi esclusivamente non vollero accettare questa donna diversa dalla donna che hanno fabbricata loro, per proprio comodo, tipo della specie....[26]

Though outwardly Neera tries to distinguish herself from her heroines, under fire she reveals the extent of her identification with their anguish. Torn between what she perceives as her womanly role on the one hand, and the "subversive" impulse to write on the other, she unconsciously projects her conflict onto the narrative plane, where it finds homologous expression in the dilemmas of her heroines caught between the equally irreconcilable extremes of sacred marital duty and adulterous sexual passion. The theme of adultery recurs so consistently in these first novels because it is the only theme capable of conveying with appropriate acuity the conflict of roles Neera herself is experiencing as a writer in this early phase of her career.

This is confirmed by the publication in 1880 of *Un nido*, which, as stated earlier, has gained Neera the dubious honour of having produced the "perfect" bourgeois novel. As opposed to preceding and subsequent works, it depicts a world in which the heroine's self-fulfillment is in perfect harmony with the myths of the prevailing order: the young farmer courting a destitute orphan girl of the aristocracy turns out to be a former poet who has abandoned the wicked literary world of the city for the serenity of cows and countryside. In the best of all possible worlds no compromises are necessary and frogs turn out to be Prince Charmings after all. It is worth emphasizing that this soppy little fairy tale – complete with cruel step-parents and all – appears shortly after the scurrilous *Addio!* which had raised so many moral eyebrows, and shortly before the ominous *Castigo*: Neera's greatest homage to the myths of her society is clearly an attempt to appease her indignant audience and hence an integral part of her dilemma as a woman writer in this phase.

Further confirmation of the connection between the adultery/punishment motif and Neera's own conflict of allegiances when she first takes up the pen is provided by the motif's sudden disappearance as soon as she enters the naturalist phase of her career. How she came to turn to naturalism at this point is something that can only be speculated upon – a contributing factor may have been Luigi Capuana's reaction to *Un nido*, which appeared in 1882:

> ... si vorrà veder uscire la Neera dal mondo un po' artifiziale dove s'è compiaciuta finora. Si vorrà vederla aprir la finestra perché in quel suo studiolo entrino e la *luce sfacciata* delle vie, com'ella dice, e il rumore assordante della vita che pur troppo non somiglia in nulla o assai di rado a quello che si sente nel delizioso nido da lei fabbricato per la sua simpatica Editta.... E' innegabile che la severità quasi

scientifica dell'arte moderna opprime, stanca, fa male al cuore. Ma dall'altro lato è anche innegabile che l'arte dove non sia passato il soffio del pensiero moderno non è più un'arte vitale e che abbia valore.[27]

Whether Capuana was responsible for Neera's sudden about-face or not, the advantages offered by his theory of "la perfetta impersonalità [dell'] opera d'arte"[28] must not have escaped her notice. For Neera, in fact, *verismo*'s view of the artist as an *impersonal* observer meant freedom from the confusion – and hence conflict – of roles that had determined the adultery/punishment motif of the early novels. The works belonging to this period – *Teresa* (1886), *Lydia* (1887), *L'indomani* (1890) – provide a far less stylized, and consequently far more authentic portrait of the lot of women in the society of her day.

Contrary to Neera's previous and subsequent fictional works, these novels lay great emphasis on the societal and environmental factors which contribute to the misfortunes of their heroines. For the first and only time in her career as a writer, Neera dares to study the dilemma of her heroines from the point of view of its relation to past conditioning: *these women are not victims of their passions, they are victims of their upbringings.* For the first and only time her characters acquire, if not great psychological depth as individuals, certainly well-documented case histories. Most of Neera's other heroines live in uncontextualized drawing rooms, their pasts consisting of the minimum number of facts necessary to justify their present situations.[29] *Their vulnerability is a given*, an assumption presented as a "universal" deriving from their womanliness. The converse of this is that those women who are not vulnerable are simply not women: a case in point is Corinna, the sister of Senio in the novel of the same name.[30]

In *Teresa, Lydia* and *L'indomani* however, the extreme vulnerability of the heroines is for the first time explored rather than assumed. These three women are as vulnerable as they are not because of their "womanliness," but because of a simple lack of alternatives. Teresa, Lydia and Marta are in three very different situations, but they share one common trait: powerlessness in the face of their own destinies.

When Neera is brave enough to paint the conflict between self-fulfillment and acquiescence to societal norms as she really sees it, and not through artificial secondary conflicts such as the one provided by the adultery motif, her writing also unleashes its own particular "poetry" – the poetry of feminine solitude, a solitude afflicting married and unmarried women alike, when their visions of love remain unfulfilled. "Le lunghe ore della solitudine femminile"[31] constitute in fact the shared experience of Lydia, Marta and Teresa, none of whom is sublimating in impossible adulterous passions or, like later heroines, in platonic platitudes. "Allevate nell'idea fissa del matrimonio, il quale, con la morale odierna è la sola porta d'uscita che esse hanno,"[32] they are caught between a dream quickly going sour and a drastic lack of socially-sanctioned alternatives, with no relief in sight. It is when she is evoking this aspect of their beings and their lives – this captivity as it were – that Neera is at her best. In *Teresa*, as Baldacci puts it, "lo studio di costume diventa studio di comportamento, ricerca positiva, arte come scienza ... e tocca profondità psicologiche che la narrativa italiana non conosceva da una ventina d'anni."[33]

Teresa tells the story of the uneventful life of a young girl of the provincial petty bourgeoisie in the second half of the nineteenth century. For reasons of temperament as well as of circumstance, Teresa is unable to give any direction to her life. She is equally inept when it comes to choosing an appropriate suitor: the young man she favours is weak and directionless himself, and unable to win her father's approval. As a result, Teresa wastes her time and energy waiting in vain for a turning point in their long-distance relationship, and loses her best years in the process.

As apparently commonplace as it may sound on the surface, this tale contains a merciless in-depth analysis of the factors which contribute to deny Teresa any real possibility of choice in life – patriarchal family, the precedence accorded to male offspring in matters of education, the subtle messages transmitted to her from her earliest years as to what constitutes femininity. As such, it merits a special place in any discussion of Neera's *oeuvre* and indeed, I have made it the subject of a separate analysis elsewhere in this volume.[34]

Lydia, published in the year immediately following the appearance of *Teresa*, transfers Teresa's tale to the upper reaches of society. One of the novel's minor characters explains this, perhaps a bit too explicitly:

> Ho letto in questi giorni un libro che analizza la vita di una fanciulla nella piccola borghesia. E' un mondo piccino, dove la fantasia e tutte le altre qualità dell'intelletto non trovano modo di svilupparsi. Quella fanciulla arriva ai trent'anni, ignorando ogni cosa, vittima rassegnata e tranquilla. La sua condizione desta pietà; ma che dire di noi, a cui

fin dalla culla l'educazione, l'esempio, le letture, la società affinano
lo spirito ed i nervi, pur imponendoci le stesse catene? (p. 193)

When we first encounter her, Lydia is an intelligent, somewhat arrogant and
impetuous young girl about to enter society:

> Che cosa aspettasse precisamente non lo sapeva nemmeno lei: ma
> era cresciuta nell'adorazione del lusso e della bellezza. Fin da piccina
> ... le parole "sta bene, è elegante, è vezzosa" le erano risuonate
> all'orecchio come promesse di una felicità futura....
> Sballottata dalla bambinaia alla governante, dal maestro di piano al
> maestro di disegno, senza un filo di connessione, senza una misura,
> con molti insegnanti ma nessun educatore, ella era cresciuta libera in
> una società dove tutto è vincolo e finzione; ... e ignorando in modo
> assoluto tutto ciò che non aveva un rapporto diretto coi sensi.
> Era figlia de' suoi tempi; aveva il sangue misto, parte di decadenza
> aristocratica e parte di insolenza borghese arrivata in alto. Molto
> intelligente, chiudeva in sé i germi del bene e del male, ma nessuno
> sviluppato, nessuno dominante. La superficialità della sua
> educazione soffocava in lei ogni tendenza individuale. (p. 197)

This lack of a well-defined value system eventually leads her to disaster. Left to
fend for herself after the death of her mother, she goes from one sterile, superficial
encounter to another, until her reputation is almost completely compromised.
"Indipendente e non maritata; vergine e già passata attraverso le corruzioni della
fantasia; non avendo mai concesso un bacio eppure vituperata dalla fama" (p. 242),
Lydia fails to realize that her only chance to find love lies in a break with her
superficial ways.

She has one chance to make this break, in an encounter with the young lawyer
Calmi, a clever and sensitive man who sees through Lydia and is attracted to her.
But Lydia is too cynical to take the necessary emotional risks and rebuffs him,
preferring to hide behind her well-cultivated mask of invulnerability and quick
repartee. Her superficial and frivolous nature makes it equally impossible for her to
find any other positive outlet for her energies. It is Lydia who, when urged by an
uncle to take up writing as a hobby, asks whether he wants to see her become "una
letterata, una di quelle orribili donne che fanno fuggire gli uomini" (p. 217).

Finally, well past the age of thirty, she thinks she has found the answer in the
person of the Austrian Count Keptsky, a newcomer to the corrupt circles in which
she moves. Blind by this time to all but her own desperate need for love, she fails
to realize that Keptsky is merely a fortune-hunter and her best friend's lover as

well. The discovery of Keptsky's true motives, revealed to her by Calmi, leads her to take her life shortly before her long-awaited wedding day.

In *L'indomani*, the relationship between upbringing and ability to cope with the subsequent vicissitudes of life is examined in the context of a highly different situation. Marta, the novel's heroine, has ostensibly found that which had always eluded Lydia: "Il sogno della sua ardente giovinezza si era avverato a puntino: un uomo giovane, simpatico, onesto, l'aveva chiesta in moglie, le aveva dato il suo nome, la conduceva con sé; l'amava dunque. Era l'amore ideale, vero, indistruttibile" (p. 324).

The novel opens just as Marta is settling down to married life. She awakens one morning, only to find her husband still deep in sleep beside her: "Marta lo guardò a lungo, intensamente, vedendo sfuggire in quel sonno ostinato una delle più antiche fantasie d'amore" (p. 323). The fall from grace however is merely beginning and is the result of Marta's failure to realize that she is projecting her dreams of love onto a man chosen for reasons having little to do with his ability to fulfill them:

> Il suo destino veniva messo a partito da parecchi mesi fra cinque o sei candidati scelti a vagliati dalle amiche della mamma ... individualità assolutamente opposte, ma che, presentandosi in forma di marito, offrivano le stesse garanzie di felicità, a detta delle amiche....
> Intanto che si discutevano le probabilità di tali matrimoni ... capitò Alberto Oriani. "Guarda," osservò una cugina, "che bella combinazione, Oriani! E Marta è Oldofredi; non cambierebbe nemmeno le iniziali." Su questa felice scoperta si incominciarono le trattative....
> Quando fu il momento di decidersi, ognuno le fece osservare ... la singolare fortuna sua nella media generale delle fanciulle; molte fra le quali si maritano tardi, spoetizzate e già avvizzite; altre non si maritano affatto; chi deve accontentarsi di un vecchio, chi di un vedovo, chi di uno un po' corto di cervello, chi di uno spiantato, o di un balbuziente o di un mezzo tisico, perché – dicono le persone assennate – tutto non si può avere. (p. 326)

The representation of Marta's life that follows, as she comes slowly and incredulously to grips with the enormous *malentendu* that her marriage has turned out to be, constitutes as devastating an indictment of bourgeois marriage as is to be found in any twentieth-century feminist tract on the subject. This from the pen of one of the most vocally anti-feminist women of her time:

Per le donne oneste ... l'amore non può essere che un dovere o un peccato; un contratto stipulato ... eguagliato ... alla vendita di un podere; oppure uno strappo alle convenienze, alle leggi, alla religione, all'onore.... Nel primo caso l'uomo furbo lo idealizza. Egli dice alle sue vittime: "Siete la gioia del focolare domestico ... le regine della nostra casa...." Potrebbe soggiungere: "Siete il minor male che noi scegliamo dopo d'aver conosciuto tutti gli altri ... il letto di riposo dopo il letto da campo, la sinecura dei nostri vecchi giorni. In cambio della vostra vita, noi che non abbiamo più né giovinezza, né candore, né ideali, vi offriamo una cosa così comune, così facile, una cosa che trovereste sul canto d'ogni via, se noi non ce ne fossimo fatto un esclusivo monopolio, accrescendone il valore col negarvene la libertà, sostituendo il decoro, il pudore, la virtù umana alle divine leggi della natura. E fin da bambine, all'età degli zuccherini, vi si fa balenare davanti agli occhi quest'altro zuccherino, ammonendovi: 'se ve lo meriterete con la docilità, la modestia, la pazienza, l'abnegazione'...." (p. 350)

Though analyses such as these are perhaps more frequent than they ought to be in fully-realized work of fiction, by no means do they represent the extent of Neera's ability to illustrate her theme. Particularly poignant – and daring – is this description of Marta's nightly vigil during her husband's absences, "le lunghe ore della sera, le ore che Alberto passava in farmacia con gli amici" :

Con le braccia inerti, svogliata Marta passava la sera sulla stessa sedia dove aveva pranzato ... dava qualche punto ... leggicchiava il giornale, sbadigliava. Le ore erano lunghe, eterne.... L'attesa, dapprima calma e rassegnata, volgeva, col volgere delle ore, ad una inquietudine generale.... Il tempo passava e dall'immobilità angosciosa, Marta entrava in uno stato di allucinazione sensuale.... Il tempo passava ancora, finché l'eccitazione, illanguidendosi, la lasciava sfinita, con le membra rotte, gli occhi pesti e vacillanti..... Alberto la sorprendeva quasi sempre distesa sul divano, pallida, inerte. E la rimproverava.... Ella non rispondeva nulla. Barcollante, terminava di svestirsi con dei brividi nelle ossa, e si cacciava sotto le lenzuola. Ma quando suo marito, avvicinandosele, mormorava: "Andiamo, via..." tutto il suo corpo si irrigidiva, si gettava indietro.
" Le donne," concludeva Alberto voltandosi dall'altra parte, "non si arriva mai a comprenderle."
E Marta, sotto le coltri, piangeva. (pp. 368-369)

Surprisingly, *L'indomani* ends on what appears to be a contradictory note – that of Marta's acceptance and joyful sublimation of her lot in motherhood. In reality, however, this conclusion is simply a prefiguration of the return to the forefront of Neera's "womanly" concerns; in fact, the following year, 1891, sees the publication of her first *scritto morale, Il libro di mio figlio*. Neera the novelist, who had been so roundly chastized by the *benpensanti* for her risqué romances, is conspicuously absent from this "libro per insegnare a pensare."[35] Says one reviewer:

> Mi trovo ... dinanzi a un libro di una delle più conosciute nostre scrittrici, ma che si presenta con una pubblicazione di un altro genere a cui mai prima si era dedicata....
> Neera autrice di romanzi letti avidamente ... ma che niente hanno a che fare con la presente [opera] ... scrisse il suo libro per insegnare a suo figlio ... gli ideali di tutte le mamme che hanno dei bambini.[36]

The "new" Neera finds consensus everywhere. The *Giornale delle donne* tells its readers that when "una madre che si chiama Neera parla a suo figlio, tutte le donne hanno l'obbligo di ascoltare."[37] Another reviewer declares the book "la miglior opera dell'insigne scrittrice, opera molto più profonda, molto più utile che non tutti i suoi ottimi e desiderati romanzi."[38]

Not surprisingly, as Neera re-establishes her credibility as a woman and a mother, she abandons the naturalist novel to return to the reassuring conventions of the *romanzo borghese*. However, the conflicts depicted in her novels now are considerably less acute than they were in her first bourgeois phase, when Neera's literary activity was limited exclusively to fiction. Moralistic and pedagogical journalism and essay-writing have provided a much-needed outlet to mediate – and mitigate – the acutely-felt conflict between authorship and womanhood. *Consequently, the situations in which her heroines find themselves become less intensely characterized, and the punishments meted out correspondingly less harsh.* The adultery/punishment motif is dropped entirely: *Senio* (1892) and *Una passione* (1903) merit particular mention in this connection.

The conflict between self-fulfillment and acquiescence to societal norms provides the basic underlying structure of these novels as of all the others: both are designed to demonstrate the impossibility of love that defies conventional morality. Clara is a young woman separated from her husband who attempts to live love outside of marriage, Lilia an unmarried woman who seeks love outside marriage and outside her milieu. Both women fail in their attempts.

However – and this is the novelty – though transgression and retribution remain the terms of the conflict, its parameters are considerably less extreme. Neither Clara nor Lilia are adulteresses and, correspondingly, neither is unduly punished; neither woman finds "love forever" but neither is left without consolation, as were the heroines of Neera's first novels. Clara returns to her previous life and finds solace in her platonic friendship with Stefano, a young doctor as sensitive as she is, who has been abandoned by his wife. Lilia has been allowed a "fling" with no dire consequences and then is granted a marriage of convenience to a rich, adoring American. The only tithe exacted from these women is the loss of their illusions, rather more a condition of being alive than an actual punishment. It is worth emphasizing that *Senio* appears in 1892, the year following the publication of *Il libro di mio figlio*, while the publication of *Una passione* (1903) coincides exactly with that of *Le idee di una donna*, in which, among other things, Neera dutifully exhorts aspiring women writers to abandon their ambitions and return to their traditional roles.

In the years following the beginning of her career as a moralist, Neera was also to find a solution to the novelistic problem of adulterous passion. *L'amor platonico*, a moral treatise published in 1897, sees the light in the same year as *L'amuleto*, a fictional representation of the theoretical positions outlined in the treatise. In this new and very different approach to the theme of adultery, the heroine gradually sublimates her attraction to a man other than her husband in the name of woman's ideal mission. Self-denial remains the order of the day but is now wedded to an ideal which raises it above the level of mere subservience to external societal norms:

> ... quasi ogni giorno rinunciavo a una gioia, a una curiosità, a una lieve soddisfazione, tendendo tutte le mie forze a raggiungere ciò che era ormai il mio unico scopo, che doveva tenermi luogo di felicità: mostrarmi degna di Lui. E mi abituavo pure a pensare la mia vita priva di Lui, a sostituire a Lui i suoi ideali, spiritualizzando la mia passione, elevandola alla dolce religiosità di un culto.... E' questo che dobbiamo fare noi donne: emulare l'uomo nelle forze spirituali, non per contendergliele, ma per aggiungervi le nostre idealità. (pp. 489-490)

With *L'amor platonico* and this tedious fictional how-to illustration of its precepts, Neera finally squares her position with the world; so much so in fact, that the American editor of *Anima sola*, writing in 1905, is able to include the following reassuring observation to Neera's readers in his introduction to the novel:

> The author of *Anima sola* who signs with the *nom de plume* Neera, in private life is Anna Zuccari, wife of Signor Radius.... While indulging in writing of glorious battles, ignoble victories, and of the

throes of a soul in the grasp of that overpowering passion, love, she is very domestic, the angel of her home – not at all the portrait of any of the heroines of her books.[39]

The novels published from this date to the end of her life present no significant new elements.[40]

Notes

[1] L. Baldacci, Introduction, *Teresa*, by Neera (Turin: Einaudi, 1976) v.

[2] For information on the various aspects of Neera's literary activity, and on the fortunes and translations of her works see G. Menasci, "Neera," *Nuova antologia di scienze lettere ed arti* 16 Sept. 1901: 263-278; also "Appendice," in Neera's *Una giovinezza del secolo XIX* (Milan: Cogliati, 1919) 263-269. For a bibliography of Neera's own publications and for a recent critical bibliography see Neera, *Monastero e altri racconti*, eds. A. Arslan and A. Folli (Milan: Libri Scheiwiller, 1987) as well as the entry on Neera by A. Arslan in *Dizionario critico della letteratura italiana* (Turin: UTET, 1986) 242-244.

[3] B. Croce, "Neera," in *Neera* (Milan: Garzanti, 1942) 932-933. This volume carries a significant selection of Neera's works, edited by Croce, and includes a complete bibliography of her works as well as two critical essays by Croce: "Neera" (932-1044), first published in *La critica* (1905): 354-368 and reprinted in *Letteratura della nuova Italia* (Bari: Laterza, 1949) vol.3, 121-140; "Prefazione all'autobiografia" (945-947), first published in *Una giovinezza del secolo XIX*, vii-xi. All future references to novels or essays included in this volume will appear in the text.

[4] R. Ghiaroni, Introduction, *Una donna*, by S. Aleramo (Turin: Loescher, 1978) 10.

[5] F. Angelini *et al.*, *Il secondo Ottocento*, Vol. 8 of *La letteratura italiana: Storia e testi* (Bari: Laterza, 1975) 588.

[6] "Neera," *Neera* 931.

[7] "Confessioni letterarie," *Neera* 896.

[8] "Prefazione all'autobiografia," *Neera* 946. For Croce's correspondance with Neera see A. Arslan and A. Folli, *Il concetto che ne informa. Benedetto Croce e Neera. Corrispondenza (1903-1917)*, (Naples: Edizioni Scientifiche Italiane,1989).

[9] B. Romani, "La narrativa borghese del secondo Ottocento," *Controcorrente tardottocentesca* (Lecce: Milella, 1974) 18.

[10] S. Pacifici, "Women Writers: Neera and Aleramo," *The Modern Italian Novel from Capuana to Tozzi* (Carbondale: Southern Illinois U. Press, 1973) 56.

[11] L. Baldacci, Foreword, *Le idee di una donna*, by Neera (Florence: Vallecchi, 1977) xviii.

[12] Baldacci, Introduction, *Teresa* vii.

[13] S. de Beauvoir, *The Second Sex*, as quoted in P. M. Spacks, *The Female Imagination* (New York: Alfred A. Knopf, 1972) 9.

[14] Neera, "Un idealista: Alberto Sormani," *Profili, impressioni e ricordi* (Milan: Cogliati, 1919) 45.

[15] *Anima sola* (Milan: Chiesa e Guindani, 1894), translated by E. L. Murison as *The Soul of an Artist* (San Francisco: Paul Elder and Co., 1905) 1.

[16] E. Showalter, *A Literature of Their Own: British Women Novelists from Brontë to Lessing* (Princeton: Princeton University Press, 1977) 96.

[17] *Addio!*, 11th ed. (Milan: Baldini e Castoldi, 1904) 4.

[18] *Addio!* 106.

[19] *Addio!* 108.

[20] *Il castigo*, 2nd ed. (Turin: Roux, 1891) 64.

[21] *Il castigo* 213.

[22] *Il castigo* 95.

[23] *Addio!* vi.

[24] *Addio!* vii.

[25] *Addio!* viii-ix.

[26] *Addio!* xiii-xiv.

[27] L. Capuana, "Neera," *Studi sulla letteratura contemporanea*, 2nd series (Catania: Giannotta, 1882) 156-157. Neera is also mentioned by Capuana in "Butti, Neera, Gualdo," *Gli "ismi" contemporanei* (Catania: Giannotta, 1898) 113-129 and in *Lettere all'assente* (Rome: Roux-Viarengo, 1904) 165-166.

[28] L. Capuana, *Studi sulla letteratura contemporanea* 140. Capuana's correspondence with Neera in these years yields no clues as to the specific influence he may have exerted on her. It has been published by A. Arslan as "Luigi Capuana and Neera: corrispondenza inedita 1881-1885," *Miscellanea di studi in onore di Vittore Branca*, Vol.5 (Florence: Olschki, 1983) 161-185.

[29] An example of this is to be found in *Rogo d'amore* (Milan: Fratelli Treves, 1914). Its heroine is called simply "la signora," and all that we are told about her, other than that she belongs to the aristocracy, is contained in the following paragraph: "Sciolta dai vincoli di famiglia, padrona di sé, semplice dinanzi a Dio che ella adorava con spirito religioso in tutte le forme del mistero, era libera, era sola; nessuna responsabilità incombeva più sulla sua coscienza, nessun compromesso coi suoi doveri...." (p. 219).

[30] "Corinna aveva un metro e settantacinque di statura, un corpo quadrato, angoloso, dall'ossatura forte, che sembrava tagliato coll'accetta, e una faccia irregolare, sparsa di peli non abbastanza folti per darle l'originalità di donna barbuta, ma pur sufficienti per togliere alle sue guancie qualsiasi attrattiva femminile. Le mancavano della femminilità poi due affermazioni caratteristiche: la mano ed il seno. L'insieme della sua corporatura mostravasi più adatto a rivestire una corazza che ad accogliere i vezzi di una donna, e la mano nerboruta allontanava l'idea delle carezze per sostituirvi il concetto di una forza virile, a cui rispondeva perfettamente l'espressione del volto.... Aveva letto una quantità di opere teologiche, filosofiche e chirurgiche.... Amava Spencer, Darwin, Nordau, Schopenhauer.... Più fortunata delle altre donne, più libera, sciolta affatto da impegni personali ... era la donna più felice del mondo" (*Senio* [Milan: Galli, 1892] 48, 50, 52).

31 "Teresa," *Neera* 43.

32 "L'indomani," *Neera* 358.

33 Baldacci, Introduction, *Teresa* ix.

34 See "The Search for Literary Mothers: Neera's *Teresa*."

35 Subtitle taken from a list of "Buoni libri per le scuole e per le famiglie," on the back cover of *Bene pei cari piccolini*, by La Marchesa Colombi (Milan: Galli, 1891).

36 R. Costanzo, review of *Il libro di mio figlio*, quoted in "Giudizi della stampa," in appendix to *Senio* 291.

37 Review of *Il libro di mio figlio*, quoted in "Giudizi della stampa" 280.

38 Review of *Il libro di mio figlio, La voce di Tunisi*, quoted in "Giudizi della stampa" 289.

39 L. D. Ventura, Preface, *The Soul of an Artist* iv.

40 Among Neera's later novels are *Il romanzo della fortuna* (1905), *Crevalcore* (1906), *Duello d'anime* (1911), *Rogo d'amore* (1914), *Crepuscoli di libertà* (1917), all written in the bourgeois vein.

The Search for Literary Mothers: Neera's *Teresa*

In Neera's most important novel, *Teresa* (1886),[1] we find the following description of a three-dimensional landscape painting-*cum*-clock:

> Ciò che dominava e schiacciava questo modesto arredamento borghese era un quadro appeso alla parete maggiore; quadro massiccio, dello spessore di un palmo, entro cui si nascondevano i segreti di una meccanica ingenua, destinata a mettere in moto contemporaneamente le braccia di un mulino a vento, l'asinello del mugnaio e l'orologio incastonato nel campanile. Orologio e asinello erano fermi da gran tempo, ma il mulino continuava ad agitare, come un fantasma irrequieto, le sue scarne braccia in mezzo agli alberi di cartone dipinto che formavano lo sfondo del paesaggio. (27)

The most striking thing about this passage is clearly the image of the windmill. Its personification, its placement at the end of the description, its designation as the only moving object left in the picture, and the comparison of its spindly arms to those of a "fantasma irrequieto," an uneasy spectre, all bring to mind an obvious question: the spectre of what? Further investigation reveals that the windmill may not be a gratuitous detail at all, and that the "spectre" to which it alludes may be that of another, far more famous nineteenth-century novel, George Eliot's *The Mill on the Floss* (1860).

The possibility of such an interpretation is supported by a direct allusion to *The Mill on the Floss* in one of Neera's essays from the volume *Le idee di una donna* (1903). The essay is entitled "La parte della donna" and contains the following remarks about George Sand as well as George Eliot:

> Le due grandi scrittrici del secolo, George Eliot e George Sand, passarono i primi trent'anni della loro vita, l'una a manipolar burro,

l'altra a fabbricar conserve: forse nessuna, ripeto, delle fanciulle che
ora si vogliono tirar su per scrittrici (povere fanciulle!) scriverà *Il
mulino sulla Floss* o *Consuelo*. Ma anche è necessario persuadersi
che migliaia di donne, le quali non scrissero romanzo alcuno, sono,
o per intelligenza o per benefico influsso delle loro anime o per ricca
sensibilità, benemerite al pari e più della Eliot e della Sand.[2]

Would Neera make a cryptic reference to Eliot's novel in *Teresa* and yet speak
so disparagingly of her elsewhere? If so, why? Before delving into the relationship
between the two writers and investigating the possibility of a further relationship
between their two novels it is necessary first to summarize *Teresa* and then to
situate it in the context of Neera's *oeuvre* as a whole.

As a young girl cloistered in the kitchen of her parents' petty-bourgeois
provincial home, Teresa knows no life other than that of domestic drudgery. Her
father is an ignorant tyrant; her mother, "avezza a tacere davanti alla voce fessa ma
imperiosa del Signor Caccia" (p. 12), is "una donnina sui quarant'anni, gracile,
patita, con la faccia lunga e terrea, pallidamente illuminata da due occhi neri, opachi,
senza lampo" (p. 11):

> Qualche cosa di stanco, come di catena lungamente trascinata, si
> appalesava in tutti i suoi movimenti. La parola aveva breve e
> titubante ... [era] senza slancio per reagire, senza spirito per
> rispondere, convinta che la prima virtù di una donna deve essere
> l'ubbidienza. (p. 12)

While Teresa is kept in the home, Carlino "il rampollo che doveva trasmettere
alle future generazioni l'ingegno dei Caccia, rimasto fino allora sconosciuto" (p.
26), is sent away to school and to university. "Giovani tutti e due e sani," very
early on brother and sister are "già differenti nell'espressione della vita interna" (p.
65). While Carlino's horizons are broadening, Teresa's are narrowing and
gradually becoming a reflection of her mother's: "Quando nelle ore di riposo ... le
due donne sedevano accanto alla eterna finestra, il loro silenzio aveva una voce" (p.
74).

The grey monotony of Teresa's existence is interrupted for the first time when
an aunt invites her to spend some time with her in a nearby town. The aunt has
fared little better than Teresa's mother:

> ... gettata a diciotto anni nelle braccia di un uomo – senza che né
> l'uno né l'altro si amassero, perché lui aveva bisogno di trovar
> moglie per accudire al negozio; e lei era una ragazza da marito ...

aveva avuto sedici o diciassette figli, ma non conosceva l'amore, non era stata amata mai. (p. 33)

Here, for the first time, Teresa ventures into the world. At a dance she meets Cecchino who flirts casually with her and ignites her already smouldering sensibility. But, significantly, later on, the thought of Cecchino "invece di essere un pensiero gaio e sorridente, le si affacciò quasi come un dolore, come una spina acutissima passata nella pelle" (pp. 46-47): in spite of her own personal inexperience, Teresa's closeness to her mother has already taught her to associate womanhood with suffering. We are first made aware of this the night Signora Caccia, about to give birth, sighs deeply in the hope that the new child will be a boy since "le ragazze, poverette che cos'hanno di buono a questo mondo?" (p. 12):

> Le poche parole della madre, pronunciate lì sull'uscio, nel turbamento di quella notte, l'avevano profondamente impressionata. Si sentiva ad un tratto fatta donna – con un presentimento improvviso di dolori lontani....
> Sembrava che in quel momento, solamente in quel momento, ella riconoscesse il proprio sesso, sentendosi scorrere nelle vene un'onda di languore non mai avvertita prima, e nel cervello sorgere una curiosità viva, pungente, la quale cessò di colpo davanti al rossore che le invadeva le guance.... (p. 15)

Her mother's incessant allusions to the helplessness of women – "Tutto è destino.... Chi sa se sarebbe fortunata" (p. 30) – are not, however, the only factors contributing to the formation of Teresa's passive nature. On her rare outings, she is usually accompanied by *la pretora*, the wife of a town official, whose cynicism seems to give voice to her own mother's resigned silence. When Teresa balks at her suggestion of a marriage of convenience, *la pretora* does nothing to spare her any illusions of future happiness:

> "Oh! le ho avute anch'io le mie disillusioni; ma quando vidi che gli anni passavano, sposai il pretore ... che di illusioni me ne poteva dar ben poche ... e che, per compenso, mi diede un figlio tutti gli anni....
> Ebbene, grullina, che pensi? Vuoi il compendio della saviezza in poche parole? Un Luminelli che sposa è sempre superiore ad un Luzzi che non sposa ... o sposa un'altra."(p. 61)

And yet, in spite of all this, "le illusioni cantavano in lei più alto, più forte della breve esperienza umana" (p. 48). By the time she meets Egidio Orlandi, a school friend of her brother's, her destiny is sealed. They begin the usual small-town courtship, consisting of furtive glances and signals exchanged in the street. Very quickly Egidio becomes Teresa's *raison d'être*, the sole receptacle of all her hopes and desires, "il...pensiero...fisso, che la accompagnava nelle sue faccende domestiche, che la seguiva per la via, che si coricava con lei tutte le sere, e ch'ella trovava, ogni mattina, per il primo sul guanciale" (p. 81).

Egidio is not without his good intentions; but Teresa's father refuses him her hand to avoid squandering his money on a dowry when he can continue to invest it in his son's education, expected to yield greater returns. Teresa hardly protests at all: "Le lunghe geremiadi economiche recitate dalla signora Soave colla sua voce rassegnata ... Teresina li aveva nel midollo delle ossa; facevano parte del suo cibo quotidiano, li respirava coll'aria" (pp.73-74). Instead, she trusts in Egidio's capacity to overcome her father's objections by proving himself in the legal profession.

However, as a man, Egidio lives in a world much larger than Teresa's and consequently is not as single-minded as she is: "Egli non aveva bisogno di quella fanciulla per essere felice, ma la trovava un complemento alla sua felicità" (p. 124). Before long, the combined attractions of journalism and of social life in the city have conspired to prevent him from achieving his goal. When he realizes this, he asks Teresa to force her father's hand by running away with him to the home of his sister. Paralyzed by the conflict between her obligations and her emotions, intimidated by the very presence of this man whom she has by now elevated to heretofore unknown heights – "L'assorbimento amoroso si manifestava con tutta la sua potenza. Dio e Orlandi" (p. 93) – Teresa has barely the strength to speak, let alone defy her father or convention:

> I dolori, le smanie, le lotte, le gelosie, le risoluzioni prese e lasciate, le estasi convulse, le malinconie isteriche, tutta la sua gioventù che se ne andava in quella lenta fiamma d'amore, non le suggerivano una sola parola. Gli stava accanto immobile, cogli occhi fissi, come un cane fedele davanti al suo padrone. (p. 160)

The inevitable ensues. Egidio detaches himself from her, while she, "sola colla sua inutile giovinezza" (p. 71), withers slowly away, all the while remaining obsessively faithful to her prince and to her dream: "... tutta sola nella cucina bassa, intenta a uffici volgari, la fanciulla ingannava l'eternità dell'aspettativa, avvinta dolcemente alla sua catena, imparando la grande virtù femminile di nascondere un tormento dietro un sorriso" (p. 87).

As Egidio's letters become less and less frequent, she begins to feel "una malinconia sottile ... un senso di isolamento, d'abbandono, come se il mondo si sfasciasse intorno a lei, ed ogni cosa viva allontanandosi, ella rimanesse sola in un gran buio freddo" (p. 108). But "tutto l'orrore del suo isolamento" (p. 129) dawns on her only when she realizes that Egidio has actually abandoned her, and that there is nothing left to connect her to the outside world: "Qualche volta, dopo una giornata di tormenti ... passiva in tanto dolore ... sentiva di trovarsi attaccata al mondo solamente per il tramite della famiglia e che intorno ci fosse una gran nebbia" (pp. 135-136).

The years pass, her brother leaves, the twins marry, Ida, the bright and studious youngest sister, leaves for the south of Italy to take a post as a *maestra*. Left alone to nurse her paralyzed father, Teresa begins to show symptoms of hysteria. Finally her father dies as well. Shortly afterwards, she receives a letter from Egidio who is now penniless and in ill health. Free at last and in what can be read as an act either of self-affirmation or of continuing self-denial, Teresa closes down the house that has been her prison for so many years, packs her bags and, ignoring the warnings of the *pretora*, leaves to join Egidio in Milan.

In the context of the development of Neera's literary career, this novel represents a rather unexpected departure from the norm since the vast majority of her novels are written in the bourgeois consolatory vein. *Teresa* and two other subsequent works, *Lydia* (1887) and *L'indomani* (1890), constitute a sort of naturalist interlude during which Neera allows herself to look frankly at the condition of women in her society. The novel is all the more surprising in the light of her extremely conservative essays and articles on the role of women. In these, not only does she discourage women who wish to write, she also suggests that in doing so they are betraying their true vocations as mothers and nurturers.

Luigi Baldacci explains this contradiction by claiming that in her essays Neera adopts an anti-feminist posture in deference to the norms of her society, while in her art she shows her true "feminist" colours.[3] Though this thesis is appealing, it is not entirely convincing: Neera's contradictions do not lend themselves to such ready classification, and in fact encompass the entire corpus of her work, fiction and non-fiction alike.[4]

Nowhere is this more evident than in the *dénouement* of *Teresa* itself, which remains ambiguous. Teresa's decision to leave home and join Egidio may well be an act of self-affirmation for *her*, but to the reader it is more like another act of submission. At this point in her life Teresa has no more family ties: one cannot help but note that she is once more going to minister to a sick and worn out man, after having nursed her father for so many years. Rebellion, Neera seems to be suggesting, is futile, since woman's lot is always the same in the end.

The truth is that it is Neera herself who, in her representation of women, does not dare to venture out of the confines of domestic parameters: it is impossible for her to develop a female character not determined exclusively by her ties to family and her function in its midst. Baldacci of course would respond to this allegation by pointing out that Neera is "sorretta da un sentimento dell'arte che la persuade a rappresentare secondo i 'colori del vero' piuttosto che a fare opera di propaganda," and that in her works "non si assegnano al personaggio compiti programmatici che siano eccedenti rispetto ai suoi limiti sociali." I, in turn, would reply using Baldacci's own words, but extending them to apply to her fiction as well as to her essays and "scritti morali": that what in fact Neera is manifesting here is a "riluttanza naturale ad accettare ... le conseguenze ultime della propria intuizione artistica."[5]

What are these consequences? Baldacci attributes Neera's ambiguity, her refusal to accept the logical conclusions of her feminist "instincts," to a refusal to accept their ideological consequences.[6] (In Italy at this time, the popular conception of feminism was that it went hand in hand with socialism, though this was not necessarily the case.) Here again, his diagnosis is questionable. Neera's misgivings are not, I believe, primarily of an ideological nature, but are far more deeply ingrained, so much so that they are projected onto a minor character, created precisely for the purpose of giving voice to them.

The character in question is Calliope, the town madwoman "quella stramba nemica degli uomini, ai quali faceva gli sberleffi, come un monello, dietro le ferriate del piano terreno" (p. 91). Calliope lives in complete isolation, ostracized by the rest of the townspeople, for whom her mysterious past is a subject of endless speculation. For Teresa, who is forced to pass by her ground-floor window whenever she goes out, Calliope functions as a living example of the fate awaiting women who deviate from prescribed feminine behaviour:

Teresina non conosceva Calliope; non l'aveva mai veduta bene, ma solamente intravista tra una sbarra e l'altra della finestra, colla faccia seminascosta sotto un ampio fazzoletto giallo, parlando da sola e dicendo improperi a tutti gli uomini che passavano.... La sua storia l'aveva sentita raccontare a brandelli, con molte lacune tra un episodio e l'altro; lacune che l'immaginazione sobria della fanciulla non si era mai data la briga di colmare.
Sapeva che era stata accolta, piccina, da una contessa, ed allevata quasi come figlia....
Vivevano allora tutte e due in un podere solitario, e già si sapeva che la Calliope aveva gusti bizzarri, uscendo sola per le campagne, coi capelli sciolti sulle spalle, un piccolo fucile ad armacollo; ardita, violenta, selvaggia. I pochi che avevano occasione di traversare il podere, la udivano zuffolare nei boschi di pioppi, imitando il canto degli uccelli, e qualche volta la vedevano correre sfrenata attraverso i campi, saltando le siepi, colle mani graffiate dalle spine e gli abiti strappati.
Era stata bella, di una bellezza virile e forte.

Seconda lacuna: Teresina aveva udito sussurrare misteriosamente, di un ufficiale francese, di fuga, di tradimento, di altre cose che non capiva bene e che non l'avevano mai interessato fino allora.
Poi balzava fuori la Calliope monaca. Era stata in convento due anni, modello di abnegazione e di penitenza; improvvisamente, alla vigilia di pronunciare i voti, sparve.
Terza e ultima lacuna; la quale abbracciava una quindicina d'anni e che aveva condotta la strana donna – rimasta sola al mondo – a chiudersi in quella casa da cui non usciva mai, e dove il paese le usava la carità di non occuparsene, lasciandola in pace colla sua pazzia inoffensiva. (pp. 25-27)

Neera's vivid and enthusiastic description of this unconventional woman doomed to social exile is all the more significant because of the uncanny resemblance it bears to well-known portraits of the notorious George Sand:

Il dottor Tavecchia, che l'aveva curata una volta, in occasione che cadendo da un albero si era fratturato un braccio, la diceva una delle più belle donne ch'egli avesse mai viste. Gli abiti bizzarri che portava, si addicevano al suo corpo da amazzone, robusto e snello. Quando si copriva il capo, lo faceva con un cappello da uomo, nero, ampio; non portava mai trine, nastri, gioielli; vestiva di nero o di bianco; spesso si cuciva tutto in giro alla gonna dei fiori freschi e tutta di fiori si fabbricava una acconciatura strana, originale, che sarebbe stata goffa per chiunque, e nella quale ella appariva incantevole. (p. 27)

It is the image of the head covered by the "capello da uomo, nero, ampio" which first alerts us to the fact that this might be a highly personal portrait of George Sand, transformed by Neera's volatile imagination into a character whose fate is emblematic of the censure that awaits women who dare to defy traditional roles.[7] The name Calliope provides the second clue, since Calliope is also the muse of epic poetry, a heroic masculine genre. And, what is more, we know that after the death of her father Sand was raised by her mother and aristocratic grandmother on the latter's estate at Nohant; that here Sand often spent her days hunting in the countryside, roaming about in male garb, with a rifle over her shoulder; that her grandmother, disturbed by her unfeminine behaviour, promptly dispatched her to a convent school in Paris, only to withdraw her when told that her grand-daughter was beginning to show signs of a vocation; that Sand then married an army officer whom she subsequently abandoned in order to join Jules Sandeau in Paris; and so on. The rest of Sand's life is too well-known to make it necessary to point out that she certainly did not end up the social outcast Neera makes of her; but it is precisely the two most celebrated facets of her life that Neera avoids mentioning completely – her adulterous affairs and her literary career.

The previous chapter, "Neera: The Literary Career of a Woman of the Nineteenth Century," demonstrates that she herself experienced writing as a transgression of normative feminine behaviour as severe as adultery, so much so that all her early novels are centered on the adultery theme, which functions as a metaphoric projection of the intensity of conflict she experienced when she first began to write. However, as soon as she finds ways to combine writing with traditional feminine values, for example through conventional anti-feminist journalism, her novels also undergo a transformation: the intensity of conflict experienced by her early heroines, torn between duty and adulterous desire, subsides precisely at the point at which Neera herself assuages her own conflicts about writing novels.[8]

The confirmation of this reading of Neera's career lies in her reluctance to acknowledge her debt and her ties to another woman writer – George Eliot. A close comparative reading of *Teresa* and *The Mill on the Floss* reveals that Teresa is none other than a Maggie Tulliver of the Italian provinces. Maggie, the protagonist of Eliot's novel, has been called "the heroine of renunciation,"[9] and it has been said that the novel exalts her suffering, depicting it as if it were a sort of feminine vocation: "*The Mill on the Floss* sympathetically analyzes the longings of an intelligent young woman in an oppressive society,but nonetheless elevates suffering into a female career."[10]

The factors that contribute to the fate of the "passive, self-destructive"[11] Maggie are obviously far more complex than those which limit Teresa's possibilities, if for no other reason than the fact that the English novel allows Maggie a far broader range of action than that ascribed to Teresa. In spite of this difference, their lives and misadventures present numerous parallels. Both grow up in the shadows of older brothers who enjoy privileges that they do not; for example, the possibility of leaving the family circle to study. In both cases the brothers experience this privilege as an imposition, since neither has the least interest in the pursuit of education. However, the fact that they are permitted luxuries denied their sisters creates situations in which Carlino and Tom come to represent for Teresa and Maggie their "windows on the world." This explains, in part, the sisters' fierce attachment to their brothers who are, by contrast, quite self-contained, shut off by what Neera, in reference to Carlino, calls "il beato egoismo d'uomo" (p. 71). Tom, says Eliot, "submitted to be kissed willingly enough, though Maggie hung on his neck in a rather strangling fashion, while his blue-grey eyes wandered toward the croft and the lambs and the river where he promised himself he would begin to fish the first thing tomorrow morning."[12] Carlino demonstrates a similar indifference when Teresa turns to him for comfort the day that a flood threatens the town. "Ma Carlino non si occupava che della piena," says Neera:

> A un tratto si accostò a suo fratello, passandogli un braccio intorno al collo, chinandosi lievemente, fino ad accarezzare colla guancia i capelli di lui, corti ed ispidi come le setole di una spazzola.
> Egli non avvertì la carezza. Tutto sporto fuori colle braccia, guardando in direzione della piazza, diceva:
> "Se venisse giù di lì! giù! uh! che fracasso...." (p. 71)

Both Maggie and Teresa form sentimental attachments to friends of their brothers and in both cases these attachments come to nought as a result of the opposition of an authoritarian father.

A last important detail linking the two novels is the flood motif. It is well known that *The Mill on the Floss* is brought to a close by the flood waters which carry both Maggie and her brother to their deaths. Maggie, unlike Teresa, runs off with Stephen in defiance of her father's wishes, only to find, however, that she has made a mistake. She returns home, having brought shame on herself and her family, with no possibility of redemption. The flood puts an end to her problems.

In *Teresa*, instead of providing closure, the flood motif opens the novel, and is used in a completely different fashion: to provide a vehicle for the "heroic" presentation of Egidio Orlandi. During the flood, Orlandi risks his life to save a child and word of his bravery reaches Teresa well before she actually meets him. Thus, when the two are finally introduced, Teresa already has a certain image of him and is predisposed to fall in love with him.

Orlandi's "heroic entrance" bears a striking resemblance to that of another male character in another well-known novel by a woman writer, a character whose courage will subsequently reveal itself to have been as illusory as Orlandi's. I am referring to Lord Nelvil, the male protagonist of Mme de Staël's seminal novel, *Corinne ou l'Italie* (1807). Nelvil, too, makes his first appearance at the very beginning of the novel in a heroic context which predisposes Corinne to fall in love with him by suggesting moral qualities which in reality have nothing to do with physical courage. In Mme de Staël's novel, however, the occasion for heroism is provided by a fire rather than a flood. Neera, by reproducing this placement and function of the "heroic entrance" connects herself to Staël as well, but to a Staël filtered through Eliot. Thus the fire becomes a flood which has the same purpose as the fire, that of presenting the male protagonist as a mythic hero for the woman. That the flood is indeed an indirect allusion to Staël's novel, is confirmed by the direct reference to *Corinne* in *The Mill on the Floss*: " 'Take back your *Corinne*,' said Maggie, drawing a book from under her shawl. 'You were right in telling me she would do me no good. But you were wrong in thinking I should wish to be like her.' "13

Eliot has no difficulty in openly acknowledging her links to another woman writer, in admitting that she is part of a female literary tradition. Neera, on the other hand, represses and even denies her sense of solidarity with other women writers in order to avoid acknowledging the break with tradition represented by her writing and by *Teresa* in particular. In this connection, it is worth calling attention to an observation made by Gilbert and Gubar in *The Madwoman in the Attic*:

> In order to define herself as an author the woman writer must redefine the terms of her socialization.... Frequently, moreover, she can begin such a struggle only by actively seeking a *female* precursor who, far from representing a threatening force to be

denied or killed, proves by example that a revolt against patriarchal literary authority is possible.[14]

The windmill in the three-dimensional picture described in the opening citation – which continues to move, like the thin flailing arms of a ghost, long after the other moving objects to which it is attached have ground to a halt ("che continuava ad agitare, come un fantasma irrequieto le sue scarne braccia in mezzo agli alberi") – is nothing other than a return of the repressed, a sign of Neera's own unacknowledged filiation anxieties.

Francesco Orlando has pointed out that "il modello della negazione freudiana è un modello formale, che può riempirsi per conto suo di contenuti svariati, e ha le caratteristiche del linguaggio dell'inconscio in quanto è una formazione linguistica di compromesso, che permette di dire nello stesso tempo sì e no, non importa a che cosa."[15] Neera is not content to have reproduced in *Teresa* the narrative scheme of Eliot's *Mill on the Floss*, nor to have paid homage to Mme de Staël through her particular use of Eliot's flood motif; the desire, or rather the need to affirm her connection to her female precursors is so strong and *yet at the same time experienced as so threatening* that only a symbol, which fulfills the double and paradoxical function of acknowledging and denying, of speaking and silencing, is capable of articulating her predicament.

Notes

[1] *Teresa* was first published in 1886 by Galli of Milan. In 1942 it was reprinted in a collection of Neera's works entitled *Neera* edited by Benedetto Croce and published by Garzanti of Milan. The most recent edition is that published by Einaudi (Turin) in 1976 with an introduction by Luigi Baldacci. The quotations which appear in this essay are all taken, however, from the Croce edition, and the page numbers in the text refer to this edition.

In addition to Baldacci's introduction to *Teresa*, I have been able to find only two other critical pieces specifically dedicated to this novel: V. Finucci, "Alienazione individuale e linguaggio ambientale: una rilettura di *Teresa* di Neera," *Misure critiche* 15. 55-57 (1985): 65-79; V. Finucci, "Between Acquiescence and Madness: Neera's *Teresa*," *Stanford Italian Review* 7.1-2 (1987): 217-239.

[2] Neera, "Le idee di una donna," *Neera*, ed. B. Croce (Milan: Garzanti, 1942) 802; also in Neera, *Le idee di una donna e confessioni letterarie* (Florence: Vallecchi, 1977) 63-67.

[3] Baldacci, Note, *Le idee di una donna e confessioni letterarie*, by Neera, xii-xx.

[4] See, in the present volume, "Neera: The Literary Career of a Woman of the Nineteenth Century."

[5] Baldacci, Note, *Le idee di una donna e confessioni letterarie* xviii.

[6] Baldacci xviii.

[7] Carlo Cattaneo, in 1863, published an essay entitled "Sul romanzo delle donne contemporanee in Italia," reprinted in his *Scritti letterari*, vol. I, ed. A. Bertani (Florence: Le Monnier, 1948) 358-389. The essay contains the following remarks on Sand, which give some idea of her image in nineteenth-century Italy: "Non possiamo certo vantare nell'arringo letterario una Sand, senza però che questa inferiorità ci desti invidia. A torto reputano alcuni che la Sand abbia esagerato l'idea dell'amore; a dir vero non fece che impiccolirla.... L'amore è la suprema moralità, non può apparire immorale se non quando è limitato, se non quando una delle sue manifestazioni si esalta a scapito dell'infinita sua essenza. Questo amore parassitario notiamo nelle eroine della Sand, ed è ciò appunto che crea per loro quello stato d'irrequietezza, quel bisogno di ribellarsi alla posizione sociale e di reclamare un'emancipazione. In esse l'amante è in lotta colla sposa, colla madre, colla sorella, coll'amica; la passione egoistica distrugge l'amor vero" (p. 363).

[8] On writing as desire in Neera, see Finucci, "Alienazione individuale e linguaggio ambientale: una rilettura di *Teresa* di Neera" 66.

[9] E. Showalter, *A Literature of Their Own: British Women Novelists from Brontë to Lessing* (Princeton: Princeton University Press, 1977) 112.

[10] Showalter 125.

[11] A.S. Byatt, Introduction, *The Mill on the Floss*, by G. Eliot (Harmondsworth: Penguin, 1979) 29.

[12] Eliot 84.

[13] Eliot 432.

[14] S. Gilbert and S. Gubar, *The Madwoman in the Attic: The Woman Writer and the Nineteenth-Century Literary Imagination* (New Haven: Yale University Press, 1979) 49.

[15] F. Orlando, *Per una teoria freudiana della letteratura*, 2nd ed. (Turin: Einaudi, 1973) 28.

The Early Matilde Serao: An Author in Search of a Character

At the time of her death in 1927, Matilde Serao was among Italy's most prolific writers and best known public figures: she had published close to forty volumes of fiction, had founded four major newspapers, three with her husband and one on her own, and had churned out thousands of pages of journalistic prose, ranging in genre from the society column to the investigative report. She had also raised five children, one of whom she bore at the age of 48, as a result of her liaison with a Neapolitan lawyer who became her companion after her separation from husband Edoardo Scarfoglio. In 1926 she came within a hair-breadth of winning the Nobel Prize for Literature, awarded at the last minute to Grazia Deledda, probably because the anti-militaristic stance Serao displayed in one of her later works displeased Mussolini. For an ugly duckling whom Giovanni Verga, her contemporary and the most important novelist of the time, had gone so far as to call a "hermaphrodite,"[1] she came as close to "having it all" as might any twentieth-century post-feminist, a feat all the more remarkable since it was accomplished in turn-of-the-century Southern Italy.

As much a regional writer as an "Italian" one, Serao exposes and examines everything from the social problems of quasi-third world Naples, to the scandalous situation of an elderly nun forced into the streets of a large city thanks to the blindness of bureaucracy and the ruthlessness of the architects of social "progress." *Il ventre di Napoli* (1884) is a collection of articles written in reaction to minister Agostino De Pretis' unfortunate suggestion that the squallor, filth and corruption of Naples might be eliminated by razing its famous *quartieri*. Serao, intimately acquainted with Naples' historical centre and its varied and colourful population, wrote some of her most impassioned prose in indignant response to what she considered a shockingly superficial and perfunctory solution to a deeply-rooted moral and social problem. *Suor Giovanna della Croce* (1901) tells the poignant story of a former nun, destitute and possessed of a child's innocence, left to fend for herself as a result of a government decision to close monasteries deemed to be too sparsely-populated to maintain efficiently.

La conquista di Roma (1885), on the other hand, is inspired by Serao's years in Rome and her intimate knowledge of the parliamentary world. Francesco San Giorgio is the newly-elected representative of a small, impoverished Southern town, proverbially struggling to survive in the big city and discovering that sex and politics in Umbertine Rome are not always what they appear to be. *Vita e avventura di Riccardo Joanna* (1887), also set in Rome, is an insider's view of the harsh underside of journalism, and of its capacity to erode those who become addicted to its occasional highs and inevitable lows. *Il paese di Cuccagna* (1891) returns to Naples and tells of another addiction, that of its inhabitants' all-consuming passion for the lottery. Impoverished aristocrats, petty-bourgeois shopkeepers and destitute lumpen-proletarians are all enslaved by superstition and the eternal human hope for a better tomorrow, in this veritable tragicomic fresco of Neapolitan mores.

The decade that sees Serao taking a close and critical look at the problems and manners of her time also sees her attempting to confront, if not quite to challenge, the portrayal of women in its literature. Italian critics have not, on the whole, been kind or fair to Serao on this (and other) counts. This is largely due to the fact that in the second part of her career, with the demise of *verismo*, she progressively abandoned the realistic, investigative treatment of themes characteristic of her early work for the guaranteed success of the popular novel, the late-Romantic *feuilleton*. (1891, the year of publication of *Il Paese di Cuccagna*, is generally considered to mark the transition, though she does have a brief, later phase, of which *Suor Giovanna della Croce* is a product, in which she attempts to return to the tone of some of her earlier work.) The conventional portrayal of women in these later novels of passion, coupled with Serao's well-known conservative stance in the face of certain feminist issues such as divorce, has led many critics to identify her position on women exclusively with this second phase and to claim that she was entirely a-critical in her approach to women's lives and as well as to their portrayal in literature.[2]

Through an analysis of one of Serao's first novels, *Fantasia* (1883), and of its relationship to two works on women that come directly after it, *La virtù di Checchina* (1884) and *Il romanzo della fanciulla* (1886), I will attempt to challenge this widely-held assumption. Moreover, we shall see that, like other women writers of her time, Serao did manage, briefly and under the influence of *verismo*, to escape the strictures of the conventional portrayal of women: *Il romanzo della fanciulla* (1886) is a collection of stories describing the difficult lives of young unmarried women, whatever their social extraction, in which she draws on such early personal experiences as those at the Normal School for Girls (*Scuola normale femminile*) and at the state telegraph offices (*Telegrafi dello stato*).

It is not by chance that this high point in her representation of women coincides with her temporary rejection of the novel as a viable genre for the exploration of feminine reality. In fact, Serao clearly saw that there was little possibility for an authentic portrayal of women within the prevailing literary tradition which she identified with this genre. She confirms this in *Fantasia* by mischievously writing herself into her own story, to remind us that the narrow typology of women in literature hardly does justice to the broad and complex spectrum of unrealized feminine possibilities:

> "Quelli sono i giornalisti," indicò Andrea a Lucia, "vi sono i corrispondenti dell'*Opinione*, del *Diritto*, della *Libertà*, del *Popolo Romano*, del *Fanfulla*, per Roma, del *Pungolo* e del *Piccolo* per Napoli."
> "Anche quella lì è una giornalista?"
> "Credo, non ne so il nome."
> "Io la invidio, se è intelligente. Ha almeno un'ambizione."
> "Bah! Preferite sempre essere una donna."
> "La gloria è bella."
> "Ma l'amore è buono," ribattè lui, serio.
> "...l'amore?"[3]

In another exchange between Lucia, the novel's *femme fatale* and her aspiring lover Andrea, Serao reiterates her dissatisfaction with the literary status quo vis-à-vis women, extending it this time to include even more naturalistic representations of women:

> Si fermarono innanzi a un gran quadro, un capolavoro di pazienza.

"Chi lo ha fatto?" chiese Lucia.
"Due signorine, figlie di un proprietario di San Leucio," rispose
Andrea.
"Che età hanno?"
"Credo, vent'otto, trent'anni."
"Belle?"
"Oh! no, ma buonissime."
"Si capisce. Vedete, in quel quadro io ci vedo un romanzo. Povere
creature, che forse hanno passato le loro solitarie serate d'inverno,
relegate in casa, distraendosi con questo antiartistico, provinciale,
umile lavoro. E forse ambedue ci si sono affaticate, sospirando su
qualche amore incompreso che l'avidità dei parenti impedisce. O
forse ci hanno lavorato, pensando di essere vecchie zitelle, una
gioventù sfiorita. Povero quadro! Lo comprerei...." (pp. 137-138)

If, however, Serao was aware of the lack of correspondence between women as
portrayed in novels and the far more complex social and psychic reality of "real"
women, she was also faced with the fact that the most widely read novels of her
time – such as Carolina Invernizio's best-selling potboilers, to cite only the most
obvious example – promoted images of women even less palatable than the
languishing virgins alluded to so condescendingly in the above passage. Verga's
Mena (*I Malavoglia*, 1881), Neera's Teresa (*Teresa*, 1886), the Marchesa
Colombi's Denza (*Un matrimonio in provincia*, 1885), for all their literary
"unreality," can hardly be considered more cliché-ridden than the *femme fatale* or
her opposite sister, the angel-of-the-house.[4] And yet, paradoxically, it is these two
latter figures – though somewhat idiosyncratically drawn – that dominate *Fantasia*.

At the time of *Fantasia*'s publication not only was the more serious, highbrow
literary product competing with the popular novel, but naturalist schemes of
representation were challenging tired romantic conventions. *Fantasia*, a novel rife
with ambiguities, documents the workings of Serao's imagination as she struggles
to forge a literary identity in the face of massive personal insecurity as well as often
conflicting commercial and artistic pressures. Where Serao stood in relation to the
literary forces of her times, the choices she perceived as being open to her, those
she finally made and their influence on her portrayal of women – these are the real
subjects of *Fantasia*.

Perhaps the single most striking feature about *Fantasia* in terms of literary
forces and choices is the reference it makes, on various levels, to Gustave
Flaubert's *Madame Bovary* (1857). Like *Madame Bovary*, *Fantasia* is a novel of

adultery, but its adulteress, Lucia Altimare, unlike Emma, plays a self-consciously derivative role: at one point in the narrative she even goes so far as to point out to her lover-to-be that their situation is curiously reminiscent of that to be found in the widely-read French novel:

> "O cara, cara, cara," mormorava Andrea, cercando di abbracciarla.
> Ella si sciolse e ridendo ironicamente, gli disse:
> "Sapete che la nostra posizione si trova nella *Madame Bovary*? E' un romanzo di Flaubert."
> "Io non l'ho letto. Come puoi essere così cattiva e dirmi queste cose?"
> "Gli è che noi facciamo del dramma borghese o del dramma provinciale, che vale lo stesso." (p. 225)

The key phrase here is "facciamo del dramma borghese": this is how Serao interprets the tale of Emma Bovary, which, in view of its notoriety, she clearly sees as a force to be contended with. However, unlike Flaubert, Serao does not focus exclusively on the "dramma borghese" of her adulteress. She introduces instead a second female protagonist, Caterina Spaccapietra, the best friend whom Lucia betrays in the course of her extramarital escapade.

The novel opens in the boarding school where the two young women first meet and where, on the eve of their graduation, Lucia convinces Caterina to enter into a blood-pact of eternal friendship. From the start, Caterina is cast as Lucia's foil, the dutiful child to Lucia's headstrong rebel, then the faithful wife to Lucia's wicked adulteress. The two young women are drawn to each other by their diametrically opposed temperaments: Lucia is depicted as imaginative, volatile, and verbose, constantly spouting one author or another in support of the various literary postures she assumes, while Caterina is presented as concrete, passive and laconic, her speech as pared down, as "essential" as her person.

Caterina neither dreams nor desires. Upon graduation, she obediently marries the man chosen for her by her family – "E' volontà di mia zia che sposi Andrea Lieti" (p. 28) – and immediately becomes the model wife, cheerful, uncomplaining, and even-tempered: "Tutta la persona aveva qualcosa di semplice e nitidamente tranquillo e allegro" (p. 57). She copes with Andrea's moods in the classical feminine way, "col silenzio, con la placidezza, con l'obbedienza" (p. 102), and appears to have no individuality or anger to suppress, no needs of her own to interfere with her ability to accommodate her husband's: "Dalla mattina alla sera si occupava del suo benessere, della casa, del pranzo, facendogli trovare il salotto fresco in estate, la camera calda in inverno, e la moglie sempre elegante, sempre serena, sempre sorridente" (p. 257).

Lucia's parabola is the very antithesis of Caterina's. At first she resists marriage as far too tame an enterprise for a woman of her far-reaching ambitions, but when she realizes how limited her choices actually are, she agrees to become the wife of her tubercular cousin Alberto: "Se fossi un uomo andrei in Africa ad esplorare le regioni sconosciute, se fossi uomo ... ma sono donna, una debole e inutile donna" (p. 30). In keeping with her tendency toward hysteria and hyperbole, she rationalizes her marriage as "un sacrificio enorme di tutta la mia gioventù ... un olocausto silenzioso che io offrirò a Dio" (p. 108).

Inevitably she soon tires of sacrifice and of Alberto, and begins to turn her energies elsewhere, to a more potentially satisfying object – Caterina's husband Andrea. As guileless as he is virile, Andrea resists Lucia's advances steadfastly at first, but in time his "healthy" love for the quietly devoted Caterina falters. Caterina's charms – and Andrea's defences – though considerable, are no match for the veritable arsenal of amorous postures unleashed by Lucia. Just as Caterina "accanto a Andrea subiva il fascino bizzarro che hanno sopra una creatura tranquilla e ragionatrice le divagazioni fantasiose" (p. 258), so Andrea "parve di essere perduto, irresistibilmente perduto per una strega maligna" (p. 259). In fact, Andrea is so taken in by Lucia's ways that it is he who actually suggests they run away together. When Caterina discovers this double betrayal, revealed to her by the sickly Alberto, she hastily arranges to close down her city home and returns to the country residence where Andrea's and Lucia's flirtation had taken place under her unsuspecting eyes. Here, she quietly takes her life in a dramatic final scene which contrasts sharply in its starkness with the Dannunzian overtones of much of the rest of the novel. In the meantime, Lucia and Andrea have made their escape unhampered. Lucia's power to manipulate, to captivate, and to deceive knows no boundaries: "Questo mostro sorridente e piangente, dalle lagrime commoventi, dalla voce incantevole, dalle flessuosità innamoranti, dalla poesia ammaliatrice della parola; questo egoismo profondo e femminile, aveva preso per sé tutto quanto aveva d'attorno" (p. 260).

The reader is left somewhat perplexed: Emma Bovary, after all, betrayed her husband and then killed *herself*. Two other equally famous adulteresses, Anna

Karenina and Effie Briest, are also punished for their transgressions despite their authors' sympathy for them: Anna throws herself under a train, Effie dies prematurely of a tragic illness. Lucia Altimare, however, in striking antithesis to her sisters-in-sin, betrays both her husband and her best friend, only to get off scot-free and with her man. And then, in a dénouement clearly meant to call attention to itself, it is the best friend who commits suicide. Why all these deviations from the norm? It is a well-known fact that the nineteenth-century realistic novel punishes heroes who threaten the stability of the social order.[5] Why is *Fantasia* the exception? Is Serao somehow endorsing adultery? And why two female protagonists instead of one?

Criticism of *Fantasia* has addressed none of these questions, largely because it has never addressed the question of the novel's relationship to *Madame Bovary*, other than at a very superficial level.[6] In fact, this relationship is not limited to the reproduction of the Emma character in Lucia. Whether Serao was aware of it or not, Caterina's most salient characteristics – ineptitude, lack of imagination, laconic speech, exasperating down-to-earthness, complete lack of visible drive and passion – all bring to mind the very traits which made Charles Bovary so intolerable to his unfortunate wife:

> La conversation de Charles était plate comme un trottoire de rue, et les idées de tout le monde y défilaient, dans leur costume ordinaire, sans exciter d'émotion, de rire ou de rêverie. Il n'avait jamais été curieux, disait-il, pendant qu'il habitait Rouen, d'aller voir au théâtre les acteurs de Paris. Il ne savait ni nager, ni faire les armes, ni tirer le pistolet, et il ne pût, un jour, lui expliquer un terme d'équitation qu'elle avait rencontré dans un roman.
> Un homme, au contraire, ne devait-il pas tout connaître, exceller en des activités multiples, vous initier aux énergies de la passion, aux raffinements de la vie, à tous les mystères? Mais il n'enseignait rien, celui-là, ne savait rien, ne souhaitait rien. Il la croyait heureuse; et elle lui en voulait de ce calme si bien assis, de cette pesanteur sereine, du bonheur même qu'elle lui donnait.[7]

What Serao had found in *Madame Bovary* were, I believe, two characters whose widely divergent styles appeared to her to epitomize the literary stereotypes of her time – the late-Romantic on the one hand (Emma), the newer stripped-down naturalist option on the other (Charles) – *and hence her own dilemma as a fledgling novelist faced with the choice between the two.* In *Fantasia*, wittingly or not, she reproduces these alternatives in the characters of Lucia and Caterina. At one level, then, *Fantasia* is a somewhat banal tale of adultery and betrayal with an unusual final twist; at another it is an exercise in the exploration of literary options by a rather insecure woman novelist in search of a literary voice at the start of her career.

In this connection, it must be kept in mind that Verga had just published *I Malavoglia* (1881), in which the character of Mena is glorified as a model of feminine passivity and self-abnegation. Inspired, I believe, by Flaubert's Emma/Charles opposition on the one hand, and by Verga's saintly creature on the other, Serao creates her own bourgeois Mena in Caterina and pits her against Lucia, *but only to find that she no more believes in Caterina's serene acquiescence and self-effacement than she does in Lucia's ridiculous language and postures.* If, as one critic has pointed out, Caterina is in her own way as artificial a creation as Lucia,[8] it is almost certainly because Serao had as many reservations about her as a character as she did about the more overtly objectionable *femme fatale.* Indeed, Caterina's saintly silence and passivity must have appeared to Serao even less "true-to-life" than Lucia's excessive verbosity and affectations. This would explain why she sometimes appears to oscillate in her allegiances to the two characters and why in the end it is Lucia who "triumphs." While Serao certainly sides with Caterina morally, the rewards and punishments meted out in *Fantasia* have nothing to do with morality and everything to do with credibility and appeal; for *Fantasia* is not, contrary to prevailing critical opinion, merely a "morality tale," but a *pastiche*, "un oggetto a doppio fondo, uno specchio deformante, ma soprattutto un grandissimo segnale letterario."[9] Consciously or not, in *Fantasia* Serao is struggling with two masculine images of women deriving from the literary trends of the time,[10] both of which she finds thoroughly unsatisfactory, but to which she is unable to offer a convincing alternative. Lucia is presented as "una creatura falsa, retorica, antipatica" (p. 92), but Caterina is little more than an anti-Lucia, with few positive characteristics of her own. Completely lacking in feminine wiles, in initiative and even in speech, she stands by passively while Lucia wrestles Andrea away from her: "Caterina ... che non trovava parole per esprimersi, il cui affetto era tranquillo e muto, che non poteva entusiasmarsi mai e che non era mai svenuta, si vergognava talvolta di amar poco. In tutto, Lucia la superava" (p. 255).

Serao's inability to propose Caterina as a convincing alternative in spite of her obvious contempt for Lucia, is dramatized in a meta-literary sub-text in which Serao also projects onto Caterina her own sense of inadequacy regarding her capacities as a writer: Caterina's "ineptitude" in life – for this is how Serao sees passivity – is, I believe, homologous to Serao's own sense of ineptitude in art.[11] *This sub-text sees Lucia and Caterina pitted against each other for control of the text, and ultimately, of the audience (Andrea), in what amounts to a tale of literary seduction.* In this tale, control derives from the ability to manipulate language to one's advantage and from having a repertoire of images on which to draw capable of "seducing" the reader. It is no accident that, unlike Emma Bovary and her lovers, Lucia and Andrea never actually consummate their adulterous passion within the bounds of the novel. In other words, what they engage in is not adultery, but the *language* of adultery. It is Lucia's "parola, lenta, precisa, seduttrice" (p. 136), that conquers Andrea, a fact which Serao refers to directly and indirectly, several times throughout the novel:

> "Voi siete forte in dialettica, voi pensate cose bizzarre, profonde e talvolta cattive, a cui io non arrivo. Sono in mano vostra; nella conversazione, m'invescate, mi prendete, mi fate soffrire." (p. 145)

> "T'ho assassinata: sono il tuo boia: sono il tuo carnefice," scriveva Andrea, che ormai aveva preso lo stile di lei e le formule, il lirismo fantastico. (p. 218)

> "Tu parli oggi come un poeta, Andrea, come un sognatore."
> "Sei tu che mi hai insegnato questo linguaggio; io non lo conoscevo: io non avevo mai sognato Lucia, vientene via con me." (p. 230)

To the extent to which she is unable to mount an offensive against Lucia's "style," Caterina is responsible for her own fate: Andrea leaves Caterina because, contrary to Lucia, "per difetto di forma, ella non trovava il modo di manifestare la sua commozione" (p. 257).

The first episode to cast the Caterina-Lucia opposition in terms of the struggle for literary hegemony appears, emblematically, almost at the very beginning of the novel: Lucia and Caterina are both asked by Galimberti, the history teacher, to read aloud their compositions on Beatrice di Tenda, wrongly accused of adultery and put to death by her husband Filippo Maria Visconti. Caterina's version of the story is a simple rendition of the facts, devoid of rhetoric, devoid of sensationalism, devoid of clichés, in a word, devoid of affect. It earns her the following reproach from her teacher:

"E' un compito molto scarso, Spaccapietra. Non è che la narrazione pura e semplice del fatto come sta nel libro di testo – anzi più semplice ancora.... Eppure siete donna.... Appunto vi ho assegnato un compito dove si poteva manifestare qualche nobile affetto, la pietà, il disprezzo per la falsa accusa ... che so io? A questo modo la storia diventa una cronologia. Il compito è arido: voi non avete fantasia, Spaccapietra." (p. 15)

Lucia's version, predictably, is as verbose, stylized and risqué as Caterina's was simple and spare. After Galimberti recovers from the initial shock of hearing a young girl speak in such provocative terms, in what is clearly an understatement, he declares simply "Il compito è lungo, Altimare, voi avete troppa fantasia" (p. 17). It goes almost without saying that, later in the novel, he falls madly in love with Lucia. His reproach to Caterina, on the other hand, is accompanied by the remark "Eppure siete donna," rendering explicit his assumption that Lucia's mode, though perhaps somewhat disturbing, is the "natural" one for a woman, while Caterina's is an aberration. The nature of the discussion that takes place among Lucia's classmates directly on the heels of the Beatrice di Tenda episode serves to illuminate this episode further. While Lucia is being officially reprimanded by the principal – though "womanly" in the eyes of Galimberti, her conduct has violated conventional standards of decorum befitting a young girl – they debate the gravity of her "crime":

"Queste cose si sanno ma non si possono dire."
"Ma scrivere che una moglie può tradire il marito, Minichini, che te ne pare?"
"Scusa, nel mondo è sempre così. La Signora Ferrari tradisce suo marito con mio cugino." (p. 19)

From there the discussion turns, not coincidentally, to novels:

"... i libri di Zola non si possono leggere," disse Giovanna Casacalenda.
"Cioè, si possono leggere," osservò Minichini: "ma non conviene dire, innanzi ai giovanotti, che si sono letti."
"Uh! quanti libri ho letto che nessuno sa," esclamò Avigliana.
"Io so di un matrimonio che non si è fatto," disse Minichini, "perché la fidanzata si lasciò sfuggire di aver letto *La Signora dalle Camelie*...."
"Minichini bella, raccontaci questa *Signora dalle Camelie*," pregò Giovanna Casacalenda con la sua dolce voce, dove soffiava la passione dell'ignoto."
"Non posso, core mio."

"Perché? Tanto è terribile? Raccontala, Minichini. Artemisia bella, raccontaci questo libro."
Le altre non parlavano. Ma negli occhi lampeggianti si leggeva la curiosità, ma sulle labbra aride il desiderio disseccava le parole. Giovanna pregava per loro, con gli occhioni supplichevoli e un sorriso languido sopra le grosse labbra. (pp. 21-22)

Serao is clearly suggesting that the confusion between life and literature, so apparent in Lucia's story, is perhaps the inevitable fate of young women whose only freedom lies in the exercise of the imagination; she is also clearly conveying her dissatisfaction with the models of feminine behaviour and possibilities literature has thus far provided. However, she feels powerless to challenge them in any active way through her own writing: hence the neutral, non-affective style – a sort of "degré zero de l'écriture" – which Serao ascribes to Caterina in the Beatrice di Tenda episode, and which she contrasts so sharply and deliberately with Lucia's flowery mannerism. Serao's failure to find a "voice" with which to counter prevailing literary representations of women is reflected over and over again in Caterina's failure to find a "voice" of her own with which to resist Lucia's imperious personality and will.

This is evident from the very beginning of their association: the first part of the novel closes with the blood pact of eternal friendship into which Lucia draws Caterina on the eve of their departure from the school. Typically, Caterina intuits that she is participating in something that is not in keeping with her own wishes, but fails to speak up, though sensing, at some level, that she ought to:

Non chiedeva neppure più, a quella insolita ora, nella notte profonda, che strano rito fossero venute a compiere nella cappella, illuminata per loro solamente.... Come quelli che sognano di voler fare una cosa e hanno una volontà sicura nel sogno, ma non la parola per esprimerla, né la forza per attuarla, così ella sentiva, in quel dormiveglia, il torpore della propria volontà. (pp. 37-38)

Another episode in this vein takes place at the beginning of part II, just after Caterina's marriage, but before Lucia's. The two young women, in the course of an outing, accidentally meet their former history teacher, Galimberti who, in the meantime, mesmerized by her seductive postures and eloquence, has fallen in love with Lucia. Caterina is struck by the impropriety of Galimberti's conduct but, again, faced with Lucia's "reading" of the event, remains mute:

"Dio mio, ecco che ci viene dietro Galimberti. E la gente che vede?
Lucia, come si fa?"
"Nulla, cara. Non glielo posso impedire. E' il magnetismo, come
capisci."
"Lui, ora manca alla sua lezione per venirci dietro."
"Non t'opporre ai Fati, Caterina."
Caterina tacque, non trovando niente da rispondere. (p. 70)

The same passivity characterizes Caterina's reaction to the first significant
encounter between her husband and Lucia. Lucia, supposedly transported by
Andrea's prowess in a fencing match tosses him her handkerchief from the
sidelines – "ma tuo marito è un glorioso Carlo d'Angiò," she tells Caterina (p. 74).
After the match, Andrea, assuming Caterina to have been the author of the dramatic
gesture, reprimands her harshly for having behaved so irrationally:

"Perché hai fatto quella cosa ridicola, Caterina?"
Ella non rispondeva, gli occhi chinati, le mani nascoste nel
manicotto.
"Tu, una donnina così ragionevole? Siamo dunque al medio evo?
Perdio, esporsi al ridicolo così!"
Caterina si mordeva le labbra, impallidiva, non potendo piangere,
non trovando filo di voce per rispondere. (p. 77)

Caterina's tragedy is that she has nothing to oppose Lucia's stereotyped,
pseudo-literary manner of interpreting and shaping experience; though she
recognizes that Lucia's manner is false and rhetorical – "E' Leopardi ancora, Lucia.
Mi avevi promesso di non leggerlo più" (p. 27), she tells Lucia after rescuing her
from a dramatically-staged suicide attempt – she has nothing with which to counter
it. Time after time, Caterina stands by speechless while Lucia draws effortlessly on
a seemingly inexhaustible supply of words, images and gestures which she uses to
"write" her life by gradually shaping ordinary events into the banal story of adultery
and betrayal that *Fantasia*, on one level, wishes to evoke: the end of her schooldays
becomes the occasion for a blood-pact of eternal friendship with Caterina; the
chance encounter with Galimberti becomes a sign from the Fates; Andrea's skill as
a fencer turns him into a dashing knight to whom she must pay homage. And at
each of these moments, that is, each time Lucia attributes "meaning" to an event,
Caterina, unable to propose an alternative meaning, consents by default.

Caterina is even given one explicit "last chance" to participate in the "writing" of
the story, to help determine the course of events at a particularly crucial moment:

Lucia, in the process of deciding whether to marry her sickly cousin Alberto, writes a long letter to Caterina, asking her advice in the matter. Caterina reads the letter aloud to Andrea; but when, in keeping with Lucia's request that Caterina speak her mind, he asks her "Tu, che ne pensi?" she answers only *"Io? Non so, non ho idee, io, non ne ho mai avute."*[12] "E che le scriverai?" insists Andrea. "Quello che mi dirai tu," answers Caterina (p. 112). That Caterina is being called upon specifically to help determine the course of events at a crucial moment is confirmed by the rest of the exchange: "Ti fo osservare," says Andrea "che l'Altimare ... non ti ha detto né di leggermi la lettera, né di chiedermi consiglio. Io non sono nominato" (p. 112). Again, however, Caterina pleads incompetence: " 'Ma tu capisci,' disse lei umiliata" (p. 112). Finally, Andrea's confusion – he has already felt the first stirrings of attraction toward Lucia – leads him to suggest that Caterina approve Lucia's marriage: " 'Scrivile che fa bene.' Lei ubbidì, poiché l'incarico suo era di trovar saggio e onesto quanto suo marito faceva" (p. 112).

It is no coincidence that this episode and these last words conclude part II of the novel. Part III begins *after* Lucia's marriage, that is, after she and her husband have taken up residence for the summer with Caterina and Andrea. It is during this extended sojourn – which would never have taken place had she not married – that Lucia's relationship with Andrea will flourish. With her silence on the subject of Lucia's marriage – with her obstinate refusal to participate in the "writing" of the story – Caterina has become the "author" of her own misfortunes: *Galeotto fu il libro e chi NON lo scrisse.* As for Lucia, she will, quite literally, have been writing all along. The confirmation comes from Alberto, once, of course, it is too late:

> "Voi non capite, è vero, come io so tutto questo? Ve lo ricordate quel romanzo che stava scrivendo Lucia ogni notte? Un'altra falsità. Non era un romanzo: era il suo *giornale*. Ogni giorno vi scriveva tutto quello che le accadeva, con tanti pensieri, con tante fantasie. Tutto l'amore vi è per filo e per segno, ogni sguardo, ogni bacio, ogni fatto. Oh vi sono brani magnifici di descrizione, vi sono cose bellissime, narrate lì dentro. E' una lettura istruttiva, e interessante. Voi ne profitterete, se volete. Leggete, leggete, che vi divertirete.... E' un bel romanzo, un bel dramma." (pp. 249-250)

Part III of the novel takes place at the agricultural fair in Caserta and is obviously inspired by the scene of the fair at Yonville to which Rodolphe takes Emma in *Madame Bovary*. Flaubert uses the agricultural fair as a means of enlarging the scope of his story: by alternating fragments of the hypocritical, rhetorical speech on agriculture and social progress made by a petty town official with Rodolphe's seduction speech to Emma, he contextualizes the moral bankruptcy of his characters and extends his indictment to the society as a whole. In *Fantasia* the fair is used in the same manner: a similar speech and similar clichés are pronounced by a fully-fledged minister brought to the fair as a government spokesman. Our attention is drawn, however, not so much to Lucia's adherence to all this empty rhetoric, as to Caterina's passive dissidence:

> Mentre la folla gridava e applaudiva, i deputati si accostarono al banco e gli strinsero la mano, felicitandolo.... Nel momento di confusione, Andrea era di nuovo accorso presso le signore.
> "Vi è piaciuto, eh? Che bella voce."
> "Egli ha detto delle cose stupende che questa folla stupida non ha intese," disse con disprezzo Lucia.
> E agitò il suo ventaglio, poiché nel gruppo dei giornalisti si parlava di lei: forse l'avrebbero nominata nelle corrispondenze.
> "Ti secchi, Caterina?" domandò Andrea.
> "No, è come alla Camera dei deputati," rispose lei, quietamente rassegnata. (pp. 121-123)

The same detachment is reflected in Caterina's lack of enthusiasm for the role she has been assigned in the fair's activities: she has been relegated to a jury made up of *signore per bene* whose task it is to award prizes for needlework and other handicrafts submitted by peasant women of the area. Instead of refusing to take part in an activity she neither believes in nor has any opportunistic social interest in pursuing, she acquiesces in resignation. Her only resistance to the world of empty words, gestures, and conventions – which the fair and all its activities, represent in a microcosm – is passive and conveyed by means of an exasperatingly detailed description of the mundane domestic preoccupations through which she escapes her role:

> Mentre la seduta continuava, accademica, in discussioni quasi famigliari ... mentre qualche relatrice leggeva la propria relazione ... mentre la scrittrice dava un consiglio pratico ... mentre il segretario leggeva le lettere di adesione ... Caterina non udiva nulla di questo. Avrebbe voluto trovarsi altrove, in casa sua, dove tutto era abbandonato in mano ai servi. Giulietta era solerte, ma non bastava. Il cuoco, poi, faceva quello che voleva. Da che aveva in casa Lucia e Alberto, per la villeggiatura, Caterina si preoccupava più che mai della colazione e del pranzo. Quei due avevano lo stomaco debole,

avevano bisogno di brodi ristretti, di vivande leggiere.... Lei e
Andrea mangiavano maccheroni e bistecche sanguinanti e insalate
refrigeranti. Anche la questione del pesce era seria, a Caserta, paese
interno, dove veniva da Gaeta o da Napoli, non sempre fresco....
A questo problema difficile pensava Caterina, mentre la principessa
Caracciolo pregava le signore di procedere alla votazione....
Caterina temeva sempre di non soddisfare i gusti di Lucia, povera
creatura nervosa, il cui stomaco era rovinato.... Bisognava
ricordarsi di scrivere a Napoli per avere del buon té, del té
Souchong.... La questione era se dirigersi da Caflisch o da Van Bol,
per questo té....
"Signora Lieti, vuol venire a votare?" interpellò dolcemente la
principessa Caracciolo.
Caterina, senza troppo sapere quello che si facesse, scrisse un nome
a caso sulla sua scheda.... Si faceva tardi: erano lì da tre ore, a
perdere tempo.
Altrove, a casa, per esempio, lo avrebbe occupato utilmente. Era
arrivata la lavandaia con un bucato immenso, e Caterina non lasciava
passare la roba alla stiratora senza rivedere pezzo per pezzo dove
mancassero i bottoni, dove si fosse staccato un nastro, dove si fosse
sfilata una guaina. La biancheria era nuova, ma ella sospettava che la
lavandaia adoperasse la potassa, per certi bucherelli che aveva
trovato nelle camicie di tela d'Olanda. Glielo aveva già detto, ma
colei aveva giurato che di questi pasticci non ne faceva e che
adoperava tutto ranno forte e sapone. (pp. 133-134)

It is clear that though Serao does identify with Caterina morally and at the
deeper meta-literary level, she does not believe in her as a character any more than
she does in Lucia; and just as Caterina senses the emptiness and the conventionality
of the activity in which she is engaged, but can protest only passively by allowing
her mind to wander to other equally empty and conventional thoughts, so Serao can
endorse neither her story nor her characters, but can come up with no convincing
alternatives. The only advantage offered by Caterina is that she is at least "agli
antipodi del bovarismo."[13] The words that translate her domestic preoccupations
stand only for what they designate – things – and not for any exalted literary worldview having no relationship whatsoever to reality.

The confirmation of *Fantasia*'s status as an exercise in literary options comes
from the novella that follows immediately on its heels. *La virtù di Checchina*
(1884)[14] contains passages of naturalistic description very similar to that cited above
in relation to Caterina. The character in question here is the "virtuous" Checchina,
whose doctor husband has invited the Marchese d'Aragona to dinner:

Ora questo marchese veniva a pranzo ed ella non sapeva che dargli da mangiare a questo nobile, avezzo alle fantasie culinarie dei grandi cuochi. Avevano un servizio di piatti solo per sei persone, comprato a una vendita da Stella, e mancava la salsiera e l'insalatiera; sarebbe bastato? E l'insalata, perché ci vuole, l'insalata in un pranzo, dove l'avrebbe messa? Ecco, gli si potevano dare li gnocchi col sugo di carne: li gnocchi li avrebbe fatti lei, Checchina, e il sugo, Susanna, che a questo era brava. Poi sarebbe venuta la carne col contorno di patate, cotte nel sugo: poi, un piatto di pesce fritto. Ma come fare, se Susanna si lamentava, sempre, che la padella era alta in mezzo e l'olio cadeva ai lati e nel mezzo il pesce diventava nero, abbruciacchiandosi? Ci voleva una padella nuova o bisognava rinunciare al fritto. Le posate d'argento erano sei, ma una forchetta aveva due rebbi storti: presto presto, in cucina, Susanna avrebbe dovuto lavarle, come i piatti, se non bastavano. E l'arrosto, l'arrosto ci voleva! Non usa il pollo, nelle case aristocratiche? come lo avrebbe arrostito, se i fornelli erano due, in cucina, e mancava il girarrosto? Questo pranzo sarebbe costato una quantità di quattrini; come dirlo a Toto, quante cose ci mancavano nella casa! (p. 870)

As we shall see, the character of Checchina is a cross between Lucia and Caterina, Serao's attempt to forge a more human and "realistic" woman than either of the two preceding prototypes, *without however abandoning the parameters they represent*. On the one hand, Checchina is full of "buon senso naturale" (p. 867). Unlike Isolina, her friend and confidante who regularly indulges in extra-marital escapades, Checchina has always been faithful to her husband. Isolina's tales of her adventures normally leave Checchina quite cold, and the contrast Serao draws between the two women is clearly reminiscent of the abyss that separated Lucia and Caterina:

"Oh! io sono innamorata più che mai."
"Di Rodolfo?"
"Ma che Rodolfo, che Rodolfo! Quello era uno stupido, un avvocatino, figurati, come mio marito! Non vi era gusto, capisci: meglio Gigio, poi. Ma questo, questo qui, è ufficiale di cavalleria, lo amo, immensamente, come non ho mai amato nessuno. O Checchina, che passione! Io ne morirò."
Mentre diceva queste parole, un fiotto di sangue le colorava il bel viso bruno, gli occhi brillavano e le labbra tumide, rosse, pareva già sentissero la golosità dei baci. Checchina la guardava con la sua aria seria di femmina senza temperamento, senza avere un fremito nella bella persona, che il goffo vestito di lana nera non arrivava a render brutta. (p. 867)

Like Caterina, Checchina is passive and respectful of the norms of feminine conduct. Under normal circumstances, her husband's avarice occasions only token outbursts on her part: "... non andavano più oltre le ribellioni della natura flemmatica e timida di Checchina. Ella ricadeva nella sua apatia, riaccomodava i suoi vecchi vestiti, li faceva tingere, li faceva lavare" (p. 881). The news of the Marchese's imminent visit to her home, however, arouses new feelings of inadequacy and new stirrings of rebellion: "Ma ora, ora, sorgeva ardente, vivissimo il desiderio di questo vestito nero" (p. 881).

The rest of the novella is an account of Checchina's anxieties, hesitations, and conflicting impulses as she struggles with her desire to accept the Marchese's invitation to visit him in his luxurious apartment. His debonair charms and the setting he offers promise a foray into the elegant world of the late-Romantic novel, but "reality," and finally her own inhibitions, interfere constantly with Checchina's ability to bring her plans to fruition. She prepares to go to her appointment with the Marchese only to find that it is raining and that she has no umbrella; then the washerwoman appears and Checchina is forced to take inventory of the week's laundry; then Susanna, her maid, decides to accompany Checchina on her "walk" since it would be unfitting for her to be seen alone in the streets. Each of these impediments occasions a long naturalistic description which undermines the story's progression toward the opposite, late-Romantic genre. Checchina eventually misses her appointment, the Marchese sends the expected note of disappointment and makes a new date. This time Checchina manages to set out on her own and even to overcome the fear of being discovered as she encounters neighbours and acquaintances sure to wonder where she is heading. However, once she finds herself in front of the building in which the Marchese's apartment is located, her nerve fails her: the building porter becomes a projection of her superego, an authority figure she would have to defy to carry out her designs. She circles the building several times, hesitates, returns, but finally gives in to her true nature:

Il portinaio leggeva un biglietto del lotto, con una cera collerica, ma non si muoveva. Ella non entrò. Per la terza volta, ritornando verso il palazzo Odescalchi, ella ripassò: egli ricaricava lentamente la pipa, premendo il tabacco col pollice – né si levava dalla soglia.
Allora Checchina abbassò il capo e se ne andò a casa rinunziando.
(p. 908)

The ironic tale of the all-too-human Checchina's adulterous non-adventures is generally considered one of Serao's more fully-realized works. Coming as it does on the heels of *Fantasia*, it is also, I believe, a confirmation of the fact that Serao was indeed aware of the radical inadequacies of literary images of women and was anxious to arrive at some compromise between these images and "reality."

If *Checchina* represents precisely this attempt at compromise then *Il romanzo della fanciulla* constitutes Serao's attempt to break out of the mold completely. Contrary to what its title suggests, the *Romanzo* is not a novel at all, but a series of stories, published as a collection in 1886, but which appeared singly in various literary magazines in 1884 and 1885. In this third and final phase of her "revolt" against the literary stereotypes of her time, Serao abandons the married woman altogether, as well as the conventions of plot and protagonist, for the collective, choral representation of the lives of young unmarried women, *fanciulle*, as seen largely from the outside and on the basis of what can be deduced from attitudes and appearance. Her settings include the *villa comunale* (*Nella lava*), a convent (*Per monaca*), a residential teachers' college (*Scuola normale femminile*), an office of the state telegraph system (*Telegrafi dello stato*). Not only do these milieux lend themselves to group portraiture, they also provide a glimpse into two aspects of female reality relatively new to literature: entry into the labour market (*Telegrafi*) and the preparation for it (*Scuola normale*).

A recent re-edition of the *Romanzo* (1985), edited by Francesco Bruni, situates it, as well as *Checchina*, in the context of Serao's ideas of the moment "circa il nesso tra l'argomento amoroso e il genere del romanzo," relating it specifically to "una sua idea sulla narrativa e sul ruolo esagerato, falso, svoltovi dalla passione amorosa":[15]

> L'idea della "fanciulla," distinta dalla donna, troppo spesso protagonista, secondo la Serao, di drammi passionali, è specificamente legata agli interessi della scrittrice entro un periodo ben circoscritto di tempo, e risulta già obliterata nell'edizione del 1895 che prende il titolo dalla prima novella della raccolta, con un sottotitolo – *Romanzo per le signore* – che indica un pubblico se non più ristretto, certo meno qualificato di quello per il quale aveva lavorato la Serao dieci anni prima.... Certo l'edizione del 1895 svende in chiave di appendice un libro serio, poco capito e apprezzato dalla critica contemporanea; ma già nell'edizione del 1893 (e poi nelle seguenti) è omessa la combattiva *Prefazione*, che

illumina sulle ragioni dell'opera e, come si è visto, si lega a vari articoli che la Serao aveva pubblicato in quel giro d'anni.[16]

Curiously enough, however, in his lengthy introduction to the volume (distinct from the "Nota al testo"), Bruni makes no mention whatsoever of these circumstances as factors contributing to Serao's unusual stylistic choices. For example, he attributes her preference for choral representation over the focus on one or two protagonists simply to the fashion of the time, to the fact that Serao "era partecipe del clima culturale del tempo."[17] And as for "il ritegno, così artistico, del libro," its lack of high drama, this is seen simply as proof of the fact that Serao situated herself "sulla linea di Manzoni e di Verga, del loro gusto per un narrare privo di svolte fondate sull'effetto passionale o sul colpo di scena."[18]

Bruni's observations, though not without foundation, add little to our knowledge of Serao and, more seriously, completely ignore a very important aspect of her literary personality: her identity as a woman and particularly as a woman writer, recognized by Serao herself in the opening sentence of her very important preface to the *Romanzo*: "La prima parola a me, per alcune semplici ed utili spiegazioni, agli uomini, cui presento una materia ad essi sconosciuta, alle donne, cui raccomando una materia ad esse ben cara."[19]

The purpose of her tales, she says, is to present a study of "la fanciulla nel vivo," an expression she uses to distinguish her own portraits of young women from that drawn by Edmond de Goncourt in *Chérie* (1883). Serao criticizes Goncourt for basing his novel not on first-hand observation but on confessions and confidences, "come se la fanciulla si confessasse mai a nessuno, madre o amica, fidanzato o romanziere sperimentale":[20]

> ... chiusa come un baco da seta in un bozzolo filato dal rispetto umano, dalla educazione strana e variabile, dalla modestia obbligatoria, dalla ignoranza imposta, dalla inconsapevolezza a ogni costo, e trascinata poi da una forza contraria d'impulsione a gravitare intorno al sole del matrimonio, la fanciulla si sviluppa in condizioni morali difficilissime....
> In questo dramma interiore ... ella diventa profonda, pensosa, maliconica spesso, scettica sempre. Nessuno più della fanciulla, apprende quotidianamente i dolori e le disfatte della lotta per l'esistenza. Essa vive guardinga, move i passi con precauzione; e la sua anima non si dà facilmente, i misteri del suo spirito restano impenetrabili....
> Ora, anch'io ho traversato questo drammatico tratto della vita, anzi la varia fortuna mi ha fatto passare, per più anni di seguito, a traverso

un meraviglioso poliorama di fanciulle d'ogni classe, d'ogni indole, d'ogni razza. Quello stupendo erbario umano, ove le sottili gramigne aristocratiche s'intrecciano coi grassi garofani borghesi, ove l'erbuccia malaticcia è sopraffatta dalla pianta florida, io l'ho visto vivere, crescere, ramificarsi, insinuandosi e penetrando dappertutto. Tutte quelle fanciulle, mi son passate accanto: son passate, si sono allontanate, sono scomparse, sono entrate nella felicità o nella morte, alcune nella felicità per la morte; ma l'immagine loro è rimasta in me, vivente.[21]

It is not simply out of deference to the naturalist credo that Serao claims to have based her portraits on young girls observed "nelle aule della Scuola normale, negli uffici del Telegrafo, ai balconi provinciali di Santa Maria ... sulle terrazze napoletane";[22] it is precisely by resorting to "memory" that she manages to justify her decision to circumvent the conventions of the novel:

Ogni volta che io tento di costruire lo schema ideale e generale della fanciulla, per farne l'eroina d'un romanzo, tutte quante le vostre voci, o amiche, felici o infelici, lontane, lontane tutte, mi risuonano nella testa, in coro.... Tutte queste voci che vengono dal passato ... mi trascinano, mi tolgono la serenità necessaria a comporre un romanzo conforme alle regole stabilite.
Perciò, io non voglio fare un romanzo, non voglio creare un tipo, non voglio risolvere un problema di psicologia sperimentale.... Invece di fabbricare una fanciulla, ho rievocato tutte le compagne della mia fanciullezza; invece di costruire un'eroina, ho rivissuto con le mie amiche del tempo lontano.[23]

If memory was able to provide her with a storehouse of feminine characters with no literary antecedents – such as the autobiographical Caterina Borelli cited earlier – it was undoubtedly more difficult to find unconventional plots to develop around these figures. This may be why she adopts a choral framework: as a means of avoiding the development of plot and character which she feared might lead her yet again down the hackneyed path of the "romanzo conforme alle regole stabilite."

That this hypothesis may indeed be a valid one is suggested by the curious "postscript" to *Scuola normale femminile*: a list of the cast of characters, each name followed by a brief description of the character's life as it was to unfold in the years following graduation. As one contemplates these capsule summaries – twenty in all – one cannot help but think of twenty little novels aborted in the early stages of gestation, by a writer only too aware of their defects. For if faithful and adulterous wives are mercifully absent from them, these plots are no less rhetorical as a result, as is evident from the following outline:

> Carmela Fiorillo non ha fatto il concorso, è stata per un anno maestra rurale a Gragnano, ma essendosi innamorato di lei il figliuolo di un ricco fabbricante di paste, ha dovuto partire dal paese e recarsi a far la maestra in un villaggio dell'Alta Savoia, con la retribuzione di quattrocento lire annue. Non essendovi casa nel villaggio dove era la Scuola, ella abitava al villaggio vicino, e doveva far quattro miglia ogni mattina e ogni sera, per andare e venire. Nell'ultimo inverno, un giorno ... ella è caduta sulla via e si è lasciata morire, per debolezza, per assideramento: gli alpigiani l'hanno raccolta due giorni dopo. Il municipio le ha decretata una piccola lapide di marmo, visto il suo zelo e l'amore alle sue umili fatiche....[24]

The fact that Matilde Serao never developed a character or a plot that seriously deviated from established parameters, notwithstanding the material available to her from her own life, had little if anything to do with her views on the role of women; she was far more intimidated by literary conventions and by an acute sense of her own personal limitations as an artist than by social or moral imperatives. If, as one critic has pointed out, "there were no Matilde-Serao-lady-journalists in her work,"[25] it was not because there were so few in real life; it was because there were none in novels. This is the hypothesis I believe explains her final capitulation to the conventions of the *feuilleton*, which, if nothing else, was to guarantee her a maximum of marketability combined with a minimum of personal and artistic risk.

Notes

[1] G. Verga, *Lettere a Paolina*, ed. G. Raya (Rome: Fermenti, 1980) 157, as quoted in F. Bruni, Introduction, *Il romanzo della fanciulla*, by M. Serao (Naples: Liguori, 1985) x. For a biography of Matilde Serao see A. Banti, *Serao* (Turin: UTET, 1965).

[2] According to W. N. Schilardi ("L'antifemminismo di Matilde Serao," *La parabola della donna nella letteratura italiana dell'Ottocento*, by G. De Donato *et al.* [Bari: Adriatica Editrice, 1983] 277-305), "la Serao è la espressione più compiuta della capacità di tenuta del progetto moderato, elaborato nella prima metà dell'Ottocento, che aveva individuato il ruolo tutto domestico e familiare della donna e che tentava con tutti i mezzi di frenare la presa di coscienza e le spinte innovatrici che anche in Italia, sia pure tardivamente nei confronti di altri paesi europei, incominciavano ad emergere. La Serao romanziera assolve perfettamente il suo ruolo: elegge le donne a protagoniste, ne evidenzia la difficoltà e la pesantezza della condizione, permette loro pure

qualche ribellione o trasgressione, sempre però naufragate o punite miseramente dal 'destino,' dalla società, da Dio; intuisce il ruolo di sopraffazione giocato dal maschio nel destino della donna, ma non solleva mai le sue eroine ad uno stato di 'ideologica consapevolezza,' non ci sono insomma nei suoi romanzi le parole lotta, rivolta, volontà di cambiamento" (pp. 280-281). For a variety of other views in this vein see G. Infusino, "Aristocrazia e popolo (Le donne negli scritti di Matilde Serao)," and D. Amato, "Femminismo e femminilità," both in M. Prisco *et al.*, *Matilde Serao tra giornalismo e letteratura*, ed. G. Infusino (Naples: Guida, 1981) 61-72 and 103-110; I. Pezzini, "Matilde Serao," *Carolina Invernizio, Matilde Serao, Liala*, by U. Eco *et al.* (Florence: La nuova Italia, 1979) 61-94; G. Buzzi, *Invito alla lettura di Matilde Serao* (Milan: Mursia, 1981) 63-88; A. Briganti, "Matilde Serao: un profilo," *Svelamento. Sibilla Aleramo: una biografia intelletuale*, eds. A. Buttafuoco and M. Zancan (Milan: Feltrinelli, 1988) 188-198.

3 *Fantasia* (Turin, 1883) now in M. Serao, *Serao*, ed. P. Pancrazi, vol. 2 (Milan: Garzanti, 1946) 119. All subsequent references to the novel will be to the Pancrazi edition, and page numbers will appear in the text.

4 According to A. Nozzoli, "dagli scenari dannuziani della Guglielminetti, attraverso i tenebrosi *pastiche* della Vivanti, sino ad arrivare al *degré zéro* di Neera, il cammino della narrativa femminile in Italia tra la fine del secolo e i primi decenni del '900 sembra così muoversi sotto la stella di un'incontrollata, aprioristica, quasi ontologica rispondenza al ruolo materno, parimenti riflessa dalle due mitologiche Eve della nostra letteratura: la 'peccatrice' e 'l'angelo del focolare,' il demone perverso e la ieratica creatura votata al parto e alla riproduzione" ("La letteratura femminile in Italia tra Ottocento e Novecento," *Tabù e coscienza: la condizione femminile nella letteratura italiana del Novecento* [Florence: La nuova Italia, 1978] 30). See also A. Arslan Veronese, *Dame, droga e galline: romanzo popolare e romanzo di consumo* (Padua: CLEUP, 1977); N. Auerbach, *Women and the Demon: The Life of a Victorian Myth* (Cambridge: Harvard University Press, 1982).

5 See L. Bersani, "Le réalisme et la peur du désir," first published in *Poétique* 6 (1975): 177-195, now in *Littérature et réalité*, by R. Barthes *et al.* (Paris: Seuil, 1982) 47-80. According to Bersani, "au XIXe siècle, les personnages qui refusent d'accepter les limites que la société impose au sujet, à sa nature et à l'étendue de ses désirs deviennent les boucs émissaires de cette société.... L'expulsion du bouc émissaire a une fonction culturelle de stabilisation.... Le roman réaliste parvient toujours à canaliser ou à punir les débordements d'énergie vitale de ses héros; il ne les tolère que dans les personnages secondaires, sous la forme dégradée d'amusantes excentricités" (pp. 70-72). See also M. Jeuland-Meynaud, "I modelli narrativi tardoromantici nella cultura meridionale," *Cultura meridionale e letteratura italiana. I modelli narrativi dell'età moderna, Atti dell'XI congresso dell'AISLII* (Naples: Loffredo, 1985) 405-445. According to Jeuland-Meynaud, in the late-Romantic novel "il motivo della giustizia, immanente o trascendente che sia, articola il sistema dei significati ideologici nella cerchia di un mondo chiuso nel quale ogni atto si tira dietro, deterministicamente, la sua ineliminabile sanzione. Tranne che in Pirandello, e del resto non sempre, l'aleatorio, il disperso, l'eterogeneo non vi hanno posto. Siamo in un universo a struttura paternalistica, e quasi mafiosa, dove al peccato, cioè allo sgarro, socialmente e culturalmente definito, segue l'espiazione, si chiami essa vendetta, castigo o giorno del giudizio, la cui ineluttabilità assicura alle opere la loro tensione morale.... Con la mitagogia della colpa-castigo, il modello tardoromantico recupera il suo significato tradizionale di *exemplum*" (pp. 421-424). Jeuland-Meynaud also notes that "punizione del vizio non significa d'altronde trionfo della virtù, soprattutto in epoca verista ... la sconfitta tocca spesso all'innocente" (p. 424). While this explains Caterina's suicide, it makes Lucia's "triumph" all the more inexplicable.

The confirmation of the rather unorthodox nature of Serao's dénouement comes from an unlikely source: a late-nineteenth century American anthology of contemporary writers of the time, which reproduces two excerpts from Serao's work, including one from *Fantasia*. (The edition cited is *Fantasy*, trans. H. Harland, American Publishers' Corporation, 1890). In the biographical introduction, the writer outlines the plot of *Fantasia* in such a way as to make it clear that either the American publishers or Serao herself at their request had taken it upon themselves to rewrite the novel's ending for this translation *in order to make it conform to conventional morality*: "This is the story of a morbid and fanatically religious invalid, who through her sickly romanticism is led into sinful feeling. She infatuates the husband of her dearest friend, and finally leaves her own husband to run away with him; but, overcome with remorse, evades her lover, and smothers herself with charcoal, to secure the happiness of the deserted wife" ("Matilde Serao," *The Warner Library*, eds. J. W. Cunliffe and A. Thorndike, vol. 22 [New York: Warner Library Company, 1917] 13134).

6 *Fantasia*'s debt to *Madame Bovary* has been seen only in the context of Serao's debt to the French novel in general, and never as a specific connection worthy of examination. See E. Scarfoglio, "Fantasie dei critici intorno alla *Fantasia* di Matilde Serao," *Nuova antologia* 16 Aug. 1883, as quoted in Banti 45; also M. G. Martin Gistucci, *L'oeuvre romanesque de Mathilde Serao* (Grenoble: Presses Universitaires de Grenoble, 1973) 483.

7 G. Flaubert, *Madame Bovary* (Paris: Gallimard, 1972) 70.

8 Buzzi takes Serao severely to task for failing to create "flesh and blood" characters: "manichini sono infatti Lucia e Caterina e i loro due maschi ... e quasi tutto di maniera è l'ambiente nel quale si muovono.... La verità è che Caterina, non meno di Lucia, è disancorata dalla realtà e dalla vita.... Il cifrario del fantasticare di Lucia non è peggiore, più astratto, più arbitrario di quello che presiede al quotidianismo di Caterina" (pp. 80-81). While Buzzi's assessment is not incorrect, he fails to perceive Serao's own ambivalence and dissatisfaction with regard to the Caterina character.

9 M. Beer, "Suicidio e inettitudine. Nota sui romanzi femminili italiani del ventennio 1880-90," *Memoria*, 2 (1981): 87. The quotation does not refer here to *Fantasia*, but to a *pastiche* of the critic's own creation. The assumption that *Fantasia* is to be read as a morality tale is not surprising since that is indeed the author's intention at a superficial level. What is surprising is that no one appears to have noticed the ambiguities and contradictions the novel presents. According to Banti, "il romanzo è a tesi: la fantasia è il male,... la normalità è il bene.... La scrittrice ovviamente parteggia per il bene e cioè per la piccola ingenua Caterina, tradita nell'amore e nell'amicizia" (p. 41). In a similar vein, Pezzini claims that "nel linguaggio della Serao, è colpa in sintesi permettere che la passione sovrasti la ragione, tesi illustrata ampiamente in uno dei suoi primi romanzi, *Fantasia*" (p. 67), with little regard for the fact that Lucia escapes unscathed and with Andrea. According to Buzzi, "il suicidio di Caterina, che si chiude in camera con un braciere acceso, conclude degnamente e secondo le attese questa vicenda che vuol essere esemplare e magistrale" (p. 79), as if Lucia's fate were of no consequence at all.

10 The only critic to suggest an interpretation even remotely akin to this one is A. Palermo, who speaks only of a possible "consapevole prova su un doppio registro" in "Le due narrative di Matilde Serao," *Da Mastriani a Viviani: per una storia della letteratura a Napoli fra Otto e Novecento* (Naples: Liguori, 1974) 47.

11 The question of the Caterina/Serao identification has been raised by Banti, but only at the moral level. Banti points out that Serao "preferisce Caterina a tal punto da identificarsi con lei, talché, in certe lettere amichevoli, la vedremo firmarsi, intenzionalmente,*Caterina*" (p. 41).

12 Emphasis added.

[13] M. P. Pozzato, *Il romanzo rosa* (Milan: Editori Europei Associati, 1982) 109. The phrase is referred here not to *Fantasia*, but, curiously enough, to the Italian feminist novel of the seventies. And yet, the entire passage might somehow be applied to Caterina/Serao's dilemma: "La dolorosa consapevolezza della difficoltà dell'espressione dei sentimenti e delle esperienze personali, intime della donna, è invece centrale nel dibattito odierno su letteratura e femminismo. In un saggio sul romanzo femminista italiano degli anni '70, Anna Nozzoli afferma: 'Una volta sancito il caparbio rifiuto dell'artificio letterario e linguistico, la voce della donna nuova sembra articolarsi sulle tracce di un linguaggio disadorno e come afono, privo di dimensioni e di colore, il cui partito preso è quello dell'indifferenza, dell'appiattimento della parola al suo elementare e irriducibile valore gnomico.'

Siamo così agli antipodi del bovarismo, l'attaccamento della donna alla nuda realtà diventa una scelta, un modo per conoscerla meglio, per appropriarsene e, forse, cambiarla. Del resto potrebbe essere un'illusione anche questa di una letteratura strettamente contenutistica, denotativa. L'esperienza 'reale' della vita non è infatti la cosa più facile da esprimere" (p. 109).

[14] *La virtù di Checchina* (Catania: Giannotta, 1884), serialized first in *Nuova Antologia* from 25 November to 16 December 1883, now in *Serao*, ed. P. Pancrazi, vol.1, 863-908. All subsequent references to the novella will be to this edition, and page numbers will appear in the text.

[15] F. Bruni, Note to the text, *Il romanzo della fanciulla* xlii.

[16] Bruni, Note to the text xlii.

[17] Bruni, Introduction xiii.

[18] Bruni, Introduction xvii.

[19] M. Serao, Preface, *Il romanzo della fanciulla* 3.

[20] Serao, Preface 3.

[21] Serao, Preface 3-4.

[22] Serao, Preface 5.

[23] Serao, Preface 5.

[24] Serao, "Scuola normale femminile," *Il romanzo della fanciulla* 181-182.

[25] J.J. Howard, "The Feminine Vision of Matilde Serao," *Italian Quarterly* 71 (1975): 68-69.

Strategies of Intertextuality in Sibilla Aleramo's
Una Donna

Of all the Italian novels written by women in the years 1880-1920, certainly the one to have enjoyed the greatest notoriety then, as now, is Sibilla Aleramo's *Una donna* (1906).[1] Its reputation has little to do with the novel's literary merit and even less with its subject matter – the dilemma of a woman in an unhappy marriage – than with the fact that at the novel's end its heroine and narrator does the unthinkable for a woman in a Catholic society: in the course of separation from her husband, though not by choice, she abandons a small child.[2]

Enough has been written about Sibilla Aleramo to make it superfluous to enter into a lengthy discussion of the circumstances leading to the publication of this novel.[3] The first chapter of Rita Guerricchio's classic *Storia di Sibilla*, entitled "Cronaca e miti," correctly identifies *Una donna* as a *confession rétrospective* with traces of traditional naturalist assumptions alongside more modern psychological influences.[4] As Guerricchio points out, the psychological novel owed its emergence partly to the perceived inadequacies of the positivist values embraced by naturalism, most notably to their inability to accommodate what she calls the "diritti dell'anima"[5] and which Maria Corti has identified in Aleramo as coinciding with the theme of the heroine's "awakening," the "nozione di risveglio di sé da parte della donna nella società del proprio tempo, nozione che non solo è ancora attuale ma trae le sue radici da atteggiamenti e riflessioni che sono del tempo del libro e in esso rispecchiati."[6]

Guerricchio's account of Aleramo's unpublished early fiction (1892-94) reveals her to have been working at first with themes and tropes typical of the bourgeois novel, with heroines largely reminiscent of the *femme fatale* so much in vogue at the time.[7] *Una donna* represents a radical departure from these early literary exercises, determined by the intervening sequence of events in Sibilla's own difficult life and by her conversion to feminist thought, which can be traced in the numerous journalistic articles she published in the years immediately preceding her return to "fiction."[8] The adoption of a feminist ideology gave Aleramo a collectivizing framework within which to place her story, so that it might read as something more significant than simply one woman's anecdotal rendering of her decision to leave her family. This intention is confirmed by the novel's title as well as by the total absence in it of place and character names: "sottratto alla determinazione storica ed ambientale intesa come mimesi descrittiva degli avvenimenti,"[9] *Una donna* underscores exemplary universal functions at the expense of detail and, occasionally, truth. The most notorious of Aleramo's departures from fact is constituted by an omission: the omission of the fact that she was already engaged in another relationship when she finally decided to leave her husband and child. This omission was to plague her for a long time to come and she later confessed it in another novel, *Il passaggio* (1919).[10]

I mention this last fact only to demonstrate how much emphasis has been placed on the autobiographical element in this novel or, more to the point, on its roots in "real life," by Aleramo herself and by her critics. Guerricchio's acute stylistic observations bring to light the novel's largely traditional chronological development (interrupted only by the occasional flashback); hence its attempt to present events as much as possible as they occurred in chronological time, and not as they occur in memory: "la dimensione del ricordo vissuto assum[e] per Sibilla i caratteri del soliloquio ad alta voce, piuttosto che del vero e proprio monologo interiore."[11] Guerricchio attributes this to Aleramo's overwhelming need to reconstruct her experience as she lived it in order to lay it to rest: "il raccontare, il rivivere, l'analizzare ... sono le tre dimensioni memoriali che sorreggono tutto il racconto."[12] The emphasis in the novel on the life-trajectory of a woman has also led to examinations of *Una donna* as an example of a Bildungsroman, the novel of development, with attempts to establish to what extent it fits into various female sub-genres of the Bildungsroman, either "the classic female novel of development [or] its evolutionary offspring, the novel of awakening."[13]

Whether they emphasize its personal or its exemplary aspects, almost all critics who have discussed this novel share the assumption that it is, above all, a revolutionary text which represents a radical departure from previous Italian novels by and about women and is therefore a milestone in the history of women's writing.[14] According to Nozzoli, in *Una donna* "si costruisce un profilo femminile inedito, emergente di volta in volta attraverso progressivi rifiuti;" it is these "rifiuti" which, ostensibly, distinguish Aleramo from other writers such as Neera, the Marchesa Colombi or Ada Negri, whose female characters are indeed oppressed but never openly rebellious.[15] Maria Antonietta Macciocchi is equally categoric: "*Una donna* spezza la catena della schiavitù. E' la rivolta. La rivolta emancipatrice contro l'umiliazione della donna sull'altare della maternità."[16]

It is important to point out that Aleramo herself contributed to this emphasis on novelty and rupture by calling repeated attention in *Una donna* to her intolerance of most women's writing of her time: "Di ideali d'ogni specie ... tutta l'opera letteraria muliebre del paese mi pareva deficiente: grandi frasi vuote, senza nesso e senza convinzione."[17] As editor at *Mulier* (the name she gives to l'*Italia femminile*, the periodical which employed her briefly in 1899) she recalls the indignation she felt "vedendo piovere in redazione libri mediocri firmati da donne, vere parodie di libri maschili più in voga dettati da una vanità ancor più sciocca di quella delle pupattole mondane di cui l'editore riproduceva in fotografia gli appartamenti *modern style*" (p. 135). Her conclusion is that "[p]oeti e romanzieri continuavano a rifare il duetto e il terzetto eterni, con complicazioni sentimentali e perversioni sensuali. Nessuno però aveva saputo creare una grande figura di donna" (p. 150). Her own ambition, by contrast, was to write

> "un libro, il libro ... che mostrasse al mondo intero l'anima femminile moderna, per la prima volta,... che recasse tradotte tutte le idee che si agitavano in me caoticamente da due anni ... e sapesse trarre da ciò la pura essenza, il capolavoro equivalente ad una vita" (p. 122).

Taken at face value, her story of separation and sacrifice, told unabashedly in the first person, (one critic has called it "an artistic rendering of Rina Pierangeli Faccio's escape from the graveyard of her fears to freedom") would seem to indicate that Aleramo really was profoundly different from other women writers of her time. It has certainly led most of her critics to believe that if she did suffer from any of the constraints or contradictions to which her literary sisters were so often subject, she had overcome them in the process of the "coming to consciousness" which her story retraces. The only dissenting voice to be heard in this chorus of feminist praise for the novel is that of Maria Corti. Her introduction to the Feltrinelli edition, while emphasizing the novel's modernity, also points out its limitations: "Di molto moderno c'è qui l'aspirazione a creare un automodello esistenziale che per ora si esprime come litote; voglio dire si esprime più per quello che si rifiuta che per quello che si propone in cambio."[18]

Corti's remarks call attention to two facts: first, to the deliberate creation in this novel of what one might call an existential "identity position" and second, to its construction on the basis of rejections of the past, rather than of projections into the future. On the basis of the interpretive strategies suggested by these observations, I would like to propose a somewhat different reading of this novel emphasizing intertextuality: by this I mean its awareness of other literary texts dealing with the same themes and operating as a sign of both rupture and continuity simultaneously.

In calling attention to *Una donna*'s respect for chronological development, Rita Guerricchio has suggested that the novel was born of Aleramo's need to relive and come to terms with her past. Again, what I would like to suggest is something slightly different: while this may indeed be the case, in the process of giving form to her experience, she found herself confronting the literary "past" as well, in the form of previous literary solutions to the dilemma of the woman in an unhappy marriage. This is repeatedly suggested by an intertextual strategy in which direct references and indirect allusions to literary models structure the text: the most significant of these is the allusion to Dante's Francesca and Paolo episode in the very first paragraph of the story.[19] Later on, as we shall see, there is repeated mention of the influence of literature in shaping her expectations and interpretations of reality. Far from being a personal, revolutionary, isolated text, unself-consciously afloat in a sea of literary and social conformity, *Una donna* is more accurately interpreted, I believe, as a text which ultimately aims at re-writing and hence disposing of these previous solutions, inscribed into the present text either through portions of the heroine's own experience, or through the vicissitudes of two important minor characters (the heroine's mother and the Norwegian designer) both of whom, in accordance with the novel's tendency to "universality," remain nameless throughout. As we break her text into its constituent parts, we shall see that it unfolds not only on a chronological axis which is a mimesis of a "real life," but also in terms of a staged tableau of already-existing literary scenarios, each of which is in turn "explored" and discarded.

In Italy, women writers had thus far treated the subject of the woman in an unhappy marriage in a manner sanctioned by Catholic morality and patriarchal norms. Neera had written about it indirectly in a series of early novels on the adultery theme and explicitly in at least two later novels, *L'Indomani* (1891) and *L'Amuleto* (1897). In *L'Indomani*, the young woman in question sublimates her unfulfilled needs in motherhood; in *L'Amuleto* she finds solace in Platonic friendship. In all cases, the family unit remains intact, notwithstanding the suffering involved. In *Una donna*, Aleramo speaks of having met "una romanziera cattolica che eccelleva nell'analizzare adulteri di desiderio coronati dal pentimento e dall'elogio del matrimonio indissolubile" (p. 147). Whether or not she was referring to Neera, it is clear that she had in mind the sort of message that Neera conveyed so effectively and so obsessively throughout most of her career.

Another well-known writer for women, the notorious Carolina Invernizio (1851-1916), also addressed the subject and also prescribed self-denial in the name of family unity. An excellent example of the values she transmitted to her readers is to be found in the model provided by the heroine of one of her most enduring gothic novels, the immensely popular *Bacio di una morta* (1887).[20] It tells the story of Clara, an innocent young woman whose marriage to a debonair aristocrat initially promises a lifetime of love and fulfillment. Instead, during his wife's pregnancy, ostensibly through no fault of his own, he falls victim to the charms of a Javanese dancer, Nara: "Non sapete di che cosa può essere capace un uomo sotto l'impero di una passione malvagia, infernale, come quella ispirata a Guido da Nara."[21] Her sensuality is so overpowering, we are told, that it gradually deprives him of all free will, so much so that he even agrees to poison his wife in order to gain control of his child's inheritance. Clara suffers greatly, but in silence and with "dignity," refusing to expose her husband for fear of tarnishing the family name. Her unfaltering love and devotion to her daughter are what keep her sane, until her husband and his mistress deceive her into swallowing the poisonous potion that sends her into a coma and allows them to abduct the child unhampered. The servants take Clara for dead and transport her to a cemetery for burial. Her brother and his wife arrive just in time to discover Clara drugged, but still alive in her coffin. The rest of the novel tells of Clara's slow recovery from her ordeal and of the plot concocted by the family notary and her brother to win back Guido's affections and restore the unity of the family. The strategy employed involves having Clara herself masquerade as a black-haired woman with whom Guido falls in love. Clara is rewarded with the recovery of her daughter and the expansion of the family unit to include her brother and his family as well.

Invernizio's "consolatory" novels clearly suggest an audience of disillusioned women for whom marriage has become at best, boring, at worst, a trial:

> La fiducia e l'amore sono i due principali elementi della donna. Posandosi più facilmente sopra le apparenze e le impressioni, ella è esposta più dell'uomo a illusioni. Quando la giovinetta comincia ad amare, crede all'eternità degli affetti, all'immortale unione delle anime, al continuo accrescimento di benevolenza, finché il disinganno non sfronda ad una ad una gran parte delle sue illusioni....
> Quanti giuramenti si fanno ... ogni giorno! Un giovane incontra una fanciulla bella, intelligente e l'ama, e crede ed è convinto nel suo cuore di non amare che lei sola, di amarla per tutta la vita....
> Si amano, sono uniti, il mondo è tutto per loro. Ma a poco a poco l'abitudine uccide quell'amore appassionato; la moglie ha nuove occupazioni, nuovi affetti: i figli. Il marito o s'ingolfa negli affari o per calmare la noia che comincia ad assediarlo ritorna all'antica vita, agli amici abbandonati.
> Eppure egli ama sempre la moglie e gli sembra di non amare alcuno più di lei; ma le sue manifestazioni si fanno così fredde che la moglie finisce col credersi ingannata, di aver dato a lui tanta gioia e tanta felicità e di riceverne in cambio lacrime ed amarezze....
> E il marito, che credeva di trovare nel santuario della casa la pace e la quiete, comincia a sentirsi inasprito; alle tristezze senza ragione della moglie, si sente offeso nel suo orgoglio....
> Ed ecco perché la vita di molti sposi, se proprio non li sostiene una gran tenerezza, una perfetta reciproca comprensione, diventa difficile, la loro convivenza poco lieta.[22]

In the context of these remarks, Clara's tale is clearly not meant to be a realistic one: the mimetic rendering of the disillusioned married woman's life makes for a totally different novelistic genre. Clara's tale is an exemplary one, in which Invernizio provides her heroine with a formidable challenge as well as a reward, and her readers with a larger-than-life role model, meant to be an inspiration as well as a consolation. Clara is glorified as a female Christ-figure, a heroine of sacrifice, who lives, dies, comes back to life, seduces her unwitting husband and even lies at his trial, all to save the family honour. Repression, patience, silence, self-denial, nurturance, manipulation, forgiveness are but a few of the typically "feminine" traits which she displays in over-abundance and which enable her to win back her husband, against all odds:

> Ormai ella non aveva più dubbi. Il suo Guido non l'amava più e si mostrava verso di lei di una freddezza crudele....
> Eppure nessun lamento uscì dalle labbra di Clara: la sua disperazione fu muta, senza lagnanze né preghiere.[23]

He, in turn, is depicted as a child, totally devoid of any responsibility for his actions, having been seduced by a woman whose evil and passionate nature have appealed to his baser instincts and deprived him of his will: "Nara sola era la colpevole della tragedia che aveva devastata la sua vita."[24] Clara's mission is to find and free him. A woman's "power" is limitless, Invernizio tells her "gentle" readers, provided she knows how to use it: such is the moral of this schematic tale of search-and-rescue by the Superwoman of Patriarchy, meant to offer its readers a warning about the dangers of unbridled sexuality, a model of virtue rewarded, and an edifying escape from their own problems.[25]

What does all this have to do with Sibilla Aleramo's *Una donna*? The heroine's unhappy marriage, which in her case leads to separation and to a new life, is not the only such situation treated in this novel. In fact, Part I of the novel, which tells of her childhood, adolescence and marriage, also tells of the deterioration of her parents' union, of her father's repeated infidelities and, in particular, of her mother's unsuccessful attempts to adapt to the situation. Unlike Invernizio's Clara or other more "realistic" heroines like Neera's Marta (*L'Indomani*), Aleramo's mother is unable to suffer in silence without serious consequences to her health and sanity: her story "ends" with a failed suicide attempt and her subsequent internment in an institution for the mentally ill. For her, passivity and resignation lead to madness.

The text deliberately presents the mother as a literary character, a stereotype rather than an individual, and one based on another literary character at that, the legendary Cinderella:

> Ella era nata in un ambiente modestissimo d'impiegati e, come la mia nonna paterna, sua madre aveva avuto molti figliuoli, di cui la maggior parte viveva sparsa pel mondo. Doveva esser cresciuta fra

le strettezze, poco amata, Cenerentola della casa. A vent'anni, ad
una festicciuola da ballo, s'era incontrata col babbo....
Quand'io ero nata, l'anno non era ancor compiuto dal dì delle nozze.
La mamma s'illuminava nel volto bianco e puro le rarissime volte
che accennava alle due stanzine coi mobili a nolo dei primi mesi di
vita coniugale. Perché non era sempre così animata? Perché era così
facile al pianto, mentre mio padre non poteva sopportare la vista
delle lagrime, e perché mostrava opinioni diverse tanto spesso da
quelle di lui, quando osava esprimerle? (pp. 21-22)

The mother's story functions here on two levels – at the autobiographical level,
as the story of Aleramo's mother, and at the metaliterary level as an exemplary
textual exploration of the sacrifice of self, proposed by other female writers as a
possible solution for the woman in an unhappy marriage:

Per diciotto anni l'infelice aveva vissuto nella casa coniugale. Come
moglie, le poche gioie le si erano mutate in infinite pene: come
madre non aveva mai goduto della riconoscenza delle sue creature.
Il suo cuore non aveva mai trovato la via dell'effusione. Era passata
nella vita incompresa da tutti....
Non una amica, non un consigliere, mai, sulla sua strada. E una
salute incerta, un organismo travagliato da lenti mali....
Amare e sacrificarsi e soccombere! Questo il destino suo e forse di
tutte le donne? (pp. 63-64)

In the third chapter, Aleramo recalls her mother's suicide attempt. This is
preceded by her recollection of her mother's only partial ability to mask the stress of
silence and her emotional pain. Unlike Invernizio's superhuman Clara – "Ma se il
viso di Clara portava le tracce delle sofferenze interne, il suo sorriso ineffabile, la
sua innata bontà non si smentivano mai."[26] – Aleramo's mother is unable to hide
the fact that, as a result of her suffering, her good humour has more than worn thin:
"Ma mi sembrava ch'ella non pervenisse a nascondere una nervosità di cui ignoravo
la cagione: notavano gli ospiti e il babbo lo sforzo che ella faceva su sé stessa per
seguire le conversazioni e i giochi?" (p. 37).

Sometimes Aleramo's character appears to be the converse of Invernizio's;
sometimes, on the contrary, she seems to mirror her. Such is the case in the
following descriptions of their respective post-suicide deliria (although Clara is
"poisoned" by her husband and his mistress, in fact, she brings this upon herself
through her silence and passivity – a figurative suicide, certainly) in which the
combination of "delirio" and "lucidità" of the first is echoed in the "assente" and
"presente" of the second: "Clara rimase assopita per molta parte del giorno....

Verso sera tornò a delirare, ma nel suo stesso delirio, aveva una specie di lucidità, che sembrava regolare le sue parole."[27] Aleramo's mother "rimase in letto due mesi in un alternarsi di febbri che minacciavano la congestione cerebrale; presente come non mai, e insieme assente, come dopo una suprema rinuncia" (p. 38).

Perhaps the myth to receive the greatest blow in Aleramo's portrait of her mother's gradual deterioration is that of the woman able to function unimpaired as a mother, independently of her own distraught emotional state. The young "Sibilla" may not understand the reasons for her mother's sadness ("Io leggevo nei libri vicende d'amore e d'odio,... credevo di saper già molte cose sulla vita, ma ero incapace di penetrare la dolorosa realtà della mia casa" [p. 33]), but she does understand that her behaviour toward her children is affected by this sadness, and that she is not, like mothers in books, able to erase her pain through the "joys" provided by her children:

> Quante volte ho visto brillare per una lagrima rattenuta i begli occhi profondi e bruni di mia madre. Saliva in me un dolore invincibile, che non era pietà, non era dolore neppure, e neppure reale umiliazione, ma piuttosto un oscuro rancore contro l'impossibilità di reagire, di far che non avvenisse ciò che avveniva. Che cosa? Non sapevo bene. Verso gli otto anni avevo lo strano timore di non possedere una mamma "vera," una di quelle mamme, dicevano i miei libri di lettura, che versano sulle figliuolette, col loro amore, una gioia ineffabile, la certezza della protezione costante. (p.22)

Aleramo, of course, had a vested interest in exploding the myth of motherhood as a panacea for all that ails women and, in Part III of the book, which tells of her final separation from husband and child, she cites an old letter of her mother's which foreshadows her own experiences. The letter is mentioned in connection with Aleramo's own admission that, like her mother, she was no longer able to dedicate herself wholeheartedly to her child in the face of her own anguish:

> Mancava a me la volontà continua della vera educatrice, la serenità di spirito per guidare la piccola esistenza; non potevo assorbirmi intera nella considerazione dei suoi bisogni, prevenirli, soddisfarli. In certi istanti per questa consapevolezza mi odiavo....
> Così era stata mia madre coi suoi bambini.... Un giorno trassi da una cassetta alcune vecchie carte di lei....
> E una lettera mi fermò il respiro. Datava da Milano: era scritta a matita, in modo quasi illeggibile, di notte. La mamma annunziava a suo padre il suo arrivo per il dì dopo; diceva di aver già pronto il

baule colle poche cose sue, di essere già stata nella camera dei
figliuoli a baciarli per l'ultima volta....
"Debbo partire ... qui impazzisco ... lui non mi ama più.... Ed io
soffro tanto che non so più voler bene ai bambini ... debbo
andarmene, andarmene.... Poveri figli miei, forse è meglio per
loro!" (pp. 180-181)

Part I of *Una donna* rewrites and discards the "novel of sacrifice" twice over:
once in the mother's story, once in Aleramo's own, since after her marriage Sibilla
repeats the passivity and resignation of her mother's life. "Torpida ... di membra
oltre che d'animo" (p. 61), she later attributes her inability to react against her
husband's abuse to her mother's example: "La sua debolezza, la sua rinuncia alla
lotta mi esacerbavano tanto più in quanto ero costretta a riconoscermi ora dei punti
di contatto nella mia rassegnazione al destino" (pp. 60-61).

The novel of sacrifice is not, however, the only sub-genre re-visited and
disposed of in Part I of *Una donna*. The novel of adultery is briefly alluded to as
well in an episode which precedes her suicide attempt and which derives, this time,
from the many novels she had read as a young girl:

> Spesso rifiutavo d'accompagnar la mamma a qualche visita e restavo
> a casa, sprofondata in un gran seggiolone, a leggere i libri più
> disparati, sovente incomprensibili per me, ma dei quali alcuni mi
> procuravano una specie d'ebbrezza dell'immaginazione e mi
> astraevano completamente da me stessa....
> Arrossivo; come arrossivo di certe pose languide che assumevo nella
> stessa poltrona, quando mi accadeva per un attimo di trasportarmi
> colla fantasia nei panni d'una bella dama piena di seduzioni. (pp. 20-
> 21)

In her own life the occasion to be "una bella dama piena di seduzioni" presents
itself with the appearance of another *forestiero* like herself, a married man whose
relatively sophisticated tastes and inclinations differ radically from those of the other
inhabitants of this small provincial town and suggest an affinity between them.
Their "courtship" begins with enigmatic glances on his part in public, progresses to
the letter-writing stage, and eventually culminates in a brief, private face-to-face
encounter, in which Aleramo rejects her suitor quite violently, overcome by nausea
at his physical advances. She then proceeds to demystify, in one paragraph, the
entire infamous tradition of the novel of bourgeois adultery:

> Lui? Era proprio lui, quell'uomo miserevole che m'era apparso, la
> sera avanti, spoglio d'ogni poesia e d'ogni illusione, brutale e

ridicolo? E un'ira folle mi prendeva contro me stessa, che cadeva subito per lasciar posto ad una vergogna profonda. Io avevo rinunciato a me stessa.... La smania di vivere m'aveva accecata. La vita che cercavo era l'errore, era l'abiezione. (p. 87)

Having undoubtedly concluded, with Antonio Gramsci, that "la donna della famiglia borghese [è] più schiava ancora quando ritrova l'unica libertà che le è consentita, la libertà della galanteria,"[28] it is at this juncture that Aleramo situates the failed suicide attempt which closes Part I. Part II tells of her convalescence and gradual "rebirth" through reading, writing, meditation and, finally, through entry into the active life as a journalist in Rome while still with her husband and child. Part II concludes with a death, as did Part I (in which the "old" Sibilla dies figuratively). This time it is a "real" death, that of the novel's other very major minor character, known simply as "the Norwegian designer" (*la disegnatrice norvegese*). These parallellisms are not coincidental. Sibilla's role model as a married woman is her mother – Part I is the story of the shedding of this model. Part II tells of the reconstitution of her personality on the basis of two new models, one provided by the Norwegian designer, the other by an older woman, a social activist whom Sibilla calls, significantly, "la buona vecchia mamma."[29] Through the fusion of these two models – the Norwegian designer is the woman who leaves an unhappy marriage, while the social activist, presented in her nurturing function, offers the example of how to live in the absence of a family – Aleramo constructs an "identity position" for herself which she feels is consonant with her own specific aims as a woman and as a writer. What exactly this "identity position" consists of can best be described beginning with the attempt to explain why Part II ends with the death of precisely the character without whose example the heroine might never have achieved her own liberation.[30]

The designer is presented as a young woman who has come to seek her fortune in Italy, having left behind a lifeless marriage in her own country, with neither guilt nor recriminations:

I suoi l'avevano data, a sedici anni, a un pastore del suo paese. "Ah che noia, mia piccola, che noia!"...
Un giorno ella gli aveva detto francamente che avrebbe desiderato "andar lontano da Dio!" Ci fu una disputa. Lui amava prima Dio, poi lei. Ella gli disse di scegliere....
E se n'era venuta sola in Italia, il paese vagheggiato sin dalla fanciullezza; aveva fatto l'istitutrice, disegnato per giornali di mode:

l'esito dei primi saggi della sua arte originale l'aveva incoraggiata a
dedicarvisi interamente. (pp. 145-146)

After some difficulty, she manages to find steady employment with the
magazine for which the heroine herself is working in Rome, prior to her separation.
The two become close friends and lend each other support in their respective
struggles. The designer is on the brink of professional and personal fulfillment –
she has just had a successful exhibition of her work and is about to marry a brilliant
young scientist in whom she has finally found a worthy companion – when
suddenly she falls ill and dies.

In discussion of this novel, critics have tended to mention this minor character
only in passing, without examining more closely the implications of her story and
its relationship to that of the heroine. Significantly, in describing her, Aleramo
remarks that "il vederla raccontare ... la sua vita di cinque anni in casa del suo santo
carceriere, fu per me la rivelazione della grande arte spontanea e profonda che mi si
manifestò di poi nei capolavori nordici" (p. 145). Moreover, the chapter in which
the designer's story is told is also the chapter in which Aleramo makes direct
reference, without naming it, to Henryk Ibsen's notorious play, *A Doll's House*
(1879), a performance of which she attends in the company of an older actress
friend:

> Una sera a teatro la vecchia attrice, nel suo palco, aveva avvertito
> due lagrime brillarmi negli occhi. Non avevo mai pianto per le
> finzioni dell'arte. Sulla scena una povera bambola di sangue e di
> nervi si rendeva ragione della propria inconsistenza, e si proponeva
> di diventar una creatura umana, partendosene dal marito e dai figli,
> per cui la sua presenza non era che un gioco e un diletto. Da
> vent'anni quella simbolica favola era uscita da un possente genio
> nordico; e ancora il pubblico, ammirando per tre atti, protestava con
> candido zelo all'ultima scena. La verità semplice e splendente
> nessuno, nessuno voleva guardarla in faccia! (p. 151)

A number of critics have called attention to the Aleramo-Ibsen connection. As
early as 1907, Alfredo Gargiulo declared that "nella *bibbia* del femminismo, al
posto della *genesi* accanto a *Casa di bambola* [doveva] ormai trovare posto *Una
donna*."[31] More recently, M. P. Pozzato has claimed that "[la] Nora Ibseniana ... fu
... il grande modello dell'Aleramo per il suo romanzo."[32] Aleramo herself, in a
piece entitled "Nucleo generatore di *Una donna*" (1901), speaking of Nora says
"senza quella voce ... non avrei lasciata la casa coniugale e mio figlio."[33] Yet, while

Aleramo uses Nora as a model, she also goes to great lengths to distinguish herself from her and to cast her own decision to leave her family in a very different light. *She does this precisely through the character of the Norwegian designer who functions, paradoxically, both as a model and as a foil: through her, Aleramo pays homage to Ibsen and contemporaneously distances herself from him.* As we shall see, it is not his solution to the dilemma of the woman in an unhappy marriage which she rejects, but his actual rendering of the situation.

Italian audiences of the period were having as much difficulty in accepting the *dénouement* of Ibsen's play as had the original Scandinavian public for whom it was written. The play was first staged in Italy in 1890 and its translator, Luigi Capuana, urged Ibsen, unsuccessfully, to re-write it with a new ending for Italian audiences. Ibsen refused and Capuana, in his preface to the translation, felt constrained to express his consternation at Nora's departure and at a female character whom he considered altogether "troppo diversa da noi":

> Per noi, il personaggio di Nora diviene un'eccezione molto strana quando si risolve ad abbandonare marito e figli, per tentare di farsi, con la propria esperienza, un'idea netta e precisa della vita e dei grandi problemi amari, senza badare a quel che dice la gente e a quel che ne predichino i libri.[34]

Aleramo's efforts to distinguish herself from Nora, were, of course, in vain: critics were generally unable to judge her book independently of its conclusion, and certainly did not perceive Aleramo's attempts to mitigate it by distancing herself from her infamous role-model. Such subtle distinctions were totally lost on them,[35] but they speak volumes to the contemporary reader. The Norwegian designer's story-within-the-story functions as a revisionist reading of Ibsen's text: this Nora comes to Italy and tries to make a new life for herself. Yet she succeeds in doing so only to die quite suddenly of rheumatic fever. In short, Aleramo subjects "Nora" to the same punishment inflicted upon other nineteenth-century heroines who have defied societal norms, from Emma Bovary to Anna Karenina. The obvious question is "why?".

In order to understand what Aleramo could not accept in Ibsen's tale – or at least what she may have wished to distance herself from – one must compare her story of a woman who leaves husband and child to his. There are two basic differences between them. The first is that Nora's tale is told in dramatic form and covers a relatively short period of time. Her decision to leave is a sudden one and is attributed to an abrupt "awakening" and not, like Aleramo's, to a progressively-acquired awareness of her oppression through suffering and cultivation of the self:

> Nora: I've never seen things so clearly and certainly as I do tonight.
> Helmer: Clearly and certainly enough to forsake your husband and your children?
> Nora: Yes.
> Helmer: There's only one possible explanation.
> Nora: What?
> Helmer: You don't love me anymore.
> Nora: No, that's just it.
> Helmer: Nora! How can you say that?
> Nora: I can hardly bear to, Torvald, because you've always been so kind to me – but I can't help it. I don't love you anymore....
> Helmer: And will you also be able to explain how I've forfeited your love?
> Nora: Yes, I can indeed. It was this evening, when the miracle didn't happen – because then I saw you weren't the man I'd always thought you.... At that moment, Torvald, I realized that for eight years I'd been living here with a strange man, and I'd borne him three children. Oh, I can't bear to think of it....[36]

Much in the same way as Manzoni objected to the unity of time in classical theatre as something which often inadvertently cast grave acts in an immoral light by not allowing for psychological development over time,[37] so I believe Aleramo did not wish her heroine to be identified with Nora's abrupt decision to leave her family. For this reason, her story, contrary to Nora's, begins almost at birth, and is told, at every level, in such a way as to provide moral justification for its ending. Her rather unusual childhood, her mother's suffering, her father's spiritual desertion of the family, her induction into marriage through rape, the physical and emotional abuse to which she is subjected by her husband, the oppressive atmosphere of the provincial town to which she is confined, her attempted suicide and the ensuing long period of convalescence, all conspire to present her final decision to leave husband and child as deeply-rooted in past injustices and as the culmination of a long and arduous process of maturation.

The second major difference between the two tales lies in the fact that, while Nora's decision is a purely individualistic one, Aleramo's is ideologically framed by political considerations. The Norwegian designer leaves her husband because her life as an ultra-religious minister's wife is boring and does not correspond to her own desire "[di] andar lontano da Dio!" (p. 146). Nora's departure in *A Doll's House* results from her discovery that she has never been "herself," only a daughter and a wife, never a person in her own right.[38] Aleramo's concern, on the other hand, is to establish what Nora Helmar takes for granted: her right to an identity for herself separate from her identity as a mother. In order to establish this she appeals to such concepts as "dignity" and "humanity" and extends her arguments well beyond the confines of her own situation:

> Perché nella maternità adoriamo il sacrificio? Donde è scesa a noi questa inumana idea dell'immolazione materna? Di madre in figlia, da secoli, si tramanda il servaggio.... Se una buona volta la fatale catena si spezzasse, e una madre non sopprimesse in sé la donna, e un figlio apprendesse dalla vita di lei un esempio di dignità? (p. 182)

Clearly, what for Nora (and for the Norwegian designer) is a marginal issue – that of putting her own fulfillment and development before that of the family[39] – constitutes a major stumbling block for Aleramo's heroine. In reviewing a performance of *A Doll's House*, Antonio Gramsci suggests why Italian audiences were incapable of feeling any "vibrazione simpatica dinanzi all'atto profondamente morale di Nora Helmar che abbandona la casa, il marito, i figli ... per adempiere ai doveri che ognuno ha verso sé stesso prima che verso gli altri":

> E' avvenuta semplicemente una rivolta del nostro costume alla morale più spiritualmente umana. E' avvenuta semplicemente una rivolta del nostro costume ... che è abito morale tradizionale della nostra borghesia grossa e piccina, fatto in gran parte di schiavitù, di sottomissione all'ambiente, di ipocrita mascheratura dell'animale uomo, fascio di nervi e di muscoli inguainati nella epidermide voluttuosamente pruriginosa, a un altro costume, a un'altra tradizione, superiore, più spirituale, meno animalesca. Un altro costume per il quale la donna e l'uomo non sono più soltanto muscoli, nervi ed epidermide, ma sono essenzialmente spirito; per il quale la famiglia non è più solo un istituto economico, ma è specialmente un mondo morale in atto...; per il quale la donna non è più solamente la femmina che nutre di sé i piccoli nati e sente per essi un amore che è fatto di spasimi della carne e di tuffi di sangue, ma è una creatura umana a sé, che ha una coscienza a sé, che ha dei bisogni interiori suoi, che ha una personalità umana tutta sua e una dignità di essere indipendente.
> Il costume della borghesia latina grossa e piccola, non comprende un mondo così fatto. L'unica forma di liberazione femminile che è consentito comprendere al nostro costume, è quella della donna che

diventa cocotte.... Non si esce fuori dal circolo morto dei nervi, dei muscoli e dell'epidermide sensibile.... La donna dei nostri paesi, la donna che ha una storia, la donna della famiglia borghese ... [r]imane la femmina che nutre di sé i piccoli nati, la bambola più cara quanto è più stupida, più diletta ed esaltata quanto più rinunzia a sé stessa, per dedicarsi agli altri, siano questi altri i suoi familiari, siano gli infermi, i detriti d'umanità che la beneficenza raccoglie e soccorre maternamente.[40]

The question of how Aleramo deals with putting her own unhappiness before duty to family and motherhood remains an interesting one, particularly because it confirms Gramsci's belief that, for the Italian woman, dedication to the family and dedication to "i detriti d'umanità che la beneficenza raccoglie e soccorre maternamente" are one and the same. In fact, while in Rome the heroine befriends not only the Norwegian designer but also an older woman whom she calls "la buona vecchia mamma dei miseri" (p. 136) and who is directly responsible for initiating her into the world of social activism:

Mazziniana fervente nella sua prima gioventù, aveva trasportato presto la sua forza rivoluzionaria nel campo sociale.... La sua pazienza nel perseguire miglioramenti parziali, riforme d'istituti benefici, aiuti degli enti pubblici, la sua tenacia nel bussare alle porte dei ricchi per ottenerne la piccola elemosina, contrastavano stranamente con la sua credenza nella necessità ultima di sconvolgere col fuoco e col ferro la massa oppressiva delle istituzioni formate dalle classi superiori. Aveva mai lasciato intravedere questo terribile pensiero a qualcuno dei giovani operai che lavoravano nella Scuola Popolare da lei fondata? (pp. 136-137)

What is important and significant about this older woman is that she becomes a new "mother" for the heroine. In other words, she provides her with a positive, active role model which legitimizes her entry into public life and which constitutes an alternative to the passive, masochistic, inward-turned example of the heroine's real mother, "assorta, chiusa come in un deserto interiore" (p. 42). Through her relationship with this woman the heroine effectively "re-parents" herself in order to complete her own re-birth:

E voi, con la persona un poco pingue e curva, con qualcosa di mia madre nei tratti del volto, voi mi chiamaste figliuola, subito, e vi prendeste sulle ginocchia il mio bimbo, e ci guardaste a lungo entrambi..... Mai, mai ho sentito, in un silenzio, tanta improvvisa compenetrazione. E quando incominciaste a parlare, a dirmi di qualcuna delle opere create in tanti anni dalla vostra meravigliosa volontà di giustizia, mi parve che un tacito convegno aveste dato alla mia anima. (p. 130)

Even more significant, however, is Aleramo's repeated insistence on the essentially maternal and nurturing vocation of this seemingly "public" woman: "Mamma mia buona e di quanti avete incontrato nella vita!" (p. 130). Though childless, she is presented as a "mother" to all those who cross her path. It is she who introduces the heroine to an older mystical philosopher whose charisma and power to fascinate her recall her earlier experience with her father. "La buona vecchia mamma," whose concrete, down-to-earth approach to life contrasts sharply with the transcendental preoccupations of this rather ethereal mystic, points out to the heroine what she sees as the limitations of his position. In so doing, she reiterates the active, nurturing aspects of her own mission, which is to improve the quality of life for the downtrodden. In turn, she herself presents a vision of life in maternal discourses : "Cara, bisogna fare che l'uomo ami la vita in quanto essa è suscettibile d'esser bella *per tutti*, materna *verso tutti*. E non è guardando oltre la morte che si può raggiungere questo scopo" (p. 140).

The metaphors attributed to this character, and used repeatedly in describing her, are obviously meant to draw an analogy between motherhood and concern for the disinherited. In other words, we are made to conclude that although she herself is childless biologically, "la buona vecchia mamma" is no less a mother because of this. Indeed, for her, the whole world is "home": "Se potessi mostrarti il mio esempio ti direi che io credo nel mistero, che ho anch'io, come si dice, le finestre aperte sul mistero. Ma non posso stare tutto il giorno alla finestra, e c'è tanto da fare in casa!" (p.141).

What are the conclusions to be drawn from all this? It is clear that Aleramo, like other women writers of the time, has internalized her society's values and, in this case, reproduces the dominant discourses around mothering. The same contradictory position which determines the need to "kill off" Nora in the person of the Norwegian designer motivates the adoption of a maternal, altruistic role model in the person of "la buona vecchia mamma." *Una donna*, in short, is not the revolutionary, autobiographical novel that we have been led to believe it is, reflecting unproblematically the author's life and uncontaminated by patriarchal literary discourses around women. Nor is it, for that matter, a genuine Bildungsroman, female or otherwise, since though it adopts, in part, the surface structure of this genre, it does so for its own purposes: to justify the heroine's final decision within the codes of the dominant culture. It remains, instead, closer in spirit to *A Doll's House*, but re-written for a Catholic society which places a heavy premium on female obedience to patriarchal authority and discourses around maternity.

As we have seen, Aleramo legitimizes her story by inserting it into an already-existing tradition of stories about women and marriage and by having her own appear to surpass its predecessors by addressing the the moral problems they leave unresolved. In other words, Aleramo organizes her story in such a way as to incorporate and provide some perspective on the "shortcomings" of previous literary discourses on the subject of the woman in an unhappy marriage. The novel of sacrifice, as lived out by her mother, is shown to leave unresolved the question of woman as subject or, as Gramsci puts it, as "una creatura umana a sé."[41] Ibsen's *Doll House* (the story of the Norwegian designer), on the other hand, is too "hedonistic" since its heroine is a woman who has totally rejected maternal values in favour of her own self-development. Aleramo's heroine, by contrast, is presented as a woman who is making her own self-development coincide, at least in part, with the "common good." What Aleramo's *Una donna* accomplishes, then, is the transformation of "desire" into "duty."

Notes

1 First published by Sten of Rome in 1906, *Una donna* has since been through numerous editions: Treves (Milan) 1919, Bemporad (Florence) 1921, Mondadori (Milan) 1930, 1938, 1944, Universale Economica (Milan) 1950, and Feltrinelli (Milan) 1973, 1981, 1982, 1983. It has been translated into Spanish (1907, 1976), French (1908, 1974), German (1908, 1977), English (1908, 1979, 1980), Swedish (1908), Dutch (1978), Slovak (1981). For complete details see B. Conti and A. Morino, *Sibilla Aleramo e il suo tempo* (Milan: Feltrinelli, 1981).

2 For a sample of reviews of the time see: S. Aleramo, *La donna e il femminismo* (Rome: Riuniti, 1978) 189-204.

3 The most recent contribution to Aleramo criticism is *Svelamento. Sibilla Aleramo: una biografia intellettuale*, eds. A. Buttafuoco and M. Zancan (Milan: Feltrinelli, 1988) which contains what appears to be a complete bibliography. Other important contributions include: R. Guerricchio, *Storia di Sibilla* (Pisa: Nistri-Lischi, 1974); M. Federzoni, I. Pezzini, M.P. Pozzato, *Sibilla Aleramo* (Florence: La nuova Italia, 1980); F. Contorbia, L. Melandri, A. Morino, eds., *Sibilla Aleramo. Coscienza e scrittura* (Milan: Feltrinelli, 1986).

[4] Guerricchio 81.

[5] Guerricchio 17; on this subject in general see Guerricchio 16-21.

[6] M. Corti, Preface, *Una donna*, by S. Aleramo (Milan: Feltrinelli, 1982) xiii-xiv.

[7] Guerricchio 21-26. On the subject of the *donna fatale*, see A. Nozzoli, "La letteratura femminile in Italia tra Ottocento e Novecento," *Tabù e coscienza. La condizione femminile nella letteratura italiana del Novecento* (Florence: La nuova Italia, 1978) 22-24.

[8] Guerricchio 33-67.

[9] Nozzoli 37.

[10] See A. Nozzoli, "L'elaborazione di *Una donna*: storia di un manoscritto," *Svelamento* 29-45.

[11] Guerricchio 92.

[12] Guerricchio 90.

[13] F. Bassanese, "*Una donna*: Autobiography as Exemplary Text," *Quaderni d'Italianistica* 11.1 (1990): 41-60. On this subject in general, see E. Abel, M. Hirsch and E. Langland, eds., *The Voyage In: Fictions of Female Development* (Hanover: University Press of New England, 1983).

[14] According to M. Zancan, "la sua figura ... si staglia dal contesto che la precede e, in parte almeno, anche dal contesto che la segue, per la continuità e la consapevole forte tensione con cui la vita e la scrittura procedono, nel suo lungo itinerario, strettamente intersecate." ("La donna," *Le Questioni*, vol. 5 of *Letteratura italiana*, ed. A. Asor Rosa [Turin: Einaudi, 1986] 825).

[15] Nozzoli, "La letteratura femminile in Italia..." 39-40.

[16] M. A. Macciocchi, Preface, *Una donna*, by S. Aleramo (Milan: Feltrinelli, 1985) 8.

[17] S. Aleramo, *Una donna* (Milan: Feltrinelli, 1985) 120. All subsequent references will be to this edition and will appear in the text.

[18] Corti xiv.

[19] Francesca's "Nessun maggior dolore/che ricordarsi del tempo felice/nella miseria" resonates in *Una donna* at several levels, according to Z. Baranski: "In *Una donna*, Aleramo ... overturns the original meaning of Dante's words ... [but] Dante's voice accentuates the pathos of her description. At the beginning of her book, she presents memories of her childhood ("e la gioia ancora grande nel ricordo") in opposition to the adult "epoca buia della mia vita"; in addition, Dante's "tempo felice" may be heard in her introduction ("Per tanto tempo, nell'epoca buia della mia vita, ho guardato a quella mia alba come qualcosa di perfetto, come la vera felicità"). ("The Power of Influence: Aspects of Dante's Presence in Twentieth-Century Italian Culture," *Strumenti critici* ns 1.3 [1983]: 353-354.)

[20] On Invernizio see M. Federzoni, "Carolina Invernizio," *Carolina Invernizio, Matilde Serao, Liala*, by U. Eco *et al.* (Florence: La nuova Italia, 1979) 29-59; see also A. Arslan Veronese, ed., *Dame, droga e galline* (Padua: CLEUP, 1976).

[21] C. Invernizio, *Il bacio di una morta* (Milan: Lucchi, 1982) 236.

[22] Invernizio lll, 113-114.

[23] Invernizio 167.

[24] Invernizio 264.

25 On this subject, see U. Eco, "Tre donne intorno al cor," *Carolina Invernizio, Mtilde Serao, Liala* 23-24.

26 Invernizio 184.

27 Invernizio 45.

28 A. Gramsci, "La morale e il costume" (*Casa di bambola* di Ibsen al Carignano)," *Letteratura e vita nazionale* (Rome: Editori Riuniti, 1977) 345.

29 This character is based on the social activist Alessandrina Ravizza (1846-1915), whom Aleramo met in 1898. See Conti and Morino 23-24.

30 The narrator describes her feelings as she stood beside the designer's deathbed in the following prophetic terms: "Le ore passate accanto alla spoglia di chi amammo non ci fanno veggenti; ma neppure ci prostrano, né ci tolgono il senso dell'esistenza che in noi continua. Sembra in quel punto di ereditare, coi doveri, anche le qualità di chi ci ha lasciati, ci si trova più ricchi, o di energia o di idealità o di amore. Ci si sente solidali coi vivi oltre che coi morti." (*Una donna* 171).

31 Quoted in Guerricchio 98.

32 M. P. Pozzato, "I romanzi e le poesie di Sibilla Aleramo," *Sibilla Aleramo*, by Federzoni *et al.* 46.

33 Quoted in Guerricchio 67.

34 L. Capuana, Preface, *Casa di bambola* (Milan: Max Kantorowicz, 1894) as quoted in L. Caretti, "Capuana, Ibsen e la Duse," *L'illusione della realtà: Studi su Luigi Capuana*, eds. M. Picone and E. Rosetti (Rome: Salerno editrice, 1990) 199-200.

35 "Ora, venendo al mio dubbio, la donna del romanzo ... per aver modo di svolgere la propria personalità abbandona il figlio (e ricordiamo che quella protagonista è una ottima madre e sente l'amor materno in tutta la sua pienezza) recide da sé un elemento certo e principale dell'individualità per poterne ritrovare altri, men certi e men vitali." (M. Bontempelli, rev. of *Una donna, Il grido del popolo* 29 December 1907, as quoted in S. Aleramo, *La donna e il femminismo* 202); "Risulta però nel libro il fatto che l'unica vittima è il figlio, e perciò non è possibile porlo ad esempio delle donne pensanti" (V. Olper Monis, rev. of *Una donna, L'Adriatico* 10 January 1907, as quoted in Aleramo, *La donna e il femminismo* 199).

36 H. Ibsen, *A Doll's House and Other Plays* (Harmondsworth: Penguin, 1965) 229-230.

37 A. Manzoni, *Lettre à M. Chauvet sur l'unité de temps et de lieu dans la tragédie* (1820).

38 Nora's exact words to her husband are the following: "When I lived at home with Papa, he used to tell his opinion about everything, and so I had the same opinion.... When I passed out of Papa's hands into yours [you] arranged everything to suit your own tastes, and so I came to have the same tastes as yours.... [Now] I must try to educate myself. And you're not the man to help me with that; I must do it alone. That's why I'm leaving you." (Ibsen 225-227)

39 When her husband says "before everything else you're a wife and mother," she is quick to respond "I don't believe that any longer. I believe that before everything else I'm a human being...." (Ibsen 228)

40 Gramsci 344-345.

41 Gramsci 345.

Pirandello and the Woman Writer: A Reading of *Suo Marito*

In 1911, Luigi Pirandello, already an established writer of novels and short stories but not yet the great dramatist we know him as today, published a very curious novel in which the central character is a woman writer. The title itself is a paradox: *Suo marito*. Pirandello withdrew the novel from circulation after the depletion of its first edition because of threats to sue from the well-known Sardinian writer Grazia Deledda, on aspects of whose life it was loosely based.[1] It was not re-published until 1941, five years after his death, partly revised and with a new title, *Giustino Roncella nato Boggiolo*.[2] The original title, *Suo marito*, alludes indirectly to the identity problems that arise for Silvia Roncella's husband as a result of her increasing fame and fortune. The later title, *Giustino Roncella nato Boggiolo*, leaves nothing to the imagination: through its deliberately provocative attribution to the husband instead of to the wife of "maiden" and "married" names, it points directly to the emasculating effects of Silvia's career on Giustino's identity and also suggests a major disturbance in the social order.

The story is a relatively simple one. Silvia Roncella is a young woman who has made a marriage of convenience to a mediocre government clerk. Silvia appears, initially, to embody all the traditional female virtues. Her one secret vice is writing. She claims to have no ambition of any sort and to write only for herself. In fact, she marries Giustino precisely because he is willing to "tolerate" her need to write. Giustino, for his part, has no understanding whatsoever of the creative process or of his wife's passion, but he does perceive that some money is perhaps to be made from it, and he urges her to attempt to market her stories. Not only does she succeed; against all odds she quickly becomes a well-known literary figure. After a while, Giustino decides that in order to maximize the opportunities for commercial gain they ought to move from his wife's native Taranto to Rome. Here, she immediately becomes the reluctant darling of the literary world, as Giustino takes on full-time the role of agent and impresario, since Silvia has also begun to write for the theatre. Gradually however, as a result of the increasing pressure and humiliation to which he unwittingly subjects Silvia in his single-minded efforts to maximize profits, relations between the two deteriorate until they finally reach the point of no return. Silvia runs off briefly with another writer, more worthy of her but not free of a previous relation. Silvia ends up alone, as does Giustino. Their child, who was being taken care of in the country by Giustino's mother, falls ill very suddenly and dies. Giustino is a broken man while Silvia's destiny remains uncertain.

Critics who have examined this novel closely, and there have not been many, taking into consideration the enormous body of Pirandello criticism generated by scholars throughout the years, have tended to focus on themes related to Pirandello's identification with Silvia as an artist – the creative process and the sharp contrast drawn between art for its own sake and art as comodity, as well as the artist's struggle to maintain control over his work in an era increasingly dominated by market values and imperatives.[3] In this reading of the novel, Silvia is seen as representing pure creativity and Giustino the attempt to channel it for commercial purposes.[4] Other critics have explored the male/female aspects of the novel – the themes of adultery, jealousy and sexuality in general.[5] But no one appears to have asked what, from another perspective, is an all-too-obvious question: why did Pirandello choose to write a novel about a *woman* writer?

The usual answer – that this is simply a *roman à clef* based on the life of Grazia Deledda seems somewhat reductive, and in any case fails to answer the question. This is clearly no more a novel about Grazia Deledda than it is a novel about a disintegrating marriage or about the tension between creativity and productivity. The last two themes could just as easily have been treated in a novel about a male writer. If the story of Grazia Deledda struck a chord, it must have done so for some very specific reasons.

The years in which Pirandello came to maturity as a writer and an intellectual were precisely the years in which women writers were becoming an increasingly visible and vocal force both in Italian society in general and, more specifically, in the world of letters. Carolina Invernizio, Neera, Matilde Serao, Grazia Deledda are only the most obvious names in a gallery of women whose works were flooding the literary marketplace in unprecedented numbers. However, precisely because of the success they enjoyed in a still highly traditional society, women writers embodied a vast and complex array of contradictions which they themselves avoided confronting. The most striking of these was their reluctance to come out in favour of the rights of women and to present clearly emancipatory messages in their novels. The intensity of conflict they experienced in connection with the act of writing, more specifically with writing novels for publication, was such that they perceived it as an essentially transgressive act. Writing entailed not only the abandonment of the self-effacing, sacrificial, nurturing role traditionally assigned to women in favour of self-expression (and ultimately self-affirmation and self-exposure); it was also the appropriation of what had long been an almost exclusively male privilege.

Moreover, the novel itself was at this time very much associated with another traditionally male privilege, adultery. The late-nineteenth-century popular novel, with which women writers were almost automatically identified, in Italy was practically synonymous with adultery: this made women who wrote novels even more suspect than those who merely read them. Add to this the fact that the literary life was thought to expose women writers to all sorts of dangers that bourgeois housewives reading in the privacy of their homes could only fantasize about, and the picture of the wanton woman novelist is complete.

As a result of the perceived conflict between virtuous womanhood and the literary life, women writers often denied or at least minimized their literary ambitions at the same time as they pursued them. In a series of essays on questions of interest to women, Neera takes a firm public stance against writing as a career for women, and even goes so far as to condemn George Sand and George Eliot for having abandoned traditional roles. Matilde Serao was a staunch anti-feminist who came out publicly against divorce, careers and even the vote for women. The Marchesa Colombi, though not as outrageously contradictory, prefaces her many volumes of short stories with coy introductions in which she portrays herself, among other things, as a desperate woman driven to the pen solely by the desire to provide her nieces and nephews with the Christmas gifts they deserve.

Needless to say, women writers never treated the subject of women writers in their own novels. Neera wrote a novel about an actress (*Anima sola*, 1894), the Marchesa Colombi a story about an amateur female painter (*Impara l'arte e mettila da parte*, 1897), Matilde Serao a novel about a male journalist (*Vita e avventure di Riccardo Joanna*, 1887), but no one had ever tackled the problems and conflicts of the woman writer head-on, at least not in fiction. It fell to Pirandello, with his personal distance from the subject and his penchant for going straight to the heart of the most painful and delicate matters, including topical ones, to be the first to write a serious novel about a woman writer.

Although *Suo marito* was first published in 1911, Pirandello's biographer, Gaspare Giudice, advances the hypothesis that the novel may actually have been written several years earlier.[6] He cites the style of the novel, as well as certain personal notes of the author regarding a minor character which date from 1903, an important year and a turning point in Pirandello's life. It is the year in which he loses his family fortune and his wife's dowry, both of which were invested in a Sicilian sulphur mine that collapsed and had to be abandoned. As a result, he was forced, for the first time, to face the realities of writing not only for himself and his peers, but also for the general reader.[7] Given these circumstances, it is reasonable to assume that he could not help but become aware that among his fiercest competitors in the commercial marketplace were women.

Moreover, in 1907 Pirandello published a review of the most notorious novel ever written by an Italian woman, Sibilla Aleramo's *Una donna*, which had appeared in 1906 and had immediately generated a heated debate on its merits and shortcomings. This autobiographical novel describes the events leading up to the heroine's decision to leave an abusive husband who is her inferior both socially and intellectually.[8] The controversy surrounding the novel derived from the fact that, given the workings of the Italian legal system, the separation necessarily entailed the abandonment of a small child as well. Contemporary critics of the novel were obsessed by one question: did a woman ever have the right to leave a child, whatever the circumstances? The debate was extremely animated and, for the most part, condemned Aleramo quite openly. Pirandello, however, did not join the chorus of detractors. His review, which appeared in Turin's *Gazzetta del Popolo* on the 27th of December 1906, is quite remarkable for the sympathy it demonstrates to Aleramo, both as a woman and as a writer:

> Non possiamo non essere d'accordo con l'autrice, non approvar le
> idee e la condotta della sua protagonista; non possiamo però non
> ammirare l'arte per cui quelle idee "vivono" veramente nel suo libro
> doloroso, e con cui quella condotta è rappresentata....9

Unlike the Deledda connection, the relationship of Aleramo's novel to Pirandello's subsequent portrayal of a woman writer is difficult to confirm.[10] However, if Aleramo owes her novel and hence her reputation as a writer precisely to the arduous decision to separate her identity as a human being from her identity as a mother, Silvia embodies Aleramo's dilemma from the very beginning. She makes her first appearance in the novel at a literary lunch being held in honor of her arrival in Rome. She arrives late and is forced to leave early, because of her fragile health. At the end of the chapter we are told that she is expecting a child and a few pages later she produces a son, coming perilously close to death in the process. Significantly, the birth of her child is made to coincide with the extremely successful opening night of her first play, which now takes place in her absence. The chapter in which both these events are located is entitled, in typically Pirandellian fashion, "Mistress Roncella: two accouchements."

The childbirth metaphor is often used to describe the artistic process, but here it is used at a first level to designate *difference* as well as affinity. It reminds us that, in the life of a woman, mind and body, creativity and procreativity, books and babies, have historically been mutually exclusive. Silvia cannot give birth to her child and be present at the "birth" of her play at the same time. The analogy between the two processes is further suggested by the very curious description of Giustino's anxieties as he awaits the audience's reaction to the performance, a description which, by evoking Silvia's absence/presence in a paradoxical, extremely powerful metaphoric re-enactment of childbirth as humiliation, also suggests that Giustino is in some way usurping Silvia's rightful place:

> Si levò il sipario, e a Giustino Boggiolo parve che gli
> scoperchiassero l'anima e che tutta quella moltitudine d'un tratto
> silenziosa s'apparecchiasse al feroce godimento del supplizio di lui,
> supplizio inaudito, quasi di vivisezione, ma con un che di
> vergognoso, come se egli fosse tutto una nudità esposta, che da un
> momento all'altro, per qualche falsa mossa impreveduta, potesse
> apparire atrocemente ridicola e sconcia. (p. 691)

If the ghost of Aleramo's dilemma lurks behind this highly stylized and symbolic rendering of Silvia's situation, then that of Henryk Ibsen constitutes an even more ascertainable presence. *Casa di bambola*, the Italian translation of *A Doll's House* (1879), resonates very clearly in the title Pirandello chooses for Silvia's first best-selling novel, *Casa dei nani*: instead of suggesting a degrading feminine condition, it suggests a masculine one.[11] That *Casa dei nani* is an explicit allusion to *A Doll's House* is confirmed at Silvia's literary lunch, when the guests suddenly notice the jarring presence among them of a curious character whom no one appears to know, "così squallido che pareva cavato di mano alla morte":

> Era evidentemente uno straniero: svedese o norvegese. Nessuno lo conosceva, nessuno sapeva chi fosse, e tutti lo guardavano con stupore e ribrezzo.
> Vedendosi guardato così, egli sorrideva e pareva dicesse a tutti, complimentoso:
> "Fratelli, si muore!" (p.612)

The fact that he is described as Swedish or Norwegian, that he appears to be Death itself incarnated, and that he is circulating in the crowd announcing to the men in particular "Brothers, we are dying" ("Fratelli, si muore"), leaves little to the imagination. Not surprisingly, he is later identified as the Swedish translator of *Casa dei nani*.

The allusion to Ibsen's infamous play is important for two reasons: first, because it strengthens the Aleramo connection, since it was a critical commonplace at the time to compare the two works; second, because it points the way quite clearly to the identification of the tradition to which I believe *Suo marito* really belongs.

This is the tradition of "the story of awakening," which recent feminist literary criticism has singled out as a female sub-genre of the Bildungsroman, the classic novel of male development.[12] In the Bildungsroman, the maturation process of the developing male always includes a sexual initiation and a coming-to-terms with the limitations of the possibilities of life followed, however, by entry into the mainstream of bourgeois society as an active and productive member. For the developing female, the range of action is obviously far more circumscribed and maturation necessarily entails an awakening to the limitations of marriage and love as a female career, and of her husband as a human being. The possibilities that ensue are resignation (as in Neera's *l'Indomani* or the Marchesa Colombi's *Matrimonio in provincia*), suicide (as in Flaubert's *Madame Bovary*, Kate Chopin's *The Awakening*), or departure (as in *A Doll's House*, *Una donna* or *Suo marito*).

In *Suo marito*, Pirandello uses the narrative patterns of the novel of awakening to deal with the conflicts of the woman writer as he saw them – but the end-product is as unconventional in its genre as the rest of his work. The first distinction between Pirandello's version of this sort of novel and others is that Silvia's "awakening" is *not* the result of a disappointment in love, since there appears to be no love as such between her and Giustino. Nor does it lead to an awakening of sexual desire. Although there is an adulterous episode, it is, as we shall see, a means to an end, and not an end in itself. Silvia's "awakening" is a result of her success in the public domain, an awakening to her own repressed ambition. The emergence of this ambition makes her husband totally dispensable, and she herself has a great deal of difficulty integrating it since there is no acceptable social discourse to legitimize it. The story of the "birth" of this part of herself is, in fact, as I hope to demonstrate, the story of her various failed attempts to contain her impulses within the framework of acceptable discourses through denial, rationalization, and displacement of her desire.

At the beginning she is described as meek and self-effacing, and totally innocent as far as ambition is concerned, guilty only of the desire to write, described here as a "demon" struggling to emerge just as she struggles to repress it:

> Più che soddisfazione, nel vedere accolto favorevolmente e lodato con molto calore il suo primo libro, ella aveva provato una gran confusione, un'ambascia, una costernazione smaniosa. Avrebbe saputo più scrivere, ora, come prima? non più per sé soltanto? Il pensiero della lode le si affacciava, e la turbava; si poneva tra lei e le cose che voleva descrivere o rappresentare. Non aveva toccato più la penna, per circa un anno. Poi ... oh come aveva ritrovato cresciuto, ingrandito quel suo demonietto, e com'egli era divenuto cattivo, malizioso, scontento.... Un demoniaccio s'era fatto, che le faceva quasi quasi paura, perché voleva parlar forte, ora, quando non doveva, e rider di certe cose che ella, come gli altri, nella pratica della vita, avrebbe voluto stimar serie. Era cominciato il combattimento interno, da allora. Poi s'era presentato Giustino....
> Ella vedeva bene che il marito non la comprendeva, o meglio, non comprendeva di lei quella parte ch'ella stessa, per non apparir singolare dalle altre, voleva tener nascosta in sé e infrenata, che ella stessa non voleva né indagare né penetrare fino in fondo. Se un giorno questa parte avesse preso in lei il sopravvento, dove la avrebbe trascinata? Dapprima, quando Giustino, pur senza comprendere, s'era messo a spingerla, a forzarla al lavoro, allettato dagli insperati guadagni, ella, sì, aveva provato un vivo

compiacimento, ma più per lui, quasi, che per sé. Avrebbe voluto,
però, che egli si fosse arrestato lì e, sopratutto, che – dopo il molto
rumore che s'era fatto attorno al romanzo *La casa dei nani* – non
avesse tanto brigato e tempestato per venire a Roma. (pp. 644-645)

As long as Silvia is able to respect Giustino as a traditional male, that is to say
as a breadwinner, she manages to contain her impulses. But when he leaves his
own position as a state archivist to take on full-time the task of managing and
promoting his wife's career, she begins to see him not only as a profiteering
philistine but, more importantly, as a parasite living off the fruits of her labour. She
quickly loses all respect for him, as well as the ability to suppress her own
ambitions. It is at this point that Pirandello speaks of "il demone malioso della
gloria." At first, the "demon" was the desire to write; now it has become the desire
for recognition, tempered only by the fear of death as a just punishment for this
desire:

> Se il trionfo era vero, in quel momento, per lei, voleva dir fastidio,
> oppressione, incubo. Ma forse ... sì, forse, in un altro momento,
> appena ella avrebbe riacquistato le forze ... se esso era vero ... chi
> sa!
> Qualcosa come un émpito immenso, tutto pungente di brividi, le si
> levava dal fondo dell'anima, turbando, sconvolgendo, strappando
> affetti e sentimenti. Era il dèmone, quell'ebbro dèmone che ella
> sentiva in sé, di cui aveva avuto sempre sgomento, a cui sempre
> s'era sforzata di contrastare ogni dominio su lei, per non farsi
> prendere e trascinar chi sa dove, lontano da quegli affetti, da quelle
> cure in cui si rifugiava e si sentiva sicura.
> Ah, faceva proprio di tutto, di tutto, il marito per gittarla in preda ad
> esso! E non gli balenava in mente che se ella...?
> No, no: ecco; contro il dèmone un altro più tremendo spettro le
> sorgeva dentro: quello della morte ... la morte che la urtava coi
> piedini del suo bimbo, che voleva vivere uccidendola. La sua morte
> e la vita del suo bambino le sorgevano dinanzi contro il dèmone
> malioso della gloria: una laidezza sanguinosa, brutale, vergognosa, e
> quel roseo d'alba lì tra i veli, quella purezza gracile e tenera, carne
> della sua carne, sangue del suo sangue. (pp. 702-703)

After her near brush with death in childbirth, Silvia retreats with her son and an
elderly uncle to Giustino's mother's mountain home, ostensibly to recover. Instead,
she undergoes a personal transformation. The newness of the surroundings and the
proximity to nature conspire to allow the relativity of things to emerge in her
perceptions, and she becomes increasingly detached from her previous life. The

change that overcomes her is such that even her child and motherhood itself begin to seem empty conventions:

> Da che s'era mossa da Roma e, con quel viaggio, tante e tante immagini nuove le avevano invaso in tumulto lo spirito, da cui già appena appena si diradavano le tenebre della morte, ella notava in sé con sgomento un distacco irreparabile da tutta la sua prima vita ... [e] il suo dèmone ne aveva profittato.... Era un dispetto atroce. Specialmente di tutte quelle cose ch'ella aveva voluto e avrebbe ancora voluto aver più care e sacre, esso si divertiva ad avventarle agli occhi la stupidità; e non rispettava neppure il suo bambino, la sua maternità! Le suggeriva che stupidi l'una e l'altro non sarebbero più stati solo a patto ch'ella, mercè lui, ne facesse una bella creazione. E che così era di quelle cose, come di tutte le altre. E che soltanto per creare ella era nata, e non già per produrre materialmente stupide cose, né per impacciarsi e perdersi tra esse. (pp. 724-725)

The arrival of the newspapers, with their triumphant headlines depicting the repeated success of her first play in theaters throughout Italy, only exacerbates her feelings as she becomes increasingly angry at Giustino for coming between her and the recognition she now so desperately craves:

> Leggendo quei giornali e quelle lettere, da cui le vampava innanzi agli occhi la visione affascinante di quei teatri, di tanta e tanta moltitudine che la acclamava, che acclamava lei, lei, l'autrice – Silvia si sentiva risollevare da quell'émpito tutto pungente di brividi già avvertito nella sala d'aspetto della stazione di Roma, allorché per la prima volta s'era trovata di fronte al suo trionfo, impreparata, prostrata, smarrita.
> Risollevata da quell'émpito, e tutta accesa ora e vibrante, domandava a sé stessa perché non doveva esser là, lei, dove la acclamavano con tanto calore, anziché qua, nascosta, appartata, messa da canto, come se non fosse lei! (p. 732)

Toward the end of her stay in the mountains, the elderly uncle who had accompanied her, and who was her last living relative, dies. With his death, she sees all her ties to the past broken and begins to feel that a "secret potency" she has always refused to recognize is about to take over her life:

> Avvertiva confusamente che non poteva e non doveva essere più qual'era stata finora; che doveva buttar via per sempre quel che d'angusto e di primitivo aveva voluto serbare alla sua esistenza, e dar campo invece e abbandonarsi a quella segreta potenza che aveva in sé e che finora non aveva voluto conoscer bene. (p. 738)

After her uncle's funeral, Silvia returns to Rome, having left her child in the care of Giustino's mother. In Rome she finds that Giustino has bought a new house with her earnings and expects her to write by day and receive their literary friends by night. Her conflict at this point is so acute that it paralyzes her. Her anger at her husband mounts daily, as does her awareness of the grotesque nature of their situation. Her thoughts are reproduced in such a way as to make it clear that her exasperation with Giustino, her insistence on wishing to escape the ridicule of others and the wish to return to her former obscurity – "Ah, poter tornare indietro, rinchiudersi nel suo guscio a lavorare quieta e ignorata!" (p. 754) – are all defences she uses to keep at bay the desire, long denied, to take charge of her life and receive the recognition she has earned. In fact, one evening as they await the guests Giustino has invited to their home in the hope of establishing a literary salon, she finds herself on the verge of blurting out her true feelings: "Basta! Lascia star tutto; non affannarti più! Vengono per me, per me soltanto! Tu non c'entri più; tu non hai più da far nulla, altro che da starti zitto, quieto, in un canto!" (p. 756).

Eventually she allows herself to think about a way of escaping her intolerable situation and finally chooses the one sanctioned by literary sources, adultery. The man with whom she decides to leave is Maurizio Gueli, a distinguished writer to whom she has been attracted since her arrival in Rome.[13] Theirs is, however, a meeting of minds rather than bodies; though they do indulge in the ritual sexual encounter, it is an aborted one and, for Silvia, simply a means to an end. It is through this brief, unconsummated affair that she definitively disengages herself not only from her husband, but also from her own unacknowledged sexuality. The description of Silvia's memory of this fleeting episode makes it clear that the desires of which she has been only marginally aware are now forever banished from her universe: "La memoria viscida di quell'unico amplesso mancato le aveva incusso una nausea invincibile, un'abominzaione, nella quale si sarebbe ormai sempre affogato ogni desiderio d'amore" (p. 864).

The definitive repression of the heroine's sexuality is not the only thing to distinguish *Suo marito* from other, more conventional novels in this genre. Equally unusual is the abrupt shift of narrative focus away from Silvia to Giustino as soon as she runs off with Maurizio Gueli. Essentially, once Silvia has left her husband, Pirandello has no more interest in her as a character. We know nothing from her point of view of her experience with Gueli or of her life afterward, except for the gossip that Giustino hears. This contrasts sharply with the unfolding of other novels such as *Madame Bovary* or *Anna Karenina*, in which the heroine's passage is followed through to its logical conclusion, typically that of her own death.

Here, instead, we are told in great detail of Giustino's devastation in the months following their separation and his return to his mother's mountain home in Piemonte. There is one particularly poignant episode that contrasts his lot and his despair with Silvia's "triumph." It is clearly intended as a counterpoint to the earlier episode in which Giustino takes credit for the success of his wife's first play the very same night she comes close to death in childbirth. This time, Giustino learns through the newspapers that a new play of Silvia's is about to open in Torino. Directionless and devoid of life, he decides on impulse to attend, hoping to make some contact with his former world. At the end of the performance the audience again clamors for the author: this time, it is Silvia herself who appears on the stage, completely transformed, at least in the eyes of Giustino:

> ... dalla vista di lei, gli era penetrato, gli s'era imposto come una convinzione assoluta: che tutto per lui era finito, perché quella non era più Silvia, no, no, quella non era più Silvia; era un'altra, a cui egli non poteva più accostarsi, lontana, irraggiungibilmente lontana, sopra di lui, sopra di tutti, per quella tristezza ond'era tutta avvolta, isolata, inalzata, così diritta e austera, com'era uscita dalla tempesta attraversata; un'altra, per cui egli non aveva più alcuna ragione d'esistere. (p. 855)

That same night, upon returning to his mother's home, Giustino finds that his son has fallen ill in his absence. Silvia is summoned to his bedside, but the child dies before her arrival. The juxtaposition of fates in the two episodes is clear: in the first, her child is born, Giustino takes credit for the success of her play and Silvia herself comes close to death; in the second, Silvia herself is "reborn" on the stage as an autonomous creature and takes credit for her own triumph, but her child dies. As for Giustino, he has become merely "redundant"; emblematically, his parting gesture when Silvia leaves after the child's funeral is to place into her hands the last vestiges he possesses of his life with her, finally acknowledging that she is now the mistress of her own destiny:

> "Ecco," le disse, porgendole le carte, "tieni.... Ormai io ... che ... che me ne faccio più? A te possono servire.... Sono ... sono recapiti di traduttori ... note mie ... appunti, calcoli ... contratti ... lettere....

> Ti potranno servire per ... per non farti ingannare.... Chi sa ... chi
> sa come ti rubano.... Tieni ... e ... addio! addio! addio!..."
> E si buttò singhiozzando tra le braccia del Prever che s'era
> avvicinato. (p. 873)

If this novel were only about the contrast between art for its own sake and art as commodity, then the final convergence of the two in Silvia would constitute an optimistic ending, as in "art defeats commercialism." Instead Silvia's transformation from an unassuming, unassertive woman who just "happens" to write, into a fully-conscious artist responsible for every aspect of her work including its commercial destiny, is made to coincide with her child's death and with her husband's defeat and humiliation.

Moreover, it is difficult, if not impossible, to reconcile the claim that Pirandello's sympathies lie entirely with Silvia, the misunderstood artist, at the expense of Giustino, the profiteering philistine, given the pathos that emerges from the total reversal of the structure of the narrative and from the description of Giustino's own emotions once his child has died and his wife has left him:

> La morte per lui non era tanto in quella piccola bara, quanto
> nell'aspetto di Silvia, nella definitiva partenza di lei. Quel ch'era
> morto di lui nel suo bimbo era ben poco a confronto di quel che di
> lui moriva con l'allontanamento della moglie. I due dolori erano per
> lui un dolore solo, inseparabile. Deponendo il bimbo nella tomba,
> egli doveva deporre insieme un'altra cosa, nelle mani di lei: gli ultimi
> resti della sua vita, ecco. (pp. 872-873)

The question that Pirandello is really raising here, and which perturbed him greatly as he contemplated the rapidly shifting position of women in turn-of-the-century Europe, is the future of the institution of marriage. The woman writer interests Pirandello both as a specific phenomenon, inasmuch as he himself is a writer, and as a symbol of the newly-emancipated woman (in this case the woman with the economic means and social prestige to make her own way in the world).[14]

On a somewhat different, though related note, the novel also suggests a profoundly disturbing consequence of the accession of women *en masse* to the literary marketplace: the feminization of culture. The novel opens on a fiercely satirical note which seems to raise precisely this issue. The setting of the opening scene is the bedroom of the grotesquely effeminate Attilio Raceni, "direttore di quella rassegna femminile (non feminista) *Le Muse*" (p. 590), which is sponsoring the lunch at which Silvia makes her first public appearance. Raceni is responsible for the "discovery" of Silvia Roncella and is now the major promoter of her work:

> ... fin dalla nascita egli era votato alla letteratura femminile, perché sua "mammà," Teresa Raceni Villardi, era stata un'esimia poetessa, e in casa di "mammà" convenivano tante scrittrici, alcune già morte, altre adesso molto anziane, su le cui ginocchia egli quasi quasi poteva dire d'esser cresciuto. E de' loro vezzi, delle loro carezze senza fine gli era rimasta quasi una patina indelebile in tutta la persona. Pareva che quelle lievi e delicate mani feminee, esperte d'ogni segreto, lisciandolo, levigandolo, lo avessero per sempre acconciato e composto in quella sua ambigua beltà artificiale. Si umettava spesso le labbra, s'inchinava sorridente ad ascoltare, si rizzava sul busto, volgeva il capo, si ravviava i capelli, tal quale come una femmina. (p. 590)

When we first encounter him, Raceni is about to set out, guest list in hand, for the home of Dora Barmis, one of his collaborators, to settle on the final arrangements for the lunch. On his way, he happens to run into a socialist demonstration in Piazza Venezia, which quickly degenerates into violence. A two-page description of Raceni's frustrated attempts to make his way through the angry crowd of demonstrators and police climaxes in an incident which highlights Raceni's humiliation as he realizes that an old man sitting on a balcony – "che stava a goderselo con la bocca aperta, sdentata, grattandosi con una mano sul mento, dal piacere, la barbetta gialliccia" – has been a mocking witness to his fear, confusion and ultimate cowardice:

> Avrebbe voluto, per riacquistare il sentimento della propria dignità mortificata, riandar lì, ricacciarsi nella mischia, afferrare per il petto a uno a uno tutti quei mascalzoni e pestarseli sotto i piedi, schiaffeggiar quella folla che lo aveva assaltato alla sprovvista così selvaggiamente, e gli aveva fatto patir l'onta della fuga, la vergogna della paura, l'inseguimento, la derisione di quel vecchio imbecille.... (p. 595)

Raceni's "unmanly" conduct and culturally feminine preoccupations in the face of the upheavals of his time – "Oh Dio, le carte, dov'erano le carte che aveva preso con sé ... la lista degli invitati ... le adesioni?" (p. 595) – mirror what Pirandello clearly saw as the moral indifference of his generation to the manly ideals of its Risorgimento ancestors. It was a theme which was to find fuller expression in another novel, *I vecchi e i giovani* (1909). Raceni's humiliation in this early episode not only prefigures Giustino's defeat at the end; it also functions as a sort of prologue which casts Giustino's fate in the broader social and historical context in which Pirandello sees it.

In conclusion, it is fair to say, I believe, that *Suo marito* is a novel of female awakening written from multiple perspectives. From Silvia's point of view, it is the story of the emergence of a woman's ambitions in the face of a mediocre husband who not only fails to understand her, but also mercilessly exploits her talents, humiliating both of them in the process. From Giustino's point of view, it is the story of a husband who generously allows and encourages his wife to develop her talents and turns them to profit only to find himself betrayed and rejected precisely for this reason. This double perspective combines to construct a story of two repressed and otherwise mismatched individuals, strangers not only to each other but also to themselves, whose marriage of convenience disintegrates when the conditions on which it was tacitly based, namely, the woman's economic and social dependence, no longer pertain. The ensuing disarray provides Pirandello with the framework within which to explore the fluctuating choreography of men and women in a critical moment in the history of gender relations.

What makes this a specifically Pirandellian structure is that the novel refuses a unitary point of view. The "truth" ultimately lies neither with the husband nor with the wife; the two points of view are as valid as they are diametrically opposed. What Silvia and Giustino share is the abyss that separates them.

Notes

1 On the Deledda connection and its consequences for the novel's publishing history see G. Macchia, ed., *Tutti i romanzi*, by L. Pirandello, Vol. 1 (Milan: Mondadori, 1973) 1048-1049. Among other things, *Suo marito* is the only one of Pirandello's novels to have escaped translation into English.

2 The new version of the novel carries a preface written by the author's son, Stefano Pirandello, justifying his decision to reprint the novel combining the first five re-written chapters with the remaining original ones.

My own analysis of this novel is based on the original text, *Suo marito*, as it appears today in *Tutti i romanzi* 587-873. All future references to the novel will be to this edition, and page numbers will be cited in the text.

As far as the new five first chapters of *Giustino Roncella nato Boggiolo* are concerned, they reflect Pirandello's interests of 1935 and not the attention to women and women's issues which characterize some of his earlier work. As a result, the character of Silvia is a far less complex one in the re-write, with many of the passages depicting her inner life and conflicts eliminated to make way for a more mechanical juxtaposition of her as "artist" with Giustino as "entrepreneur."

3 For specific criticism of this novel see: S. D'Alberti, *Pirandello romanziere* (Palermo: S.F. Flaccovio, 1967) 99-113; M. Ricciardi, "Il posto di *Suo marito* nel romanzo pirandelliano," *Il romanzo di Pirandello*, ed. E. Lauretta (Palermo: Palumbo, 1976) 109-124; C. Micocci, "Silvia Roncella e-o Giustino Boggiolo," *Il romanzo di Pirandello* 125-141; R. Dombroski, "Il dramma della produzione," *La totalità dell'artificio: Ideologia e forma nel romanzo di Pirandello* (Padua: Liviana, 1978) 81-102; R. Scrivano, *Finzioni teatrali: Da Ariosto a Pirandello* (Messina-Florence: G. D'Anna, 1982) 253-266; E. Gioanola, *Pirandello la follia* (Genoa: Il Melangolo, 1983) 194-199; L. Martinelli, "Silvia Roncella (Una lettura di *Suo marito* di Luigi Pirandello)," *Letteratura siciliana al femminile: donne scrittrici e donne personaggio*, ed. S. Zappulla Muscarà (Caltanisetta: Salvatore Sciascia, 1984) 103-123; R. Barilli, *Pirandello. Una rivoluzione culturale* (Milan: Mursia, 1986) 100-109.

4 See Ricciardi, Micocci, Barilli, Dombroski, Martinelli.

5 See D'Alberti, Gioanola (for a psychoanalytic reading), Dombroski, Martinelli.

6 G. Giudice, *Pirandello* (Turin: UTET, 1963) 150.

7 See M. Costanzo, "Cronologia della vita e delle opere di Luigi Pirandello," *Tutti i romanzi* lxi.

8 See, in this volume, "Strategies of Intertextuality in Sibilla Aleramo's *Una donna*."

9 L. Pirandello, *"Una donna,"* reprinted in S. Zappulla Muscarà, *Pirandello in guanti gialli* (Caltanisetta-Rome: Salvatore Sciascia, 1983) 219-225. The passage cited in my text appears on pp. 221-222. For more information on the debate surrounding Aleramo's novel see my essay in this volume.

10 The possibility of an Aleramo connection has also been suggested by F. Angelini, "Un nome e una donna," *Svelamento. Sibilla Aleramo: una biografia intellettuale*, eds. A. Buttafuoco and M. Zancan (Milan: Feltrinelli, 1988) 69.

11 First published in Norway in 1879, *A Doll's House* tells the story of Nora Helmar, the wife of a respected small-town bank manager who realizes, one day, that her husband is not the morally upright man she thought he was and that she herself has never been "herself," only a daughter, a wife and a mother. The depiction of Nora's "coming to consciousness" and ultimate abandonment of her family for the pursuit of her own self-development caused the play to be received with much consternation all over Europe, and no more so than in Italy. Here, it was first staged in 1890 and Ibsen was actually asked by his translator, Luigi Capuana, to re-write it with a new ending, in order to spare Italian audiences the outrage of seeing a woman literally close the door behind her on everything they considered sacred. (See Ibsen's letter of 23 January 1891 to Moritz Prozor in *The Correspondence of Henrik Ibsen*, ed. M. Morison [New York: Haskell House, 1970] 436-437.)

Curiously enough, the Ibsen connection seems to have eluded Italian critics, and Renato Barilli even goes so far as to insist that "nessuno ... potrà vedere nella Roncella una sorta di eroina ibseniana delle rivendicazioni femminili contro i privilegi del maschio" (Barilli 103). It is certainly true that Silvia is not consciously acting out that sort of role, but that Pirandello himself does cast her in it is undeniable - she is a sort of Nora *malgré elle*.

[12] See M. Hirsch, Introduction, *The Voyage In. Fictions of Female Development*, eds. E. Abel, M. Hirsch and E. Langland (Hanover: University Press of New England, 1983) 3-19; also, S. J. Rosowski, "The Novel of Awakening," *The Voyage In* 49-68.

[13] It is perhaps worth pointing out that Maurizio Gueli, as distinguished a writer as he may be, is described as not having written a word for over ten years. He is also in the clutches of a violently jealous woman (in whom critics have seen the tragic figure of Antonietta Portulano, Pirandello's wife) who, when informed of his betrayal of her, attacks him with a knife. As a result of this attack Gueli is forced to have his right arm amputated: I leave the myriad interpretative possibilities here to the reader.

[14] That Pirandello was in fact sensitive to these issues at this time is testified to by a novella entitled *Pari*, written in 1907 and published for the first time in *La vita nuda* (1911), and now in *Novelle per un anno*, Vol. 1 (Milan: Mondadori, 1952) 377-385. I quote from the novella: "Nelle loro conversazioni serali, Barbi e Pagliocco avevano definito insieme il *femminismo* questione essenzialmente economica. Ma sì, perché le donne, poverine, avevano compreso bene la ragione per cui diventava loro di giorno in giorno più difficile trovar marito. Il veder frustrata la loro naturale aspirazione, il dover soffocare il loro smanioso bisogno istintivo, le aveva esasperate e le faceva un po' farneticare. Ma tutta quella loro rivolta ideale contro i così detti pregiudizi sociali, tutte quelle loro prediche fervorose per la così detta emancipazione della donna, che altro erano in fondo se non una sdegnosa mascheratura del bisogno fisiologico, che urlava sotto? Le donne desiderano gli uomini e non lo possono dire; poverine. E volevano lavorare per trovar marito, ecco. Era un rimedio, questo, suggerito dal loro naturale buon senso. Ma, ahimé, il buon senso è nemico della poesia! E anche questo capivano le donne: capivano cioè che una donna, la quale lavori come un uomo, fra uomini, fuori di casa, non è più considerata dalla maggioranza degli uomini come l'ideale delle mogli, e si ribellavano contro a questo modo di considerare, che frustrava il loro rimedio, e lo chiamavano pregiudizio.

Ecco il torto. Pregiudizio il supporre che la donna, praticando di continuo con gli uomini, si sarebbe alla fine immascolinata troppo? Pregiudizio il prevedere che la casa, senza più le cure assidue, intelligenti, amorose della donna, avrebbe perduto quella poesia intima e cara, che è la maggiore attrattiva del matrimonio per l'uomo? Pregiudizio il supporre che la donna, cooperando anch'essa col proprio guadagno al mantenimento della casa, non avrebbe più avuto per l'uomo quella divozione e quel rispetto, di cui tanto esso si compiace? Ingiusto, questo rispetto? Ma perché allora, dal canto suo, voleva esser tanto rispettata la donna? Via! via! Se l'uomo e la donna non erano stati fatti da natura allo stesso modo, segno era che una cosa deve far l'uomo e un'altra la donna, e che pari dunque non possono essere.

Mai e poi mai Barbi e Pagliocco avrebbero sposato una donna emancipata, impiegata, padrona di sé. Non perché volessero schiava la moglie, ma perché tenevano alla loro dignità maschile e non avrebbero saputo tollerare che questa, di fronte ai guadagni della moglie, restasse anche minimamente diminuita. Metter su casa, d'altra parte, con lo scarso stipendio di segretario, sarebbe stata una vera e propria pazzia, e dunque niente: non ci pensavano nemmeno." (381-382)

Selected Bibliography

This bibliography includes only works which I have consulted directly. Relatively recent comprehensive bibliographies exist for Neera, Sibilla Aleramo and Matilde Serao in the following publications: Arslan, Antonia. "Neera." *Dizionario critico della letteratura italiana.* Turin: UTET, 1986; Buttafuoco, Annarita and Marina Zancan, eds. *Svelamento. Sibilla Aleramo: una biografia intellettuale.* Milan: Feltrinelli, 1988; Maria Grazia Martin Gistucci. *L'oeuvre romanesque de Matilde Serao.* Grenoble: Presses Universitaires de Grenoble, 1973. I have not found a comprehensive bibliography for the Marchesa Colombi. Also cited amongst the secondary sources are those works of feminist criticism and theory which have most influenced my approach to these writers.

Primary Sources

Aleramo, Sibilla. *Una donna.* Milan: Feltrinelli, 1985.

---. *La donna e il femminismo.* Rome: Riuniti, 1978.

Capuana, Luigi. *Profili di donne.* 2nd ed. Milan: Brigola, 1877.

Eliot, George. *The Mill on the Floss.* Ed. A.S. Byatt. Harmondsworth: Penguin, 1979.

Flaubert, Gustave. *Madame Bovary.* Paris: Gallimard, 1972.

Ibsen, Henrik. *A Doll's House and Other Plays.* Trans. P. Watts. Harmondsworth: Penguin, 1965.

Invernizio, Carolina. *Il bacio di una morta.* Milan: Lucchi, 1982.

Marchesa Colombi. *Dopo il caffè*. 2nd ed. Bologna: Zanichelli, 1880.

---. *Il tramonto di un ideale*. 2nd.ed. Milan: Galli, 1896.

---. *La cartella no.4*. Milan: Baldini e Castoldi, 1901.

---. *Prima morire*. 5th ed. Milan: Galli, 1896.

---. *Prima morire*. Rome: Lucarini, 1988.

---. *Serate d'inverno*. 2nd ed. Milan: Galli, 1887.

---. *Un matrimonio in provincia*. Turin: Einuadi, 1973.

Neera. *Addio!* 11th ed. Milan: Baldini e Castoldi, 1904.

---. *Anima sola*. Milan: Chiesa e Guindani, 1894.

---. *Crepuscoli di libertà*. Milan: Fratelli Treves, 1917.

---. *Il castigo*. 2nd ed. Turin: Roux, 1891.

---. *Il marito dell' amica*. 1885. Milan: Galli, 1891.

---. *Le idee di una donna*. Florence: Vallecchi, 1977.

---. *Monastero e altri racconti*. Eds. A. Arslan and A. Folli. Milan: Libri Scheiwiller, 1987.

---. *Neera*. Ed. B. Croce. Milan: Garzanti, 1942.

---. *Profili, impressioni e ricordi*. Milan: Cogliati, 1919.

---. *Rogo d'amore*. Milan: Fratelli Treves, 1914.

---. *Senio*. Milan: Galli, 1892.

---. *Teresa*. Turin: Einaudi, 1976.

---. *Un nido*. 5th ed. Milan: Baldini e Castoldi, 1913.

---. *Una giovinezza del secolo XIX*. Milan: Feltrinelli, 1980.

---. *Una passione*. Milan: Remo Sandron, 1903.

Serao, Matilde. *Il romanzo della fanciulla. La virtù di Checchina*. Ed. F. Bruni. Naples: Liguori, 1985.

---. *Serao*. Ed. P. Pancrazi. 2 vols. Milan: Garzanti, 1946.

Pirandello, Luigi. *Giustino Roncella nato Boggiolo*. Milan: Mondadori, 1973.

---. *"Suo marito."* *Tutti i romanzi*. Eds. G. Macchia and M. Costanzo. Vol.1. Milan: Mondadori, 1973. 587-873.

---. *"Pari."* *Novelle per un anno*. Vol.1. Milan: Mondadori, 1952. 377-385.

Secondary Sources

Abel, Elizabeth, Marianne Hirsch and Elizabeth Langland. Introduction. *The Voyage In: Fictions of Female Development*. Eds. E. Abel, M. Hirsch. E. Langland. Hanover: University Press of New England, 1983. 3-19.

Angelini, Franca *et al. Il secondo Ottocento*. Vol. 8 of *La letteratura italiana: Storia e testi* . Bari: Laterza, 1975.

Arslan, Antonia, ed. *Dame, droga e galline. Romanzo popolare e romanzo di consumo fra Ottocento e Novecento*. Milan: Unicopli, 1986.

---. "Luigi Capuana e Neera: corrispondenza inedita 1881-1885." *Miscellanea di studi in onore di Vittore Branca*. Vol. 5. Florence: Olschki, 1983. 161-185.

---. "Neera." *Dizionario critico della letteratura italiana*. Turin: UTET, 1986. 242-244.

--- and Anna Folli. *Il concetto che ne informa. Benedetto Croce e Neera. Corrispondenza (1903-1917)*. Naples: Edizioni Scientifiche Italiane, 1989.

Auerbach, Nina. *Woman and the Demon: The Life of a Victorian Myth*. Cambridge: Harvard University Press, 1982.

Baldacci, Luigi. Introduction. *Teresa*. By Neera. Turin: Einaudi, 1976. v-xii.

---. Note. *Le idee di una donna*. By Neera. Florence: Vallecchi, 1977. xvii-xx.

Baldacci, Maria Bruna and Stefania Biagioni, eds. *Soggetto donna: dalla Bibliografia Nazionale Italiana 1975-1984. Memoria* 14 (1985).

Banti, Anna. *Matilde Serao*. Turin: UTET, 1965.

Baranski, Zygmunt G. "The Power of Influence: Aspects of Dante's Presence in Twentieth-Century Italian Culture." *Strumenti critici* ns 1.3 (1986): 343-376

Barilli, Renato. *Pirandello. Una rivoluzione culturale*. Milan: Mursia, 1986.

Bassanese, Fiora A. *"Una donna*: Autobiography as Exemplary Text." *Donna. Women in Italian Culture*. Ed. A. Testaferri. University of Toronto Italian

Studies 7. Ottawa: Dovehouse Editions, 1989. 131-152. Also in *Quaderni d'Italianistica* 11.1 (1990): 41-60.

Beer, Marina. "Nota sui romanzi femminili italiani del ventennio 1880-90." *Memoria* 2 (1981): 76-88.

Bersani, Leo. "Le réalisme e la peur du désir," in Roland Barthes *et al.*, *Littérature et réalité*. Paris: Seuil, 1982. 47-80. (First published in *Poétique* 22 April 1975.)

Blelloch, Paola. *Quel mondo dei guanti e delle stoffe*. Verona: Essedue, 1987.

Bonghi, Ruggero. *Lettere critiche: Perché la letteratura italiana non sia poplare in Italia*. Ed. E. Villa. Milan: Marzorati, 1971.

Bruni, Francesco. Introduction. *Il romanzo della fanciulla*. By Matilde Serao. Ed. F. Bruni. Naples: Liguori, 1985. I-LVII.

Buttafucoco, Annarita and Marina Zancan, eds. *Svelamento. Sibilla Aleramo: una biografia intellettuale*. Milan: Feltrinelli, 1988.

Buzzi, Giancarlo. *Invito alla lettura di Matilde Serao*. Milan: Mursia, 1981.

Byatt, Antonia Susan. Introduction. *The Mill on the Floss*. By George Eliot. Harmondsworth: Penguin, 1979. 7-40.

Capuana, Luigi. *Letteratura femminile*. Ed. Giovanna Finocchiaro Chimirri. Catania: C.U.E.C.M., 1988. (First published as an article in *Nuova antologia* 1 January 1907).

---. "Neera." *Studi sulla letteratura contemporanea*. 2nd. series. Catania, 1882. 145-157.

---. "Butti, Neera, Gualdo." *Gli "ismi" contemporanei*. Catania, 1898. 113-129.

Caretti, Laura. "Capuana, Ibsen e la Duse." *L'illusione della realtà: studi su Luigi Capuana*. Eds. M. Picone and E. Rossetti. Rome: Salerno editrice, 1990. 185-203.

Cattaneo, Carlo. "Sul romanzo delle donne contemporanee in Italia" (1863). *Scritti letterari, artistici, linguistici e vari*. Vol. I. Ed. Agostino Bertani. Florence: Le Monnier, 1948. 358-389.

Cavalli Pasini, Annamaria. "La donna *fin-de-siècle* tra isteria e misticismo." *La scienza del romanzo. Romanzo e cultura scientifica tra Ottocento e Novecento*. Bologna: Patron, 1982. 203-257.

Chiavola Birnbaum, Lucia. *Liberazione della donna. Feminism in Italy*. Middletown, Connecticut: Wesleyan University Press, 1986.

Conti, Bruna and Alba Morino. *Sibilla Aleramo e il suo tempo*. Milan: Feltrinelli, 1981.

Contorbia, Franca, Lea Melandri and Alba Morino, eds. *Sibilla Aleramo. Coscienza e scrittura*. Milan: Feltrinelli, 1986.

Corti, Maria. Preface. *Una donna*. By Sibilla Aleramo. Milan: Feltrinelli, 1982. vii-xvi.

Croce, Benedetto. *Letteratura della nuova Italia*. Bari: Laterza, 1949.

---. "Neera." *La critica* (1905): 354-368. Rpt. in *Neera*. By Neera. Ed. B. Croce. Milan: Garzanti, 1942. 932-944. Also rpt. in *Letteratura della nuova Italia*. Vol.3. 121-140.

---. "Prefazione all'autobiografia." *Una giovinezza del secolo XIX*. Milan, 1919. vii-xi. Rpt. in *Neera*. By Neera. Ed. B. Croce. Milan: Garzanti, 1942. 945-947.

---. *Storia d'Italia dal 1871 al 1915*. Bari: Laterza, 1953.

D'Alberti, Sara. *Pirandello romanziere*. Palermo: S.F. Flaccovio, 1967.

De Donato, Gigliola, *et al*. *La parabola della donna nella letteratura italiana dell' Ottocento*. Bari: Adriatica editrice, 1983.

Dombroski, Robert S. "Il dramma della produzione." *La totalità dell'artificio: Ideologia e forma nel romanzo di Pirandello*. Padua: Liviana, 1978. 81-102.

Drake, Richard. Introduction. *A Woman*. By Sibilla Aleramo. Berkeley and Los Angeles: University of California Press, 1980. v-xxxvi.

Eco, Umberto, *et al*. *Carolina Invernizio, Matilde Serao, Liala*. Florence: La nuova Italia, 1979.

Eliot, George. "Silly Novels by Lady Novelists." *Westminster Review* October 1856: 442-461. Rpt. in *Essays of George Eliot*. Ed. T. Pinney. New York: Columbia University Press, 1963. 300-324.

Federzoni, Marina, Isabella Pezzini and Maria Pia Pozzato. *Sibilla Aleramo*. Florence: La nuova Italia, 1980.

Folli, Anna. "Le arpe eoli. Lettura di Neera." *La Rassegna della letteratura italiana* Jan.-April 1987: 98-120.

Finucci, Valeria. "Una rilettura di *Teresa* di Neera." *Misure Critiche* 15.55-57 (1985): 65-79.

---. "Between Acquiescence and Madness: Neera's *Teresa*." *Stanford Italian Review* 7.1-2 (1987): 217-239.

Friedman, Susan Stanford. "Creativity and the Childbirth Metaphor: Gender Difference in Literary Discourse." *Speaking of Gender*. Ed. E. Showalter. New York: Routledge, 1989. 73-100.

Gardiner, Judith Kegan. "On Female Identity and Writing by Women." *Critical Inquiry* 8.2 (1981): 347-362.

Ghiaroni, Rosanna. Introduction. *Una donna*. By Sibilla Aleramo. Turin: Loescher, 1978. 7-13.

Gilbert, Sandra and Susan Gubar. *The Madwoman in the Attic: The Woman Writer and the Nineteenth-Century Literary Imagination*. New Haven: Yale University Press, 1979.

---. "Tradition and the Female Talent." *The Poetics of Gender*. Ed. Nancy K. Miller. New York: Columbia University Press, 1986. 183-207. Rpt. in *No Man's Land: The Place of the Woman Writer in the Twentieth Century*. Vol. 1. By Sandra Gilbert and Susan Gubar. New Haven: Yale University Press, 1987. 125-162.

Ginzburg, Natalia. Introduction. *Un matrimonio in provincia*. By the Marchesa Colombi. Turin: Einaudi, 1973. v-x.

Gioanola, Elio. *Pirandello la follia*. Genoa: Il Melangolo, 1983.

Giudice, Giovanni. *Pirandello*. Turin: UTET, 1963.

Goldmann, Lucien. *Pour une sociologie du roman*. Paris: Gallimard, 1964.

Golini, Vera. "Critical Perspectives on Italian Women Writers at the Turn of the Century." *Tra due secoli: il tardo Ottocento e il primo Novecento nella critica italiana dell'ultimo ventennio*. Vol. 4 of Biblioteca di Quaderni d'italianistica. Ottawa:The Canadian Society for Italian Studies & Groupe de Recherches International "1900," 1988. 143-168.

Gramsci, Antonio. "La morale e il costume. *Casa di bambola* di Ibsen al Carignano." *Letteratura e vita nazionale*. Rome: Editori Riuniti, 1975. 343-346.

Guerricchio, Rita. *Storia di Sibilla*. Pisa: Nistri-Lischi, 1974.

Howard, Judith Jeffrey. "The Feminine Vision of Matilde Serao." *Italian Quarterly* 71 (1975): 55-77.

---. "The Civil Code of 1865 and the Origins of the Feminist Movement in Italy." *The Italian Immigrant Woman in North America*. Proceedings of the Tenth Annual Conference of the American Italian Historical Society. Eds. B.B. Caroli, R.F. Harney and L.F. Tomasi. Toronto: The Multicultural History Society of Ontario, 1978. 14-22.

---. "Patriot Mothers in the Post-Risorgimento: Women after the Italian Revolution." *Women, War, and Revolution.* Eds. C.R. Berkin and C.M. Lovett. New York: Holmes and Meier, 1980. 237-258.

Ibsen, Henrik. *The Correspondence of Henrik Ibsen.* Ed. M. Mirson. New York: Haskell House, 1970.

Jeuland-Meynaud, Maryse. "I modelli narrativi tardo-romantici nella cultura meridionale." *Cultura meridionale e letteratura italiana. I modelli narrativi dell'età moderna.* Atti dell'XI congresso dell'AISLLI. Naples: Loffredo, 1985. 405-445.

Kennard, John Spencer. "La femme dans le roman italien." *The Colonnade* 14 (1922): 3-32. First delivered as a lecture in 1904.

"La satira e Parini." *Dizionario letterario Bompiani.* Vol.6. Milan: Bompiani, 1972.

Leavis, Q.D. "The Englishness of the English Novel." *Collected Essays.* Ed. G. Singh. Cambridge: Cambridge University Press, 1983. 303-327.

Macciocchi, Maria Antonietta. Preface. *Una Donna.* By Sibilla Aleramo. Milan: Feltrinelli, 1985. 5-12.

Martin Gistucci, Maria Grazia. *L'oeuvre romanesque de Matilde Serao.* Grenoble: Presses Universitaires de Grenoble, 1973.

Martinelli, Luciana. "Silvia Roncella (Una lettura di *Suo marito* di Pirandello)." *Letteratura siciliana al femminile: donne scrittrici e donne personaggio.* Ed. S. Zapulla Muscarà. Caltanisetta: Salvatore Sciascia, 1984. 103-123.

"Matilde Serao." *The Warner Library.* Eds. J.W. Cunliffe and A. Thorndike. Vol.22. New York: Warner Library Company, 1917.

Menasci, Guido. "Neera." *Nuova antologia* 16 Sept. 1901: 263-278.

Miccoci, Claudia. "Silvia Roncella e-o Giustino Boggiolo." *Il romanzo di Pirandello.* Palermo: Palumbo, 1976. 125-141.

Miller, Nancy K. "Emphasis Added: Plots and Plausibilities in Women's Fiction." *PMLA* 96.1 (1981): 36-48. Rpt. in *The New Feminist Criticism: Essays on Women, Literature and Theory.* Ed. E. Showalter. New York: Pantheon, 1985. 339-360.

Moi, Toril. *Sexual/Textual Politics: Feminist Literary Theory.* London: Methuen, 1985.

Morandini, Giuliana. *La voce che è in lei. Antologia della narrativa femminile italiana fra '800 e '900.* Milan: Bompiani, 1980.

---. Preface. *Prima morire.* By the Marchesa Colombi. Rome: Lucarini, 1988. ix-xvi.

Nozzoli, Anna. "La letteratura femminile in Italia tra Ottocento e Novecento." *Tabù e coscienza: la condizione femminile nella letteratura italiana del Novecento.* Florence: La nuova Italia, 1978. 1-40.

Orlando, Francesco. *Per una teoria freudiana della letteratura.* Turin: Einaudi, 1973.

Pacifici, Sergio. "Women Writers: Neera and Aleramo." *The Modern Italian Novel from Capuana to Tozzi.* Carbondale: Southern Illinois University Press. 49-67.

Palermo, Antonio. "Le due narrative di Matilde Serao." *Da Mastriani a Viviani: per una storia della letteratura a Napoli fra Ottocento e Novecento.* Naples: Liguori, 1974. 33-65.

"Paolo Ferrari." *Enciclopedia dello spettacolo.* Vol.5. Rome: Le Maschere.

Parca, Gabriella. *L'avventurosa storia del femminismo.* Milan: Mondadori, 1976.

Pieroni Bortolotti, Franca. *Sul movimento politico delle donne. Scritti inediti.* Ed. A. Buttafuoco. Rome: Cooperativa UTOPIA, 1987.

---. *All'origine del movimento femminile in Italia (1848-1892).* 1963. Turin: Einaudi, 1975.

Pirandello, Luigi. Review of *Una donna. Gazzetta del popolo.* 27 December 1906. Rpt. in *Pirandello in guanti gialli.* By S. Zappulla Muscarà. Caltanisetta: Salvatore Sciascia, 1983.

Pozzato, Maria Pia. *Il romanzo rosa.* Milan: Editori Europei Associati, 1982.

Prisco, Michele *et al. Matilde Serao tra giornalismo e letteratura.* Ed. G. Infusino. Naples: Guida, 1981.

Ricciardi, Mario. "Il posto di *Suo marito* nel romanzo pirandelliano." *Il romanzo di Pirandello.* Ed. E. Lauretta. Palermo: Palumbo, 1976. 109-124.

Romani, Bruno. "La narrativa borghese del secondo Ottocento. *Controcorrente tardottocentesca.* Lecce: Milella, 1974. 9-26.

Rosowski, Susan J. "The Novel of Awakening." *The Voyage In: Fictions of Female Development.* Eds. E. Abel, M. Hirsch, E. Langland. Hanover: University Press of New England, 1983. 49-68.

Russ, Joanna. *How to Suppress Women's Writing.* London: The Women's Press, 1984.

Ruthven, K.K. *Feminist Literary Studies: An Introduction.* Cambridge: Cambridge University Press, 1984.

Santoro, Anna. *Narratrici italiane dell'Ottocento.* Naples: Federico e Ardia, 1987.

Scrivano, Riccardo. *Finzioni teatrali: Da Ariosto a Pirandello*. Messina: G. D'Anna, 1982.

Serao, Matilde. *Ricordando Neera*. Milan: Treves, 1920.

Showalter, Elaine. *A Literature of Their Own: British Women Novelists from Brontë to Lessing*. Princeton: Princeton University Press, 1976.

---. "Toward a Feminist Poetics." *Women's Writing and Writing About Women*. London: Croom Helm, 1979. Rpt. in *The New Feminist Criticism: Essays on Women, Literature and Theory*. Ed. E. Showalter. New York: Pantheon, 1985. 125-143.

---. "Feminist Criticism in the Wilderness." *Critical Inquiry* 8.2 (1981): 179-206. Rpt. in *The New Feminist Criticism. Essays on Women, Literature and Theory*. Ed. E. Showalter. New York: Pantheon, 1985. 243-270.

Spacks, Patricia Meyer. *The Female Imagination*. New York: Alfred A. Knopf, 1972.

Todd, Janet. *Feminist Literary History*. New York: Routledge, 1988.

Ventura, L.D. Preface. *The Soul of an Artist*. By Neera. Trans E.L. Murison. San Francisco: Paul Elder and Co., 1905.

Weigel, Sigrid. "Double Focus: On the History of Women's Writing." *Feminist Aesthetics*. Ed. G. Ecker. Trans H. Anderson. Boston: Beacon Press, 1986. 59-80.

Zancan, Marina. "La donna." *Le questioni*. Vol.5 of *Letteratura italiana*. Ed. A. Asor Rosa. Turin: Einaudi, 1986. 765-827.